Cardiff Papers in Qualitative Research

About the Series

The Cardiff School of Social Sciences at Cardiff University is well known for the breadth and quality of its empirical research in various major areas of sociology and social policy. In particular, it enjoys an international reputation for research using qualitative methodology, including qualitative approaches to data collection and analysis.

This series publishes original sociological research that reflects the tradition of qualitative and ethnographic inquiry developed at Cardiff in recent years. The series includes monographs reporting on empirical research, collections of papers reporting research on particular themes and other monographs or edited collections on methodological developments and issues.

Realizing Qualitative Research into Higher Education

Edited by

CRAIG PRICHARD
PAUL TROWLER

From the books for

CONTEMPORARY SOCIOLOGY

Editors
JoAnn Miller and Robert Perrucci

ASHGATE

Published by
Ashgate Publishing Limited
Gower House
Croft Road
Aldershot
Hants GU11 3HR
England

Ashgate Publishing Company
Suite 420
101 Cherry Street
Burlington, VT 05401-4405
USA

Ashgate website: http://www.ashgate.com

British Library Cataloguing in Publication Data
Realizing qualitative research into higher education. -
    (Cardiff papers in qualitative research)
    1. Education, Higher - Congresses
    I. Prichard, Craig, 1962- II. Trowler, Paul III. Cardiff
    University. School of Social and Administration Studies
    IV. Higher Education Close Up Conference (2nd : 2001 :
    Lancaster University, England)
    378

Library of Congress Cataloging-in-Publication Data
Realizing qualitative research into higher education / edited by Craig Prichard and Paul Trowler.
        p. cm. -- (Cardiff papers in qualitative research)
    Includes bibliographical references and index.
    ISBN 0-7546-3270-9
    1. Education, Higher--Research--Methodology. 2. Qualitative research. I. Prichard,
Craig, 1962- II. Trowler, Paul. III. Series.

LB2326.3.R43 2003
378'.007'2--dc21

2002043966

ISBN 0 7546 3270 9

Printed and bound by Athenaeum Press, Ltd.,
Gateshead, Tyne & Wear.

Contents

PART I: STUDENT LEARNING IN HIGHER EDUCATION

PART II: TEACHING PRACTICES IN HIGHER EDUCATION

PART III: ORGANIZING AND MANAGING HIGHER EDUCATION

List of Tables

List of Figures

List of Contributors

David I. Bell is a South African psychologist and educator. His work has encompassed community empowerment and social transformation in both formal and non-formal education in Southern Africa. Currently, he is a Professor of International Development and Social Change at Clark University in the United States.

Sara Delamont is Reader in Sociology at Cardiff University (Wales). She was the first woman president of the British Education Research Association, and is the author of *Knowledgeable Women* (originally published in 1989 and now a Routledge e-book).

Veerle Hulpiau is a scientific staff member at the Educational Support Office of the University of Leuven (Belgium). Her work and research focuses on educational policy, educational evaluations and quality assurance.

Josep M. Masjuan is Professor in the Department of Sociology at Universitat Autònoma de Barcelona (Spain). He has long been working in Sociology of Education and Educational Institutions, contributing to actual changes carried out in schools. He currently has research interests in supporting university evaluation processes, organizational changes in higher education institutions and transition from studies to work.

Rob Moore is a senior lecturer in the Centre for Higher Education Development at the University of Cape Town (South Africa). His interests include institutional research, curriculum, and the professional development of academic staff.

Jane McEldowney Jensen is an anthropologist and Assistant Professor of Educational Policy Studies and Evaluation at the University of Kentucky (USA). She is the author of *Post-secondary Education on the Edge: Self-Improvement and Community Development in a Cape Breton Coal Town.*

Moragh Paxton is Senior Lecturer in the Centre for Higher Education Development at the University of Cape Town (South Africa). She is currently completing her PhD in Applied Linguistics.

Tom Phillips was until recently, Head of Health and Social Studies at Bolton Institute (England). He is now an independent researcher and doctorate supervisor for the Bolton Institute and the Open University. He has a particular interest in showing how cultural theory can illumine classroom practices at whatever level of education.

Tony Potts is head of Education Studies and co-ordinates the PhD and MEd (Research) programmes in education at La Trobe University, Bendigo (Australia). The current chapter is part of a larger study on civic leaders and the university.

Craig Prichard is senior lecturer in the Department of Management at Massey University Palmerston North (New Zealand). The Open University Press published an adaptation of his PhD research on the development of managers in UK further and higher education under the title *Making Managers in Universities and Colleges* (2000).

Helena Troiano works as a researcher and associate lecturer in the Department of Sociology at Universitat Autònoma de Barcelona (Spain). Her main areas of interest are centred on higher education: transition from studies to work, implementation of curricular innovations, organizational changes and changing academic culture.

Paul Trowler is senior lecturer in education in the Department of Educational Research, Lancaster University (England). There he leads the Doctoral Programme in Educational Research and pursues research interests in change processes in higher education.

Kim Waeytens is professor in the Educational Support Office of the University of Leuven (Belgium). Her work and research focuses on educational policy, educational evaluations and staff development.

Catherine Watts is a senior lecturer in the School of Languages, University of Brighton (England) where she teaches German, TESOL and Education. She was awarded her Doctorate in Education (EdD) in June 2002 by King's College, University of London. Her doctoral thesis explored the decline in the take-up of modern foreign languages at degree level in the UK.

Acknowledgements

This collection would not have made it to this point without the help and enthusiasm of Kerry Gibson, Terry Wareham and Amanda Westwell of Lancaster University's Higher Education Development Centre, and Josie Grace of the Department of Management at Massey University.

Introduction

Craig Prichard and Paul Trowler

The book before you is built around the conviction that one of the best ways for qualitative researchers to develop their craft is to read and critically examine the work of others. With this in mind we have assembled ten pieces of work that not only tackle some of the most contentious issues confronting higher education around the world (e.g. massification, democratization, globalization, managerialization), but also do so from a range of methodological positions from across the qualitative research field (e.g. ethnographic, evaluative, historical and critical traditions). To further support the reader's engagement with research practice each chapter begins with a short narrative by the authors. Here each reflects on one of the issues that they confronted in actually undertaking their work. The authors discuss gaining access to research sites, recruiting research participants, undertaking interviews and methods of textual analysis.

Alongside this desire to offer qualitative researchers working in the higher education field a range of research exemplars, we hope this collection also makes a contribution to the long stand debate across the social sciences surrounding qualitative methodologies. Before laying out our position on this we want to briefly provide some background to the collection.

Each of the chapters here was presented at the second Higher Education Close up (HECU) Conference at Lancaster University in July 2001. The conference was designed to provide a forum for researchers across the world who see value in fine-grained qualitative study of higher education. The first conference had been held at Preston in 1998 and had been so successful that it was inevitable that a second would be held.

Clearly these conferences fulfilled a need. Previously, higher education's 'close up' researchers had formed a small minority at general education conferences. This was the case even in those conferences devoted solely to the study of higher education, such as the annual conference of the Society for Research into Higher Education (SRHE). With the launch of the HECU series they now had a forum at which they could share findings, network, improve the theory and practice of close up higher education research and discuss their common methodological, ethical and other issues which close up research gives rise to.

The need for more fine-grained, hermeneutically grounded studies in HE has not gone unrecognized. The importance and the scarcity of such research approaches in the HE domain has been identified by many theorists, including Tony Becher (1989), Geoffrey Walford (1992) and Rob Cuthbert (1996). Sheldon Rothblatt for example noted that while we are 'inundated with information about nearly every aspect of higher education, we lack sustained discussion of the changing inner culture of universities' (Rothblatt, 1996, p 18). Writing at about the same time John Smyth made the point that:

> It is so obvious it hardly even deserves a mention: higher education around the world is undergoing massive and unprecedented changes, and herein lies its major problem! Most of what is happening is going ahead largely unexamined, and certainly unopposed.... What is most surprising, given the nature of the 'animal', is that there are so few attempts to document systematically what is happening to it, or to explain it theoretically. That is curious given the predisposition of academics towards working on and explaining other people's lives and worlds. That we devote so little time to analyzing what it is we do...must be one of the great unexamined educational issues of our times. (Smyth, 1995, p. 1)

The HECU conferences and subsequent publications were events whose time had clearly come.

Just days before the second HECU conference began Paul Trowler's telephone rang. The education correspondent from *The Guardian* newspaper was interested in the conference and wanted to ask some questions. Paraphrased, they were: 'what do we mean by "close up" research; what good are its results and why should funders devote more resources to this style of research?'.

At the time we found the questions somewhat irritating. *Of course* close up research is 'for the good', *of course* funding agencies should devote *more* resources to it, and *of course* such work contributes to improving higher education for students, staff and communities generally.

But how does it do this? In what areas? To what extent? And how could it be done 'better'? We deal with both these sets of questions in the discussion below. As we do we will introduce the exemplary pieces of qualitative research on various features of higher education that make up this book. But before we get to these we need to address the Guardian correspondent's question about what we mean by 'close up' research into higher education.

The Nature of Close Up Research

There are two senses of 'close-upness'. The first relates to professional practice. The second is more straightforwardly methodological. In terms of professional practice, close up research comes from the concerns and issues raised in the daily practice of higher education. It comes from the ground, not from the research agendas generated by governments or funding agencies. 'Why are my students behaving like this?' 'Why is there such conflict among my colleagues?' Why doesn't this course operate in the way we expect it to?' 'Why are the outcomes of this policy so different from the intentions which underpinned it?'. These and many other questions like them bubble to the surface in higher education every day. Answering them properly needs good research approaches, founded in good theory. They are important, 'real' questions, and the chances of getting sensible answers to them which then yield improvements in practice are greater than for 'far off' research alone which often addresses questions of more significance to policy-makers than to professionals on the ground. Moreover these 'improvements' themselves have more chance of being defined as such by practitioners and students themselves, because the original questions came from their daily lives.

We concur, then, with the SRHE's response to the National Educational Research Forum's (NERF) consultation attempts to tie educational research and education policy together more closely:

> The best research comes 'bottom-up'...Much of the work that we believe should be promoted and disseminated has little or no direct funding...Research by their peers carries credibility with practitioners. (SRHE, 2001)

The best research comes from people who are 'close to the action'. Their research often arises organically from their work and is also more likely to make an impact on higher education in the longer term. This is precisely the strength of many of the chapters in the collection. For instance in our first section on student learning Moragh Paxton (chapter two) shows how detailed textual analysis of student assignments provides important insights into the social-cultural processes in which higher education is engaged, and how particular disciplines maintain control of the 'kind' of students they promote. While not addressed directly, this chapter provides insights into the kind of practices that might be used to inform reviews of course content and delivery formats for programmes as they confront a broader range of students.

Likewise in our second section on teaching practice Tom Phillips (chapter five) uses a self-ethnographic method to explore his own classroom practice. The value here is that he is able to extract and examine in detail the different modes by which he performs as a teacher. Again there are important pedagogical insights to be had here for the development of courses and programmes.

Turning now to the second source of 'close up-ness', the methodological one. Close up research is methodologically part of an explosion of qualitative research right across the social sciences that mirrors a retreat from quantitative natural science methodologies. This movement has spurred the development of a huge range of methodological programmes – some of which appear in this book. While many such programmes hold competing positions on a number of research grounds each in different ways appreciates the complex, culturally and historically specific character of human practice as it is lived out in higher education institutions. In higher education fine-grained qualitative research is concerned with what might seem to some to be the 'private lives' (Trow, 1975) of students, cooks, cleaners, teachers, researchers, vice-chancellors and all who make up these rich institutional territories and terrains. Fine-grained research is committed in other words to a detailed analysis of institutional 'undergrowth'. It eschews reductionism and aims to appreciate the complex character of social life, its construction and how it is lived out.

Moving now to our Guardian correspondent's second question, 'what good are the results of close up research?'. Our argument in summary is that their chief value is in the illumination of social reality, of the everyday processes of daily life. Their significance, and their impact, is brought alive as research goes underneath the taken-for-granted, surfaces the tacit and questions the assumptions on which practices are based. At its best it questions the 'problems' that are presented by others (policy-makers, higher education managers) and considers why they are being presented as problems in the first place. Its questions are authentic ones, rooted in professional practice.

However, a number of problems plague such research. First, it will rarely claim to have found the 'right' answer, as more positivist-oriented approaches tend to do. Very often the conclusions of close up research are littered with more questions than answers. But they are higher-grade questions than would have been asked without that research; more subtle, more penetrating. Yet to policy makers and managers this is merely irritating. They don't want subtle questions, they tend to want simple answers to simple questions such as: 'what and where are the levers of change, and when should I pull them?'. Invidious comparisons are made with large scale quantitative studies which do appear to offer short, simple answers: 'X% of the population think and do this, and Y% would feel this way if that happened'. However, as Stephen Ball says, in his 'bilious' response to the NERF consultation, such thinking sees educational research as:

> ...simply a set of technical-rational procedures unbeset by uncertainty and unmarked by any kind of epistemological reflexivity. This is what Hammersley (1997) calls the 'engineering model' of research. Research which works upon but is not part of a social world. In this vision research ceases to be an intellectual exercise either for its practitioners or for its readers. It is simply about providing accounts of 'what works' for unselfconscious classroom drones to implement... Atkinson (2000) proposes a different view of the role of research in 'the possibility of promoting and extending critical discourse among both researchers and teachers, and of opening up channels for debate and consideration of a *range* of solutions to classroom problems' (p. 322). In other words, she sees research as an educative process that could contribute to teachers' reflection, decision-making and judgements about their practice; not tell them what to do. In such a conception research is invigorating and empowering. Such a conception treats the teacher with respect and the purposes of education as debatable and contestable. (Ball, 2001, 266)

In answering our Guardian correspondent in this way, though, we must beware of falling into one of the traps of media spin; the generation of conflict where there is none – because conflict is more interesting than consensus. We do not wish to situate close up research and other forms of HE research as in opposition to each other, as strict alternatives. Rather they are complementary approaches to understanding HE better and usually work best when in tandem. Much of the research reported in the chapters here uses a range of methods, and those studies are the better for them. For example the action-learning project presented in chapter four by Joseph Masjuan and Helena Troiano relies on data from a large sample telephone survey of graduates four years on from the completion of their studies. Data from this was used to engage university staff and external representatives in problem focused dialogue aimed at better alignment between university provision and labour market demands.

A second doubt about close up research relates to the question of generalization of results. Such research uses a microscope rather than a telescope. As a result its field of vision is limited. The obvious question, then, is precisely that of our Guardian correspondent – 'what good are its results [if they are based on the study of a very small part of social reality]?'. This is particularly troublesome because universities, even within the UK, are so different, one from another:

> It is the good luck of the universities that there are so many of them, that there are no two exactly alike, and that inside every university there is a mind-boggling variety of departments, schools, styles of thoughts, styles of conversation, and even styles of stylistic concerns. It is the good luck of the universities that despite all the efforts of the self-proclaimed saviours, know-betters and well-wishers to prove the contrary, they are not comparable, not measurable by the same yardstick and – most important of all – not speaking in unison. (Bauman, 1997, p 25)

As Walford (2001) notes, there are several standard answers to this question about generalization to be found in an extensive literature (Becker, 1990; Schofield, 1990; Stake, 1995). The first is that a sufficiently 'thick description' of a case allows readers to evaluate for themselves its applicability to other contexts with which they are familiar. Here, then, the answer to the correspondent's question lies in the thickness of the description close up research can offer: it allows the reader to more fully know and appreciate the object of research than is possible through other research approaches.

The second response is to argue that generalization is to *theory* rather than from cases to larger populations or other contexts. Thus the details of the case are used to develop more sophisticated theory about the issue at hand (for example, the enhancement of teaching and learning). It is the value of this theory rather than the details of the case itself where the value of close up research lies. Stones imagines what this might ideally look like. It would be:

> ...constructed in such a way that the findings of a case study would feed back into a precise body of theory about that type of case study. This body of theory would act as a storehouse of more or less hermeneutically sensitive case studies of conjectural events and processes that have addressed specifically phrased questions. (Stones, 1996, pp. 71-2)

A third response is to reject the aim of generalization at all and to simply claim value and interest in close up studies for themselves. Here, though, the claim is a limited one, because inevitably a claim for a study as being important and interesting in itself could only be justified for some people. Higher education managers may find one study interesting and valuable, but another not. Geography lecturers, educational developers and vice chancellors will each have their own ideas of what is intrinsically worth studying and what is not.

We would offer each of these answers to our inquisitive Guardian correspondent, and emphasize that they are not alternatives but are compatible. Together they make the point we began with, that close up research is 'illuminative': it helps us think better about questions we have, it casts light in previously dark places and it turns up the contrast level, helping us to make distinctions more clearly.

Two further issues are also frequently said to beset close up research, and hence limit their value: the problems of myopia and of non-cumulation, that is the fact that they focus on the ground and cannot see the higher level influences on actors there, and that they do not allow social science to progress beyond the particular.

To deal with the myopia issue first: ground level studies are often accused of being short-sighted, of only being able to see things that are close at hand, not those further away that actually connected to them in important ways. In the field of public policy studies, for example, Sabatier (1986) and Marsh and Rhodes (1992) summarize the critique of ground level studies of policy implementation with the following points:

i.   Bottom-up approaches overestimate the discretion of the lower level actors and fail to recognize sufficiently the constraints on their behaviour.

ii. They do not explain the sources of actors' definitions of the situation, perceptions of the their own interests etc. In fact these may come, directly or indirectly, from above, beyond the scope of close up studies.

iii. The upper levels (for example governments) set the ground rules for negotiation and this is not recognized by close up studies. (adapted from Sabatier, 1986, pp. 35-6)

The first is a criticism Marxists and others have levelled at interactionist and other phenomenologically-oriented perspectives that adopt a micro rather than macro level of analysis. Clearly there is always a danger of losing sight of structural constraints on behaviour when studying social action at the ground level, but this is not an intrinsic flaw of all studies at that level as, for example, Corrigan's (1981) study amply demonstrates and as Ozga (1990) argues more generally. The second, though, could be levelled at many ground level studies and provides a criterion against which to judge studies. The third is closely related to the first and, like that one, is not necessarily a characteristic of bottom-up approaches.

Moving to the second problem, which concerns cumulation. Close up research is often accused of producing nothing more than a series of interesting but essentially non-cumulative case studies (LeCompte, 1979; Finch, 1986; Lester et al, 1987). Social science, it is argued, cannot progress on the basis of such studies because they have nothing to say to each other: each might be interesting but essentially stands alone.

One response to this is to develop techniques for the synthesis of qualitative studies in this tradition (e.g. Noblit and Hare, 1988). Another is to attempt to draw generic issues out of disparate studies, as many book editors attempt to do. We argue, however, that this should not be necessary. Such studies are often strong on description but weaker on theory, a frequent characteristic of ethnographic approaches which Finch (1986), Hammersley, Scarth and Webb (1985), Woods (1984) and others consider to be a major deficiency in that approach. Adding a more sophisticated, and transparent, theoretical substructure to underpin the description means that theory provides the cumulative 'glue' in this form of research. It allows the researcher to produce more than just description of a single site: a 'stand alone' descriptive study. With this theoretical substructure it is both possible to create significant comparisons with other studies in much the way that Finch (1986) recommends.

All this helps answer the Guardian reporter's final question: why should funders devote more resources to this style of research? It has value, as the chapters in this book demonstrate, but it is not a cheap option. Close up research takes time, both the time of the researcher and, very often that of the researched. Ethnographic research in particular is a lengthy and costly business. Not enough of it is done nowadays for this reason. The incentives are for research that is cheap, quick and from which publications can be quickly generated in order to contribute to the scores achieved in research evaluation exercises like the British Research Assessment Exercise. Evaluation regimes such as that which exists in the UK and in many other countries, based on bibliometric exercises, mean that close up research is frequently squeezed out.

Structure of the Book

As noted the chapters in this collection draw on a range of methodological positions. In order to give some balance and coherence to the collection, and to each section of the book, we have included works that can be located within three main methodological traditions: the evaluative, the interpretive and the critical. Such categorization – while useful for theoretical or methodological discussion – does not always represent the depth and detailed work found in each chapter however. What these labels do identify is the general intent or primary objective of each piece of research as it is presented here. For instance the evaluative pieces, found in chapters three, four, five and eight, have as their primary aim the evaluation of particular forms of higher education activity. The interpretive works meanwhile aim to contribute more generally to our understanding of particular issues and processes – see chapters six, seven, nine and ten. The critical works – see chapters one, two and six – are inevitably evaluative and interpretive, but their focus is more specifically on questions, and the questioning, of power, politics and interest.

More substantively we have arranged the book in three sections that reflect the three primary fields of activity and research into higher education – student learning, teaching practice and management and organization. Each of the chapters in these sections explores a contemporary and, we think, compelling issue in these fields. The remainder of this introduction briefly introduces each of these chapters.

In part I section the chapters explore four key issues in the broad field of student learning. In each case student learning is not treated as an insular process internal to the university. Rather it is explored in relation to, industrial decline, academic disciplines, part-time paid work by full time students, and graduate employment.

Beginning with a deliberately broad view of student learning in higher education, chapter one provides a compelling picture of the place of higher education in the social and economic history of a small community. Here Jane Jensen's analysis of life history interviews highlights the importance of higher education for social and economic mobility against the backdrop of industrial decline. At the same time her research identifies the dilemmas for people and the consequences for communities of this higher learning. A key consequence is that it seemingly contributes – like the decline in traditional industry – to the demise of small communities, and the decline of people's local ties to family and community.

Chapter two meanwhile moves to explore learning practices within the university. Here Moragh Paxton provides a detailed textual analysis of student assignments from an economics course. Through this she brings to light the complex discursive processes by which students 'learn' a subject. By counter posing the assignment work of two students, one who embraces the ideational resources provided by this academic discipline, and the other who attempts to import resources from other disciplines to counter this discipline's claims, the chapter is able to highlight in a detailed way the political nature of higher education learning.

Chapters three and four investigate the links between student learning and the external working lives of students and graduates. In chapter three Catherine Watts explores the characteristics, and evaluates the effects for full-time students, of part-time paid work. Chapter four turns to the relations between student learning and their subsequent experiences in full-time employment. This chapter at the same time provides an example of a piece of action research whose aim was to connect organizational change within one university and labour market restructuring.

The three chapters in part II explore teaching practices. Tom Phillips opens with a careful self-ethnography of his own teaching practice. Here he highlights incisively one of perhaps the most taken-for-granted feature of teaching – that it is a rhetorical and often dramatic performance. Chapter six meanwhile turns to compare teaching practices between academic disciplines. In this case Sara Delamont discusses the strong differences between disciplines with respect to PhD supervision. And given these differences, it is perhaps not surprising that we find in the last chapter of this section research that highlights the intense difficulties of producing cross-disciplinary teaching activities in response to external and institutional pressure.

This last chapter leads us neatly to part III on the management and organization of higher education. Again our selection of chapters here has been driven by our concern to reflect in this collection some of the more difficult and current issues confronting higher education. Given this it is unsurprising perhaps that this section opens with research into the effectiveness of quality audit processes. Chapter eight, from Veerle Hulpiau and Kim Waeytens, offers what might be regarded as a detailed analysis of the relative failure of external audit processes to influence internal institutional processes which could be said to bear on teaching quality. To explain this lack of action the chapter draws on a sophisticated multiple perspective analytical framework and concludes by offering a series of pointers as to how change with respect to improving such linkages between audit and institutional processes might be directed. Change, meanwhile, is at the core of chapter nine. Here David I. Bell provides a detailed discursive analysis of interviews with vice-chancellors from South Africa's historically black universities. Set in the context of post-apartheid political aspirations and education policy the chapter asks to what extent the transformational discourse at the core of post-apartheid agenda appears in the perceptions of institutional leaders. The results provide an interesting commentary on the contextual nature of university leadership. The final chapter in this section and indeed the collection turns to the relations between universities, their locales and local stakeholders. Here Tony Potts provides an analysis of interviews with local civic leaders, and plots the multiple and at points contradictory dimensions of the university's relations with its nearest neighbours. The chapter highlights how universities in their post-industrial massified forms have become important sources of economic stability and even growth for local communities. At the same time local communities look to universities to provide more traditional forms of inputs in the form of locally-related research and teaching activity. This, inevitably, can run counter to both the national and international agendas by which universities garner legitimacy and support. By returning to issues of the contribution of universities to local communities this last chapter turns us, in some respects, to the issues raised in the first chapter of the collection. Likewise we hope that this collection will also make a contribution to our own community. In this we include the community of researchers and practitioners engaged in the close up analysis and development of higher education.

References

Atkinson, E. (2000), In Defence of Ideas, or why 'what works' is not enough. *British Journal of Sociology of Education*, vol. 21(3), pp. 317-330.

Ball, S. (2001), 'You've been NERFed!' Dumbing down the academy: National Educational Research Forum: 'a national strategy - consultation paper': a brief and bilious response. *Journal of Education Policy*, vol. 16(3), pp. 265-268.

Bauman, Z. (1997), Universities: Old, New and Different. In A. Smith and F. Webster (eds) *The Postmodern University?: Contested Visions of Higher Education in Society*. Buckingham: Open University Press/SRHE, pp. 17-26.

Becher, T. (1989), *Academic Tribes and Territories*. Buckingham: Open University Press/SRHE.

Becker, H. S. (1990), Generalising from Case Studies, in E. Eisner and A. Peshkin (eds) *Qualitative Inquiry in Education*. New York: Teachers' College Press.

Corrigan, P. (1981), *Schooling the Smash Street Kids*. London: Macmillan.

Cuthbert, R. (ed.) (1996), *Working in Higher Education*. Buckingham: Open University Press/SRHE.

Finch, J. (1986), *Research and Policy: the uses of qualitative methods in social and educational research*. Lewes: Falmer.

Hammersley, M. (1997), Educational Research and Teaching: a response to David Hargreaves' TTA lecture. *British Educational Research Journal*, vol. 23(2), pp. 141-162.

Hammersley, M. Scarth, J. and Webb, S. (1985), Developing and Testing Theory: the case of research on student learning and examinations, in R. Burgess (ed.) *Issues in Educational Research: qualitative methods*. Lewes: Falmer.

LeCompte, M. (1979), Less Than Meets the Eye. in M. Wax (ed.) *Desegregated Schools: an intimate portrait based on five ethnographic studies*. Washington DC: National Institute of Education.

Lester, J. P. et al (1987), Public Policy Implementation: evolution of the filed and agenda for future research, *Policy Studies Review*, vol. 7(1), pp. 200-216.

Marsh, D. and Rhodes, R. A. W. (1992), *Implementing Thatcherite Policies*. Buckingham: The Society for Research into Higher Education and Open University Press.

Noblit, G. W. and Hare, R. D. (1988), *Meta-Ethnography: synthesising qualitative studies*. Newbury Park, California: Sage.

Ozga, J. (1990), Policy Research and Policy Theory: a comment on Halpin and Fitz, *Journal of Education Policy*, vol. 5, pp. 359-362.

Rothblatt, S. (1996), Inner Life of Don-Dom, *Times Higher*, March 22, 18.

Sabatier, P. (1986), Top-Down and Bottom-Up Approaches to Policy Implementation Research, *Journal of Public Policy,* vol. 6, pp. 21-48.

Schofield, J. (1990), Increasing the Generalizablity of Case Study Research, in E. Eisner and A. Peshkin (eds) *Qualitative Inquiry in Education*. New York: Teachers' College Press.

Smyth, J. (1995), *Academic Work*. Buckingham: Open University Press/SRHE.

Society for Research into Higher Education (2001), *Response to the National Educational Research Forum Consultation*. London: SRHE.

Stake, R. (1995), *The Art of the Case Study*. Sage: London.

Stones, R. (1996), *Sociological Reasoning: towards a post-modern sociology*. London: Macmillan.

Trow, M. (1975), The Public and Private Lives of Higher Education, *Daedalus*, vol. 104, pp. 113-127.

Walford G. (1992), The Reform of Higher Education in Arnot, M. and Barton, L. *Voicing Concerns*. Wallingford: Triangle.

Walford, G. (2001), Site Selection Within Comparative Case Study and Ethnographic Research. *Compare*, vol. 31(2), pp. 151-164.

Woods, P. (1984), Ethnography and Theory Construction in Educational Research. in R. G. Burgess (ed.) *Field Methods in Educational Research*. Lewes: Falmer.

PART I
STUDENT LEARNING IN HIGHER EDUCATION

Chapter 1

Going to University: Family Histories and Post-Secondary Credentialing

Jane McEldowney Jensen

Reflection on Method: Interviewing

Getting people to talk about education is easy. There is a great deal of educational rhetoric readily available to any segment of the population and it is a safe topic of discussion. My research requires more than a discussion of the merits of education or a critique of current or past practices. I want to know how individuals' educational values are constructed and how they have changed over time. I want to know how people *feel* about education, particularly post-secondary education and learning experiences.

Life history interviews provide the opportunity to gain this kind of information. Life histories are a kind of narrative interview. We demonstrate, in the stories we tell, what we think is important and why. Narrative interviews, especially those that chronicle the shared experiences of a group of people, are a good method for exploring the cultural values of a community or organization. Excellent examples of the use of this method can be found in Barbara Myerhoff's (1992) work with Jewish seniors living in Venice Beach, California and John Bodnar's (1989) study of the closing of the Studebaker plan in South Bend, Indiana.

My ethnographic research in Cape Breton includes focused life history interviews as one of a set of methodological tools. I started each interview explaining that I wanted to understand the ways the people of the community valued post-secondary education given their own experiences and circumstances. This usually elicited blank stares or encouraging, but uncomprehending, smiles and nods. I learned in one of my first interviews to stop and say no more about schools or educational policy because one of my explanatory comments about Canada's changing policies toward retraining sent one of my interview participants off on a two-hour tirade about the coal company and workman's compensation. To avoid this kind of abstract critique of public policy and focus on individual experiences, I learned to follow my introduction by simply asking, 'When was the first time you remember learning something important?'. Every question after that was a probe to encourage the interviewee to continue his or her story of learning.

Many of the participants in my research began by talking about their pre-school childhood. These stories set the desired tone for the rest of the interview. As soon as this narrative style of interview seemed established, I would probe further about what happened after formal schooling beginning with the decision to finish high school (if that was appropriate) and then what kind of learning, formal and informal, had taken place since. I sometimes used worksheets such as maps of the town or a blank timeline to encourage discussion if the interviewee was shy or unsure of what to say. By teaching me about the town using the map or indicating on the timeline major changes in their lifetime individuals took an active role in the telling of their story. In this way I collected narratives of life experiences with learning both in and out of school.

Introduction

This chapter presents, through the histories of two extended families, how educational aspirations and attitudes toward the efficacy of education have changed from one generation to the next in Glace Bay, Nova Scotia – a Canadian coal-mining town now facing the end of an industrial economy. I follow three generations of Glace Bay residents beginning with two senior citizens who survived the labour strikes of the 1920s, their children who experienced the closing of the mines in the 1960s, and their grandchildren who face an uncertain future in an industrial region that no longer has any industry. These stories of Frank, a retired civil servant; Millie, a retired nurse; and conversations with their friends and families offer narratives that build our understanding of education and social mobility in de-industrializing communities.

Setting

The community studied is a coal-mining town on Cape Breton Island, Nova Scotia. Although much of the island is rural, the area surrounding Glace Bay was developed in the early part of the twentieth century by large coal and steel corporations located off-island, first in Britain and later in central Canada. Unlike mining in the mountains and hills of the United States, the coal and steel industry in Cape Breton has never been locally owned and operated therefore animosity between labour and management has been concentrated between local residents and external authority figures (Obermiller, P.J. and Philliber, W. W., 1994). Founded in 1901, Glace Bay originated as a company town populated by workers with a strong history of labour activism, cooperative initiatives, and economic upheaval. Glace Bay is also known for its fishing industry, primarily in-shore fishermen who harvest lobster and, until recently, cod. The decline of cod stock in the Atlantic fishery has meant substantial downsizing of fishing in the area resulting in the loss of jobs for both fishermen and those who work in local fish packing plants. In the summer of 2001, the most recent owner of the coal industry in the region, a government entity called Cape Breton Development Corporation (DEVCO), closed all of the remaining coalmines in industrial Cape Breton. By then, Glace Bay as a political unit had already ceased to exist having been amalgamated into the Municipality of Cape Breton in 1996 along with a number of neighbouring colliery communities. While small groups of individuals in Cape Breton still talk about reviving the coal industry, this story is literally about the end of an era for an industrial region.

Research Questions

My research focuses on the ways that the people of Glace Bay have interpreted the modern ideology of achievement. An achievement ideology rewards individual aspirations for success and requires confidence in the meritocratic potential of educational credentials for economic opportunity. The town of Glace Bay has had a strong heritage of solidarity and self-sufficiency that simultaneously accepts the potential of formal education while publicly eschewing individual ambitions that compete with a perceived ethic of cooperation. In interviews, residents of the town spoke proudly of the educational achievements of their children, but cynically of the potential of entrepreneurial efforts saying, 'They'll pull you down if you try to climb up'. In this chapter, I ask how this paradox of individual versus community ambition is resolved. External ownership of the coal mines and fisheries production has allowed few opportunities for the building of a diversified economy, despite the relative success of local residents. How is the hegemonic weight of an ideology of success born by a community that has been and continues to be economically marginalized? As requirements for educational credentials have changed over the last century, how has educational decision-making changed from one generation to the next? In what ways have community members' understandings of self-improvement, family, community, and knowledge changed as the mines and fisheries have closed and the government has become the primary, albeit downsizing, employer?

This study draws upon two conceptual frameworks, cultural production and theories of credentialism. These theoretical constructions overlap in the study of educational decision-making; especially in the ways individuals understand the efficacy of post-compulsory education. In contrast to studies that examine how students resist the normative structure of educational settings, I ask what happens to those individuals who *do* go along with society's rules, those who assimilate, who finish the programmes, who acquire the credentials and who sometimes succeed, but also fail. What happens to the schoolboys in Paul Willis' (1979) study of working-class children who chose to accommodate rather than resist the exchange of their mental labour for social status? What happens to the high school students in Jay MacLeod's (1995) study of an inner-city neighbourhood who dream of professional careers, but lack the resources to articulate those dreams within an educational system that has already passed them by? Unlike some students who are conscious participants in the post-secondary credentialing game for the benefit of their home communities (Brayboy, in press), I believe most individuals who acquiesce to the increasing educational requirements of the new economy are not aware of the structural inequalities inherent in that system.

This is, in fact, what defines hegemonic ideologies as 'actively constituted...in a variety of specific places' (Apple, 1982, p.12). While self-conscious, in the Marxist sense, of their working-class identity, individuals from Glace Bay seeking to survive in the 'new economy' often do not see or are not conscious of the stratification of outcomes *within* post-secondary education. Gray (in Hogan, 1982) might refer to this as the way 'subordinate classes follow a "negotiated version" of ruling-class values' (p. 37). In other words, individuals who are successful in the educational system but who do not recognize the hidden curriculum of status within that system may find themselves with educational credentials that are ill-suited to their local economy or inadequate for finding dignified work, despite the promise of those credentials.

What happens to those who succeed at school and manage to climb the ladder, if only a little? What happens to those who experience educational success, but then fail to succeed economically or to use that education in ways that are meaningful to them? In places where deindustrialization has resulted in severe economic stress and politicians and educators alike offer education or retraining as the solution, these questions are particularly important. In Glace Bay, as increasing numbers of each generation have achieved progressively higher educational credentials, concurrent economic success has occurred for some but not all players. Higher education thus reproduces social stratification by increasing the social and economic capital of some more than others. At the same time, however, higher education provides an opportunity to overcome that stratification thus reasserting the relative truth of the ideology of success.

Methods

I completed the main body of fieldwork for this study in 1995 with follow-up visits to Glace Bay over the last five years. Based on twelve months of ethnographic fieldwork, my research includes participant observation, focused life history interviews, and historical document reviews. This chapter reflects the intersection of biography and history wherein we learn not only what residents believed to have happened in their town, but also what they were doing at the time – the decisions they made and the ways that they interpreted the options and obstacles before them.[1] I recruited individuals for interviews through a variety of methods. These included snowball sampling (following one lead to the next, especially from one family member to the next), and convenience sampling (seizing opportunities to talk to local residents in public venues such as coffee shops, the library, the bingo halls, my landlady's kitchen, etc.). I also contacted alumni from one of the two high schools in town (now consolidated into one institution) from a reunion mailing list. Using this fieldwork and interviews, I created, for this chapter, two fictitious

---

[1] See Watson, L. and Watson-Franke, M.B. (1985) for a discussion of the use of life history interviews.

families. These are composite families, made up of pieces of stories of real individuals who are not related. They are, however, family histories that would be familiar to any Glace Bay resident. They are representative of the kinds of family stories I heard and recorded. Pseudonyms and slight changes to the facts are intended to protect the privacy of these citizens.

Visiting Frank

I first met Frank in his home, a renovated company house two blocks away from the house in which he had lived most of his life. Frank went to St. John's Elementary School in the neighbourhood of New Aberdeen and then to St. Anne's High School in the 1930s. To get to school, Frank and his brothers crossed the cluster of streets that made up his neighbourhood; past another community called Tablehead, and finally up Chapell Hill. Glace Bay is made up of over fifteen such neighbourhoods, most of which once surrounded mine heads, the tops of 'deeps' tunnelling beneath the town's streets and out under the Atlantic ocean into one of three coal seams that wrap the southeastern shore of Cape Breton Island. When Frank was in school, miners, fishermen, and their families populated the town. Some merchants lived near their small businesses, but most professionals and managers lived in Sydney about twenty minutes away on today's roads.

Frank did not finish high school. As a teenager, he worked in a bootleg mine, one of many small enterprises dug into the cliffs surrounding the town or burrowed down from a mine head hidden in a backyard shed. I asked why the company allowed these bootleg mines to continue and he laughed.

> They [company officials] would come and blow up the entrance every once in a while, but it only took a few days to get back to where you were before. We'd steal timbers from the company and some of the older miners would check our work and make sure we were keeping our lines straight and safe.

When he was seventeen, Frank went with his father and brothers to sign on with the coal company. 'I tried several times to get on at the mine', Frank said, 'but with three brothers and a father in the mine, I think they thought that was enough from one family'. While listening, I realized that Frank had told this story many times. For a man of his age, growing up in a company house, in a company town, to have avoided a life in the mine required explanation. It had not been his choice to avoid the mine, his story told, but that of the mine managers. If he had not had three older brothers or if the overmen (on site supervisors) had been more pressed for labour he might have become a professional miner. Given different circumstances, he might have begun a job that would require him to work twelve hour days (or more), going to and from work in darkness most of the year, with very little pay or time off, in dangerous working conditions. If he had become a miner, he might have joined a fraternity that offered a common bond with the men in his family and community. Frank talked about that bond wistfully.

Instead of going into the deeps, Frank went into the Navy in the fall of 1936. Six months later he was sent to Europe as part of the Canadian fleet sent to protect the English Channel. Although of the age to enlist, his brothers stayed in the mine. Coal was needed for the war effort and many Cape Breton miners were asked to stay on their jobs, despite their willingness to serve overseas. In fact, the need for coal required them to work even harder, despite the low pay and working conditions. After almost thirty years of largely unsuccessful union activity and strikes against the absentee coal company management, any movement to strike was squelched by the weight of patriotism. Union activism in the mines became an abstract ideal engineered by organizers outside of the area resulting in a stronger union organization (the United Mine Workers), but relinquishing the fight for better conditions to the progress of time and technology. Of Frank's three brothers, two remained underground miners until they retired, and one became a diesel mechanic at the steel mill in Sydney.

When he returned from the war, Frank took the civil service exam. 'I had the second highest score that year', he told me proudly. He went to work for the government and stayed in that civil service until his retirement in the 1980s. Frank was ahead of his time. In 1950, when he was 35 years old, the town population was 23,000. 12,000 of those people were miners. Frank worked above ground in a clean job that paid decently and allowed him to come and go from work in daylight most of the year. His work experience was categorically different from that of the other men in his family, his classmates at school, and most of the men in his neighbourhood. Coal was king in Glace Bay during this time and Frank talked about the miners coming home shoulder to shoulder across the sidewalks, packing the town on Saturday night, providing most of the coal for Nova Scotia and Central Canada. 25 years later, however, the town population was still over 20,000 but only 3000 men worked in the mines. Frank's brother and son were laid off as the mines closed. Frank had been promoted. He was one of a growing number of people who worked for the government in civil and social service jobs; above ground jobs that paid decently, although not extravagantly, and offered few occupational hazards. Frank was lucky here too, retiring just before major downsizing occurred in government jobs in the 1980s and 1990s.

Despite his very different career path, Frank was typical of many Glace Bay residents in his generation. He was an avid reader.[2] He pushed his seven children to finish school, citing his Scottish heritage as giving him respect for learning. He worked hard and saved enough to improve his home in New Aberdeen and buy a summer bungalow on the Mira River. He kept his family as close as he could, but mourned the fact that most of his children lived away in Central and Western Canada. He followed local politics closely and kept up with local gossip sitting with his friends, many of them old school friends, down at the Tim Horton's coffee

---

[2] I conducted a survey of patrons at the Glace Bay Library, finding that they represented an even sample of residents including all economic and occupational groups. Their answers to questions regarding reading habits among their families and friends indicated a strong value for reading in the town.

shop. He complained about the closing of St. Joseph's hospital and what he called a decline in medical services, but applauded the building of a new high school that he believes will help close the gap between Catholics and Protestants in the town. And he told stories of the old days: the pit ponies, the strikes, the bootleg mines, and the days when miners filled the sidewalks of the town shoulder to shoulder with blackened faces on their way home from work.

Frank spoke proudly of his nine children. Two died as young men, one in the Navy and the other in a fishing accident. Three of his daughters have college degrees and live away. Two others went to work in the Northwest Territories after high school and still live out west. One son went to work for the company after dropping out of a training programme and one lives nearby and works as a hospital administrator. I asked Frank what he thought the future held for his grandchildren who live in Cape Breton. He sighed and said:

> When I was growing up, I thought we were as worse off as anyone, but the young people now have it worse. We had anarchy, burning the pluck-me stores, soldiers in the streets, and the labour wars, but now the prospects for work are so bad. It's not just political but economic. It's even harder for people to deal.

Frank spoke with pride when describing the history of his town, but with frustration when talking about its future. He was most upset when talking about the lack of opportunities for young people in the town and the ways that many of his children's generation find it difficult to come home.

Millie's Story

Millie lived on the other side of town from Frank in a new house, built for her by her son (a doctor) but still less than a mile from the company house in which she grew up. Eastern European Jews, Millie's family lived in a neighbourhood that was a mix of nationalities: Italian, Belarussian, Polish, and Ukrainian. Although it did not have a reputation for being culturally different, community clubs in the language and culture of the European immigrants' home regions were more persistent on Millie's side of town than Frank's neighbourhood. Most of the houses in Glace Bay are company structures like Frank's, clustered together in rows on numbered streets around the mine heads, and sold to their owners by the coal company in the 1960s. In contrast, newer houses like Millie's popped up along the connecting roads between the mines and on the roads leading out of town, creating suburban streets of split-level ranches and colonials between the older neighbourhoods.

Millie's father had been a clerk at a company store in Caledonia, one of the oldest mines in Glace Bay. Millie's family was luckier than most as her father's job in the store made him less likely to be laid off by the company during strikes and downsizing. She was visibly upset, however, when she talked about the strikes of her childhood when the coal company put families in her neighbourhood out in the street and how many of her classmates were often hungry. Millie graduated in 1939 from Morrison High School, the public school that served most of the non-Catholic students in town. She went to nursing school in Montreal for a year and then returned to train on-the-job at the public hospital on South Street.

Millie was proud of her education and her family. 'When you went to college in the forties', she began, 'it was a big deal! My mother stood on the step of the house and cried!'. She went on to talk about how important it had been to her to 'get out' of Glace Bay. 'I couldn't wait! To get away from this close knit clannishness.' Millie spoke both fondly and with bitterness about the closeness of her family and those of her neighbours. She explained that what she called clannishness extended beyond the Scottish families that made up the largest ethnic group in the town and reduced the antagonism that might have existed between ethnic and religious groups. 'It helped us survive', she exclaimed. 'We knew too much to ignore each other's pain.'

Millie and her sisters and brothers all went to college, which was somewhat unusual, but not unheard of in Glace Bay. Two of her sisters became teachers, one brother moved away to 'the Boston States' and went into business and the other became a doctor. 'My parents lived for three things: food, shelter, and education', she exclaimed. Millie and her husband, a clerk for the coal company, carried on this educational tradition sending their son to college in Halifax and later on to medical school in New York. Their daughter also went to college, but dropped out of school and works in Sydney for a training company.

In addition to her nursing, Millie was active in community outreach, sometimes working with extension workers from 'Little X' in Sydney, the junior college campus of St. Francis Xavier University in Antigonish. At the time, both the Catholic Church and the labour movement supported grassroots educational activities based on a philosophy of cooperation. Later called the Antigonish Movement, Millie worked with the people's school that taught grass-roots development and self-help programmes, especially literacy, home economics, and the benefits of cooperatives. Millie talked about how she appreciated the principles implied by the popular education movement. 'The principles of self dignity are still important', Millie sighed, 'just harder to place in today's world'. I asked Millie the same questions about the future that I asked of Frank. She responded that she had recently had the same conversation with her sisters now living in Boston:

> When my sisters ask me 'Mil, what are they doing in Glace Bay?' I say, 'It's a welfare state'. They can't believe it.

Frank and Millie lived through the period of the town's history when immigrants struggled with the company and children were sent to school with the hopes of getting them out of the mines and into something better. They both remembered those hard days fondly, with more than a little nostalgia. This is typical in Glace Bay where any introduction to the town is a history lesson. Frank and Millie's stories also reinforce the notion that for this generation, post-secondary education was an opportunity rather than a necessity. While the costs of attending college were significant, they were not insurmountable. One of Frank and Millie's peers explained how booster clubs, local community organizations, and the

Catholic Church would often provide the scholarships young people needed to continue their education.[3] Ethnicity played a role in family values toward education, but differences in the type of education pursued (university degrees versus technical certification for example) were not as stratified for this generation as they would later become. For this town of immigrants, the emphasis was on survival.

Frank and Millie also both commented on the working-class nature of the town. When I asked how it was possible for almost everyone to describe themselves as 'working-class' despite census evidence of some affluence in the town today, they referred me back to the town's history. 'We had to pull together to survive', Millie explained, 'and now that things are better, we still identify with that'. Frank was a little more cynical:

> The union meetings used to be entertainment for people. There was nothing else to do. You see? Now there's some that have pools in the backyard and TVs in every room and some that don't, but we got in the habit of saying we're all the same, that we're all together. We cling to that now even if it means dragging the young ones down with us.

For Glace Bay residents in Frank and Millie's generation, the idea of community and solidarity is easier to uphold than in today's climate of haves and have nots. Despite her education and training, Millie feels comfortable in her card group. Frank is a regular down at the donut shop waxing eloquently about Maritime history with friends who went to university and friends who dropped out of grade school to go into the mines. Their children, however, have a more difficult time maintaining that sense of place.

Teachers, Nurses, Miners, and the Pogie

Frank and Millie's children came of age in a very different economy. Coal was still 'king', but the mines were closing. New technology in the mines reduced the number of miners needed and required more technical training for those who continued to work the deeps. The professionalization of nursing and teaching meant more credentials were necessary to be eligible for jobs. Increases in government services – education, healthcare, and social services meant new kinds of jobs, but not enough for all of Glace Bay's children. Perhaps most importantly, changes in the local labour market from industry to service meant that different kinds of social norms were expected of Glace Bay workers. Not only forced to leave physically to find work, Frank and Millie's children's generation often had to

---

[3] I have not, due to the constraints of space, highlighted the differences between American and Canadian higher education. There are many similarities, especially with regard to the extent of support by civic organizations for scholarships that offsets the rigidity of class lines more common in the UK and Europe (Axelrod, 1990; Lipset, 1990).

'leave' behind the social norms of their parents, or juggle between two worlds in order to be successful on the job.

These changes in the job market affected Frank and Millie's peers as well as their children. Frank and Millie's friends and classmates had already established themselves in their career paths when the mines started to close. When the shut downs started, many took their families and moved away to find work in the mills and plants of Central Canada and the United States where their versatile skills were appreciated. To offset the displacement of workers, the Canadian government sponsored retraining programmes and grant projects such as the excavation and building of the historic Fortress at Louisbourg. A small group of government-sponsored miners went to university and became teachers. Thus, at least two generations faced the closing of the mines in the 1960s and 1970s: immigrants to Glace Bay who had not yet retired, and the children of the town's founding population. The older generation had to relocate or retool and the younger generation had to imagine what a future without coal might hold.

Frank's son Dave described his high school years in the late 1950s as full of excitement. His was the first class at the new St. Michael's High School and there were new post-secondary institutions and programmes opening in the area. Economic times were tough, however, and he credited the threat of mine closures as part of the excitement for his peer group:

> We were on a wave. Our parents were afraid for us because everything was changing, but to us it seemed like there was so much possibility. We didn't have the choice of 'the mines or else' that our fathers had. Maybe because there was nothing here we felt like anything could happen!

Dave went on to talk about how his younger siblings who went to high school after the takeover of the mines and steel mill by the government in the 1970s did not have the same excitement. 'They were passive about everything', he said. In fact, his younger siblings were less successful in school; only one finished college and two of the others barely finished secondary. By the time they reached high school, the king was dead and the government was bailing out the coal company. This marks the beginning of the region's dependency on government transfer payments, subsidies, and grants.

Dave and his classmates faced a very different set of educational choices when they came of age than Millie and Frank. Graduating from high school in the 1950s and 1960s, they had access to the junior college in Sydney, opportunities for technical education at a government technical college, and the choice of a variety of new proprietary training institutions. Although they still had to leave Cape Breton to complete a four-year degree, government funding for post-secondary education was increasing and local institutions provided more options to more students. Employment was a problem, however. The traditional occupations in Glace Bay required more education than in Frank and Millie's day and there were fewer jobs to be had. Many of Dave's generation left Glace Bay – some before finishing high school. There were jobs in the factories in central Canada and in the fledgling oil industry of western Canada. Job opportunities were also available in the Northwest Territories. Many students, however, chose to stay in school and use education to help them find work at home. These students became the teachers, nurses, and government workers raising their families in Glace Bay today.

The 'Aspirations' page of Morrison High School's 1957 yearbook lists social work, teaching, nursing, secretarial, accounting, engineering, law enforcement, and the military as the dreams of its senior class. Frank's son, Dave, who went to parochial St. Michael's High School, about the same time, agreed that the list also represented his group's goals although he admitted wryly that students at Morrison had better test scores for getting into university than St. Michael's students. Dave went away to college and later finished a Masters in Public Administration in Toronto. He returned to work in Cape Breton when his mother died to be closer to his father, taking a cut in pay to do so. Dave came home, but only in part. Because his job required a different set of values than those used in community spaces like the coffee shop and legion hall, Dave talked about sometimes feeling like an outsider in his own hometown.

Dave's sister Karen went to teacher's college a few years after Dave left home. She also talked about the excitement she felt as a high school senior. 'There was doom and gloom every day in the papers', she explained, 'but we were as good as anyone!'. She talked about the number of teachers across Canada from Cape Breton. 'We went [to university] to get out, but we also wanted to come home again someday. Teaching made leaving possible, but some of us never came home.' For example, Karen's friend Trudy still lives in Toronto. Trudy talked about living away from the island:

> It was pretty lonesome at first. Most of our friends are Maritimers or from BC [British Columbia]. We talk about moving back, but if we hadn't left when we did, our children would have left us. We go home every two or three years, usually during lobster season.

Trudy believed that she and her husband, who works for the RCMP, would eventually retire to Cape Breton, but not to Glace Bay. 'We'll get a nice country house on the lake', she mused admitting her reluctance to be 'so close' to her old neighbourhood, but wanting to be home in Cape Breton.

Millie's daughter Rachel graduated from Morrison High School in the early 1960s and went away to an American college. She dropped out when she couldn't 'find herself'. 'I went because I was expected to, but I didn't know what I wanted to do', she explained, 'and I missed being home'. Returning to Nova Scotia Rachel went to work for a proprietary school first in Halifax and later in Cape Breton conducting life skills training courses. Her company provided upgrading and skills classes for government clients and was known for being 'on the inside' of economic development initiatives.

Rachel talked about her mother's interest in the cooperative movement and how it affected her desire to pursue a career that included 'helping people'. I asked if she had ever wanted to go back to school and become an educator and she shook her head and said that she had attended workshops on entrepreneurship and marketing. 'Training people without teaching them how to think like business people doesn't change things', she said. 'As an educator I can do more to help my students if I have the business know-how than I would if I just taught them subjects.' Rachel's job requires her to develop partnerships with businesses and she stated she was interested in building entrepreneurship programmes in schools. 'They [the children] need to learn independence. Their parents are too far gone in the dependency mind frame.' Rachel clearly distinguished between status groups saying 'us' when referring to her family and business colleagues and 'them' when referring to her clients, often under-educated adults receiving government assistance. Despite her own lack of post-secondary credentials, Rachel seemed to feel confident in her ability to navigate the world of business education.

Rachel's older brother Josh also talked about wanting to work in a field where he could 'help people'. He finished medical school in the United States and then returned to Nova Scotia after working in central Canada for ten years. We talked about his decision to go to college and his decision to go on to medical school. 'I always knew I'd go on', he said. He did not think of himself as an overly academic student or particularly successful, but he reflected on the differences between his family and those of his classmates:

> In the old days, the people were self-educated. They would discuss politics, listen to the radio, and follow the union debates. It didn't matter whether my mother went to college or not...her friends were just as educated from books and conversation as she was. But they [his parents] pushed at us, and some of the people I went to school with didn't get pushed. That made a difference.

Alistair, a friend of Josh's, gave another perspective on the influence of family. When he wanted to excel academically, his father objected to his academic interests. 'My dad used to say, "University is for doctor and lawyer's sons"', Alistair explained. 'My dad didn't come to my graduation', Alistair added quietly, 'he said that reading and studying would just make it harder to go into the mines when the time came'. He said his mother, however, would have 'done anything' to help him achieve his dreams and she supported his efforts to go to college and later graduate school. Josh and Alistair were in high school when working in the mines was still possible – assuming you could get into the company's apprenticeship training programme. Both felt lucky to have mothers who pushed them to continue their education, but they made these choices in a climate that did not always encourage formal post-secondary educational ambitions. Although many of Josh and Alistair's classmates and their parents had finished high school and valued post-secondary education, there were still many residents who had not.

For example, unlike the group described above, Frank's nephew John did not go on to college. He dropped out of high school and went to Ontario to work for a tool and die plant with a group of his classmates. Later, a friend from Glace Bay encouraged him to come back and he went to work for the coal company in 1972. The mine he was working closed, and John went to work for the steel mill with Frank's youngest son until they were both laid off in 1989. Unemployed since that time, when we spoke he was working a variety of odd jobs and occasionally crewing on a lobster boat. Trained on-the-job and through upgrading classes at the

Adult Vocational Training Center (AVTC), John is a licensed diesel mechanic and can run a variety of heavy equipment. Divorced, he lives with his ageing father and mother and helps supplement their pension income. John laughed when I asked him about leaving to find work. 'I guess you could say I'm one of them Cape Bretoners who just likes living on the pogie [unemployment]', he joked. In all seriousness, he talked about wanting to stay close to his children and parents and how he did not think that he could do any better living away. 'I'm from the Bay, you see and here that means something. There, I'd just be another John.' I asked about whether he thought he might return to school. 'For what?' he answered, 'I'd only get a degree that I'd have to use away and I'm too old to become something I'm not'.

The cultural capital of some of the first wave of immigrants – a love of reading, belief in the efficacy of formal education, and an appreciation for seeking out knowledge – has become economic and social capital for their children. With their degrees, Dave, Karen, Josh, and Rachel participate in a wide system that includes physical as well as social mobility. In many ways they are always leaving even if they live at home. They have to navigate between the different cultures of their professional work and their local community. John, however, makes the conscious choice to stay in Glace Bay. He rejects opportunities for continuing his education and maintains deep local ties.

The High School on the Highway

Millie and Frank's grandchildren have grown up in an industrial Cape Breton that has little to no industry. While a certain percentage of every generation has always left the island to find work and seek broader opportunities, the continuing severity of the economic conditions in Cape Breton means that a larger and larger portion of young people have been forced to leave or face unemployment. As the perceived efficacy of post-secondary credentials for local work has declined, cynicism about and, in some cases, resistance to external requirements for education have increased. Students in the class of 1995 at Glace Bay High School responded 'we have to go' and 'it's required now' in answer to my questions about their post-secondary aspirations.[4] When referring to the University College of Cape Breton, Millie's granddaughter talked unenthusiastically about going to the 'high-school on the highway' and then away to find work. For her, post-secondary education was a necessary next step after high school rather than the opportunity it was for her

---

[4] I surveyed 98 juniors and seniors at Glace Bay High School in the spring of 1995. As a result of scheduling, these students were a mix of both the general (college prep) and careers (vocational) programmes. I asked whether I was missing any particular group of students using this method and was told that the only students not in those study hall classes were those out sick that day. Further conversations with parents of low-income students revealed that a number of students would have been suspended or on probation, thus this survey probably did miss some students most at risk of not completing high school.

grandmother and father. Many of her classmates said they would 'have to go away', but that they also wanted to return someday.

The pressure to acquire credentials and perhaps leave the island is not restricted to young adults. Frank's youngest son, now in his late forties, told of attending mandatory 'life-skills development' sessions after he and his cousin John were laid off from the steel mill in the early 1990s. For him, further education became a prescription rather than the personal pursuit of knowledge his father enjoyed.

The career aspirations of young people in industrial Cape Breton have not changed since their parents graduated from high school. The table below shows the similarities in aspirations from one generation to the next.

Table 1.1 Student career aspirations

Glace Bay H.S. 1995 & 1996 Student Survey	Morrison H.S. 1957 Year Book
social work	social work
teaching	teaching
nursing/medicine	nursing/medicine
secretarial	secretarial/accounting
law, criminal justice	RCMP (police)/law
trade (electrician, plumber, etc.)	engineer/electrician
business	military

The most popular choices for both generations were those in the social services (teaching and nursing) and in some kind of business. What has changed, however, are the educational requirements to succeed in these jobs and the potential for employment in these fields locally. Successful college graduates continue to leave Cape Breton to find work – even those who planned on staying. If post-secondary education no longer provides opportunities to be successful in Cape Breton, what new roles does post-secondary education play today?

Conclusion

During the first half of the twentieth century, education did reproduce social differences in Glace Bay, but because of the similarities in circumstances from one immigrant family to the next, the playing field was remarkably level. For Glace Bay residents, the changing educational requirements in the job market played a far greater role than the economic and social capital of families in the ways that economic inequality came to be produced. With each generation the symbolic claims of educational credentials, especially those of four-year liberal arts degrees and graduate professional education became more and more economically valuable. Millie and Frank's families were more successful than many of their neighbours not because of differences in their positions within the production of capital, but because their family values for education were rewarded in later generations when credentials became valued commodities. Ethnicity and religious affiliation influences these values. But within these groups differences are similar to differences between groups. This indicates that the economic context in which individuals made decisions has remained primary.[5]

The crucial shift, it seems, for this community, came during the 1960s when the economy made a dramatic swing away from coal mining and the state began to play a leading role in economic development. It was at this moment that post-secondary education not only became more accessible but also more important to getting and maintaining positions within the bureaucratic cultures of teaching, nursing, and government agencies – the most stable occupations available in the area. This shift also meant balancing a community-based knowledge system useful for negotiating everyday interactions in Glace Bay with a wider sense of 'the game' in the new economy. Frank and Millie's children, while pursuing the credentials and economic mobility of a de-industrializing economy still tried to define themselves within the local structures of family, neighbourhood, and community– even when living 'away'. Frank and Millie's grandchildren, however, share less of that loyalty to place. Their success is measured more and more by their ability to play the global game rather than the local.

I end this generational analysis with the story of Frank's granddaughter, Amelia. Amelia, of all the characters introduced here, has reached the most transformational of results from her educational experiences. Amelia's father did not go to college, but at her uncle's prodding she finished high school and attended a year of college at the Nova Scotia School of Design. When her Celtic inspired creations started selling in galleries across North America, she dropped out of college and moved back to Cape Breton. For this young woman, the commodification of heritage, especially the folk heritage of the Gaelic highlanders of Cape Breton, has produced a market in which creative ability and craftsmanship are once again rewarded over institutional credentials.

Unlike her cousins, Amelia's entrepreneurship, despite her lack of educational credentials, has made it possible for her to stay in Cape Breton. She uses the sensibilities of middle-class cultural consumerism to find success. The educational credentials of others, which contribute to their participation in 'the game' of the larger economy, also contribute to the success of a consumer heritage industry in Cape Breton. With an ironic ethnographic twist, Amelia is able to make the familiar cultural symbols of Cape Breton 'strange' and valuable – and make a living despite her lack of post-secondary credentials. As towns like Glace Bay become

---

[5] The Jewish community is perhaps the exception in that almost all of the Jewish families in town sent their children on to post-secondary education. Their success, however, resulted in their disappearance as members of the community as there are no Jewish children left in Glace Bay schools; their successful parents are living away in places where their credentials can be used.

further marginalized economically by the closing of the last of the coalmines in the area, successful citizens begin to align themselves with the more romantic image of Cape Breton and reduce their allegiance to 'the Bay'. Amelia is successful in this climate because of her cultural capital, her ability to 'read' and reproduce that romantic Cape Breton image.

Each generation of Glace Bay families have achieved successively higher educational credentials but the quality of those credentials has not remained constant. Some individuals have received educational experiences that have provided economic and social capital in the form of professional careers and entrepreneurial opportunities. Others have received training that allows them to compete for specific jobs, but is useless if those jobs are scarce. In earlier generations these differences were less noticeable, but with changes in the economy, some post-secondary graduates fare better than others. The efficacy of post-secondary education does not seem to be in question, although it is clear that the hierarchy of degrees, certificates, and 'life-skills' diplomas offer very different opportunities.

So what happens to those that succeed in post-secondary education? It depends. It depends on the kind of degree they attain and what they are able to do with it. Post-secondary education is a requirement in today's economy. Security, however, also requires a willingness to be mobile, a loyalty to vocation or profession rather than place. The acquisition of post-secondary credentials does not, in itself, change economic conditions; therefore, success for the individual does not necessarily mean success for the community unless that individual success is accompanied by structural changes. The ideology of success is based on an individual not community development. Therefore this story raises questions of what happens to communities like Glace Bay when success means leaving. Amelia's experience may provide one hopeful answer. By recognizing the value of their island home in a global context, the descendents of this coal mining community may be able to imagine a future for themselves as members of a regional economy that keeps rather than exports its human capital.

References

Apple, M.W. (1982), 'Reproduction and Contradiction in Education: An Introduction' in M. Apple (ed.), *Cultural and Economic Reproduction in Education: Essays on Class, Ideology, and the State*, Routledge, Boston.

Axelrod, P. (1990), *Making a Middle-class: Student Life in English Canada During the Thirties*, McGill-Queen's University Press, Montreal.

Bodnar, J. (1989), 'Power and Memory in Oral History: Workers and Managers at Studebaker', *The Journal of American History, vol. 75*(4), pp. 1201-1221.

Brayboy, B. (2001), Playing in the Ivy: American Indian Ivy League college graduates use of capital for empowerment and liberation. Paper presented at the *Higher Education Close Up-2* Conference in Lancaster, England.

Hogan, D. (1982), 'Education and Class Formation: The Peculiarities of the Americans' in M. Apple (ed.), *Cultural and Economic Reproduction in Education: Essays on Class, Ideology, and the State*, Routledge, Boston.

Lipset, S.M. (1990), *Continental Divide: The Values and Institutions of the United States and Canada*, Routledge, New York.

MacLeod, J. (1995), *Ain't no makin' it: Aspirations and attainment in a low-income neighbourhood*, Boulder, CO: Westview Press.

Myerhoff, B. (1992), *Remembering lives: The work of ritual, storytelling, and growing older*, Ann Arbor, MI: University of Michigan Press.

Obermiller, P.J. and Philliber, W.W. (1994), *Appalachia in an international context: Cross-national comparisons of developing regions*, Westport, CT: Praeger Publishing.

Watson, L. and Watson-Franke, M.B. (1985), *Interpreting Life Histories: an Anthropological Inquiry*, Rutgers University Press, New Brunswick, NJ.

Willis, P. (1977), *Learning to Labor*, Gower, Aldershot.

Chapter 2

Ways in which Students Gain Access to University Discourses: The Intersection of the Academic Curriculum with Student Voices

Moragh Paxton

Reflection on Method: Analysis

Linguistically oriented discourse analysis along Hallidayan lines is a powerful tool. It has allowed me to 'get inside' the texts to analyze the patterns in the language and to begin to identify the connections between form and meaning. However, I cannot assume that my interpretations and assumptions are correct. Many of the case study students come from very different sociocultural contexts and I need to be asking questions about who they are and why they are using language in particular ways. Attempting to answer questions like these would be impossible without reference to the students themselves, who when prompted, have been able to explain and interpret aspects of their texts. Therefore the students have become partners in the research process. One student, Sizwe himself has been able to explain his intertextual references such as his use of the hunting metaphor in the first paragraph of his economics assignment or his difficulty in achieving coherence when he was drawing on information from a variety of different websites. This has provided me with critical insights into the process of production of his text and the context in which it was produced (Figure 2.1 Fairclough's middle layer).

Secondly, the analysis needs to be linked to the broader dimensions of society (Fairclough's outer layer). This is particularly important in the South African context where students' difficulties with English and with academic writing are often a consequence of language inequality and apartheid schooling. Therefore I have interviewed students about their home and school background to develop a richer understanding of their socio-cultural histories. I am interested then in whether the academic context serves to further disempower these students. Does the academic register serve the interests of only the powerful group in universities and in society and does this mean that these learners are marginalized? Whose interests are being served by curriculum design and choice of textbooks? In order to find the answers to these questions it has been necessary to understand the politics of the institution, the faculty and the department and to get insights into the power play behind their decisions. This has meant interviewing key decision makers in the economics department and beyond.

What makes Fairclough's work powerful is that he has brought a linguistic perspective to discourse and social theory. Also he provides multiple points of entry for analysis – description of the textual analysis, interpretation of the analysis assisted by students themselves and explanation in terms of the wider social context. However, critical discourse analysis (CDA) has been critiqued by Blommaert (2001) because he says the treatment of context in some CDA work could be regarded as largely backgrounding and narrative. Blommaert feels that contextual information that needs critical scrutiny is often simply accepted as fact to frame the discourse samples that are to be analyzed; he cites examples of a priori statements on power relations, such as 'politicians are manipulators' 'power is bad' (2001: p. 15), which are used to frame the discourse analysis and says that it leads to highly simplified models of social structures and patterns of actions. In my research I have attempted to avoid this pitfall by trying to understand and critique the contexts more fully. This I believe has been achieved by lengthy interviews with the students to understand more about the social context in which they are writing as well as the social contexts from which they come. Then I have interviewed the key players in the economics department to understand decisions about teaching methodology, course content etc.

Introduction

This chapter describes the pilot study for a larger research project exploring the interaction between the academic curriculum and student voices, particularly the ways in which students from different communities and cultural practices begin the process of appropriating the discourses and cultures of the university. The project focuses on the acquisition of one particular discourse, that of economics.

In the pilot study, I identified two case studies and collected and analyzed the assignments that were the final products of an online writing project run in the second semester of the language and communications tutorials in first year economics. The pilot project will feed into the larger project, as these two case study students will be followed through their university careers and in their third year they will be asked to reflect on the process of acquisition through interviews and the writing of a literacy narrative.

The pilot looks at a snapshot rather than change over a period of time and therefore it was unable to get at the *process* of adjustment/appropriation. However, it has been very generative because, while analyzing the data for the pilot, I became interested in ways in which students begin to take on discoursal identities and in the ways in which identity is linked to learning.

The chapter is divided into four parts. Firstly, I will briefly review the literature on literacy and socio-cultural theory. Secondly I will describe the computer-based project which provided the context for the student writing which is to be analyzed. I will then describe a methodological framework for text analysis drawing on the work of Fairclough (1992) and Ivanic (1997 and 1998) and finally I draw on Ivanic's framework for analyzing two case studies.

Literature review

Much of the recent work in literacy studies has focused on developing a strong theoretical framework for understanding the socio-cultural implications of literacy. Research has shown that discourse patterns or ways of using language reflect world views or 'forms of consciousness' of particular cultures and that discourse patterns are expressions of culture and identity (Scollon and Scollon, 1981, Heath, 1983). Discourse theorists argue that change in a person's discourse patterns may involve change in identity and this may conflict with the person's initial acculturation and socialization (Gee, 1996: p.189). Students entering the university experience these conflicts as they start to become members of the new Discourses of the university and to take on new identities and they find their other social worlds are juxtaposed with the academic world (Clark and Ivanic 1998). Clark and Ivanic explore what the compromise between a personal history on the one hand and the requirements of convention and the history of the discipline means and what sorts of consequences this adjustment might have for people's sense of self (1998: p. 135). This is a fascinating framework in which to analyze the two case studies that follow.

In terms of learning theory, I am most interested in a language based theory of learning, therefore I have drawn on the sociocultural theory of knowledge construction which originates in the work of Vygotsky (1978), and has been extended and developed by theorists from a number of different disciplines.[6] Vygotsky says that learning is mediated by culturally inherited semiotic tools and that language-based social interaction is the most important of these tools. The discourse one engages with 'intermentally' with others becomes internalized as 'inner speech' for intramental functioning such as problem solving and reflection. Thus, socio-cultural theorists emphasize that knowledge construction is social and cultural in nature. The educational theorist, Wells, points out that Halliday's work in functional linguistics and his understanding of language as a 'social semiotic' compliments the work of Vygotsky. Halliday says 'language is the essential condition of knowing, the process by which experience becomes knowledge' (1993: p. 94).

Wells takes this one stage further when he says that learning is certainly a semiotic process but, 'it involves learning to *do* as well as to mean' (1999: p. 48) and that the goal of this learning is

...not just the development of the learner's meaning potential, conceived as the construction of discipline based knowledge but the development of the *resources of*

---

[6] Bruner (1971), Moll (1991), Wertsch (1991), Wells (1992), Halliday (1978, 1993).

action, speech, and thinking that enable the learner to participate effectively and creatively in further practical, social and intellectual activity.

Wells emphasizes that it is important that students construct their own understanding by using what they already know to make sense of new information so that a learner's transformed understanding is a personal reconstruction (1992: p. 281) i.e. it is accommodated within the learner's emerging identity.

In the context of the bridging course in economics at UCT, this is an issue, which we need to understand more clearly. The discourse of economics is highly valued by first year students from disadvantaged backgrounds who are hoping to make a career in economics. However, most students struggle with understanding and expressing the new concepts appropriately and resort to using the words of the textbook when they answer questions in the weekly tutorial assignment or in the economics essays. This 'borrowing' has the effect of censoring their own discourses and often means that they have not fully made sense of the concepts and 'made them their own'. This may lead to learning problems later on.

In my study I have become interested in the relationship between identity and learning. As Wells says,

> It is not simply our view of the world that is constructed in the discourses in which we participate but our view of ourselves, our values and our very identities. (Wells, 1999: p. 120)

Also, in the context in which we work in South Africa, students' socio-cultural histories, particularly their schooling histories, may have shaped the way they learnt to make meaning and to build understanding. But, the possibilities for self are open to contestation and change. When students enter the higher education community and encounter new discourses they come under the influence of new and powerful ideologies and these impact on identity and position them in new ways. They may also encounter new ways of making meaning, which may shift their ways of learning and understanding.

The Industry Research Project

In the language and communications tutorials linked to the economics course, we encourage students to explore economic understandings through discussion and through informal and formal writing. The Industry Research Project was a project based extension of these tutorials and I believe that its success lay in the fact that it gave students the opportunity to talk and write about the learning that had happened in economics in a computer based 'community of inquiry' (Wells 1999) where they had to reinvent and reconstruct those theories in a new setting i.e. the gold industry.

I became interested in computer-based online writing because researchers of online writing say that it promotes active learning as students become active shapers of knowledge [Hill Duin and Hansen, (1994) and Snyder (1998)] and that it is a more interactive medium encouraging both reflection and interaction (Warschauer 1997). Because writing is permanent, it provides a powerful mediating technology – it can be reviewed, rethought and revised but writing lacks the immediacy of responsive interchange that characterizes speech. Computer mediated discussion seems to do both – the text is permanently archived and at the same time students get immediate responses to their writing. Because computer mediated discussion forums reduce the necessity for face-to-face interaction, they encourage the participation of voices that may otherwise be marginalized because of race, ethnicity, gender, disability or other factors such as shyness (Snyder, 1998, Warschauer, 1997).

The extended first year course in economics, ECO110h, has a very diverse student population consisting of 150 students on the four year Academic Development Programme (ADP) in Commerce and students on the extended 'gateway' programme in Humanities. In the questionnaire sent out, 39 per cent of the students said English was not their first language and they identified eight other South African languages and Portuguese as home languages. The aim of the project was to expose students to real world issues with the hope that they would apply the economic concepts they had learned to the investigation of three SA industries i.e. clothing and textile, gold, or oil industries. Students divided themselves into small groups and selected an industry of their choice; each individual in the group then selected one of six topics[7] within the industry to focus on for their research. Students had to conduct research and each produce a feature article for a newspaper and then, as a team, prepare a twenty minute oral presentation in which each member participated. A project website was developed with information on each industry, and links to useful websites. Six of the eleven tutorials were computer-based.

Students were introduced to the gold industry by means of two Excel tutorials, designed to give them insights into the dynamics of the South African gold industry. These included a number of activities and questions to lead students to a better understanding of how a South African industry operates e.g. what influences fluctuations in the gold price and the ways in which companies react to these. The final activity in these tutorials was a share trading game where each student was allocated R1000 to invest in three gold mining companies.

The task that followed the Excel tutorials called on students to introduce themselves on the Web Crossing discussion forum and then to create a newspaper style heading and first paragraph on the industry they had chosen. This was a brainstorm or 'free write' to kick off the writing process. The next step was for students to get started on their research so that, working in their teams, they could come up with a set of questions for the Experts (lecturers and experts in particular

---

[7] The topics for selection were as follows: The history of the industry, The current situation in the industry, Labour practices, Price determination, A company, Impact of the industry on you, your family and your community.

industries). Once the experts had responded, students were to type the first drafts of their newspaper reports onto the Web for feedback from peers and tutors. Final drafts of these reports were handed in in hard copy during the period of preparation for the group oral presentations, which took place in the classrooms, although a number of groups chose to make further use of the technology to do power point presentations.

The project turned out to be demanding and quite time consuming for students and the convenor of the first year economics course felt that it took time away from and distracted students from learning and focusing on the central microeconomic concepts. Therefore it was decided that in 2001, the Industry Research Project would not be repeated as a component of the first year Microeconomics course. The Multimedia Education Group and the Academic Development Programme are now developing the Project further with the hope of offering it as a credit-bearing generic skills course. This course would build on conceptual learning in Economics and Accounting, while continuing to emphasize both oral and written communication skills.

A Methodology for analyzing student writing

I have used Fairclough's (1989) three dimensional framework for understanding the context of production of the writing.

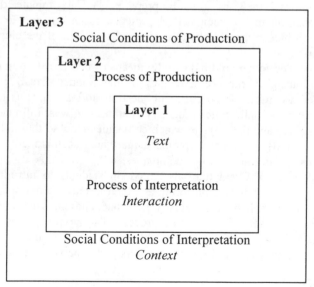

Figure 2.1 Ivanic's adaptation of the Fairclough model (Ivanic 1997: p. 41)

The inner layer is the actual student text and the middle layer represents the processes of production and interpretation of the text. In my analysis this refers to what the students were doing and thinking in the process of reading, interacting and producing their assignments online. It would also refer to the interpretation process they went through in reading from other texts in order to produce their own (I will return to this when I discuss Fairclough's definitions of intertextuality). During the distribution process, the students' articles were posted to the Web and organized into their topic areas by the systems operator so that tutors could post their feedback.

The outer layer of Fairclough's diagram refers to the social context which influences the production and interpretation of the discourse. These are the contesting systems of values, beliefs, norms, conventions and power relations which impact on what is written and spoken. The outer layer can be seen as sets of cultural contexts i.e. the global, the national, institutional and departmental contexts that impact on production of students' texts.

Values and beliefs may constrain what can be said within particular cultural contexts and what is said then reinforces and reproduces established beliefs. For instance, in the context of university writing, particularly writing for 'marks', many students from more disadvantaged backgrounds feel strong pressure to conform to the dominant values of the department, the faculty and the university because they see this as a route to success and, in so doing, they will then reinforce disciplinary values. However, texts not only reproduce social relations but also oppose them, as we will see when we look at Daniel's text below. Fairclough's outer layer points to the importance of understanding students' social histories when analyzing their texts so that we understand the context of culture in which they are produced.

Fairclough uses the term intertextuality[8] in interesting ways which seems crucial to my framework because it is in the interaction with other texts that students make meaning and acquire new discourses. Fairclough says an intertextual perspective points to the 'historicity' (Fairclough, 1992: p. 84) of text; a new text is shaped by existing 'chains of speech communications' (Bakhtin, 1984: p. 94, quoted in Fairclough, 1992) and is responding to these earlier texts. In online writing the process of text production is very visible and it is 'archived' from the moment it goes on the Web, therefore this helps to provide insights into the context of text production or the 'historicity'. Fairclough subdivides intertextuality into 'manifest intertextuality' and 'interdiscursivity'. In 'manifest intertextuality' the other texts are explicitly present and may or may not be signalled by quotation marks. Ivanic says that the key difference between these two types of intertextuality is that in interdiscursivity 'the echo in the new text is not of another specific text but of a recognizable abstract text type or set of conventions; a pattern or template of language use, rather than a sample of it' (1997: p. 48). This might be the language of the church or in our case the language of economics.

The notion of intertextuality originated with Bakhtin (1981) and Bakhtin's description of all language as 'hybridized' or 'multivoiced' seem a very powerful metaphor for understanding interdiscursivity in our students' texts. Bakhtin says

---

[8] The term intertextuality was coined by Kristeva (1986a) to describe Bakhtin's 'translinguistic' approach to text analysis.

that writers play a unique role in shaping their own texts but that they are 'interanimated' by 'social languages and speech genres'.

But as Recchio (1991) points out, writers not only draw on the discourses of the community they are seeking to enter, but on the discourses they bring with them. I think that if we can identify the different voices that are embedded in students texts, we come closer to understanding how they are constructing meaning.

Ivanic (1997 and 1998) has used Fairclough's and Halliday's view of language to develop a framework for analyzing identity in students' text, she says:

> When a writer words something in a particular way, by a particular choice of words and structures, they are aligning themselves with others who use such words and structures and hence making a statement of identity about themselves. (1997: p. 45)

Ivanic has developed what she calls the 'clover leaf' consisting of three aspects of identity i.e. the 'autobiographical' self, or the writer's personal history, the 'discoursal' self or the way people represent themselves in text 'through their practices and the discourse types they draw on' and the 'authorial self', or the way in which people own their ideas.

> viewing oneself as an author – feeling authoritative and feeling the right to exert a presence in the text is often related to the sense of power and status writers bring with them from their life history. (1997: p. 153)

Ivanic bases her research on adults who are first language speakers of English, therefore while the framework is useful, I believe it needs to be expanded for use in my particular context. Many of the texts I am looking at are written by second language speakers of English, therefore my access to how students articulate their identity is only through what they say and write in English, not their mother tongue and I think it is important to bear this in mind when looking at the discoursal identity of some of the case studies. There may be instances of language 'breakdown' that obscure meaning and therefore my interpretations of their meaning needs to be constantly referred back to the students for checking.

Moreover, because my analysis focuses on one discipline at the first year level, I have tried to look in more depth at the ways in which these first year students are learning and making meaning in economics. I see this in terms of the relative authority students take on or not in their writing and in terms of how they choose to position themselves in relation to something they read or to a new concept. The authorial self can be linked to the gender, class, ethnicity and maturity of the writer, and first year students, particularly those who are writing in their second language often do not have the confidence to take an authoritative position in relation to a particular idea. They feel that in writing an academic essay, they have nothing worth saying, that they have 'no voice'.

People construct identities as they become part of a community and make sense with a particular epistemology. However, as Ivanic points out, acquisition is not an initiation into a fixed set of discourse practices; writers negotiate an identity from a range of possibilities for 'self-hood'. Nevertheless, I think it must be noted that a writer is not in full control in the 'choice' of an identity. Pedagogical practices provide sites for the articulation of discourses and the process of acquiring a new discourse and identity is a subconscious process and it is *socially constrained*. Students' identities as learners are shaped by their life histories. South Africa's apartheid history has meant that students entering university have come from very diverse schools and diverse literacy and learning practices. Many of these students have not been adequately prepared for tertiary studies. They may have come from homes where there are very few books, and from schools where they may have been taught to learn by rote or they may have had to teach themselves from the textbook and this will have shaped their learning processes i.e. whether they have learned to simply reproduce concepts or to understand them thoroughly so as to be able to apply them in new contexts. Some of these students find that they are positioned by the social opportunities that have been available to them and they simply do not have the personal resources to catch up. And yet it is always surprising that others from the very same background will grow in confidence and assume identities as achievers.

The two assignments that have been selected for analysis have been chosen so as to provide insights into writers with contrasting life histories and backgrounds in terms of race, gender and socio-economic background. In addition the assignments selected show a range of abilities.

Sizwe

Autobiographical self

Sizwe is a Xhosa speaker from Alice, a small rural town in the Eastern Cape where he studied at Phandulwazi Agricultural High School. This is a school disadvantaged during the apartheid era and still quite poorly resourced. It offers a very limited academic curriculum, and yet because Sizwe was a top student, he gained sufficient points to gain admission to the Commerce faculty at UCT. He studied English as a second language, Afrikaans and Xhosa. His school did not offer commercial subjects, so he studied agricultural science and biology and mathematics (only offered on the standard grade), obtaining an A for Xhosa and Mathematics. In his interview he told me that his uncle had a supermarket in the village and he had worked for him and become interested in the world of commerce and decided to study at university. For Sizwe, there is a lot at stake. He wants to become a Chartered Accountant (CA), which will mean at least five years of study on the Commerce Academic Development Programme. Although he is receiving Financial Aid, it would not cover his costs at university and he will have to raise the extra money himself, because his family is not able to support him. This will have to be done through vacation work or by raising money in his community and it puts students under a lot of stress. I think it is important to understand the social and contextual pressures these students have to cope with – this powerful pull of a commerce degree. This is part of Fairclough's outer layer –

the context of culture within which Sizwe and many of his fellow students are operating.

Initially rather quiet and withdrawn, he has gained in confidence as the year progressed, Sizwe has formed a peer study group and worked very hard so that, despite his disadvantaged school background, he was one of the top ten performers in economics, and on the project, his group put on one of the best group presentations.

He is a typical achiever. He is very motivated and keen to succeed and therefore he is willing to conform to the dominant values of the department and the faculty. He sees appropriating the privileged discourse of economics as crucial and, as I show, he tries to use it in his assignment, although it was never a stated requirement for the project.

Discoursal Self

Writers choose from alternatives and although, sometimes, these choices are subconscious, they are 'an important component of the discoursal construction of identity' (Ivanic, 1998: p. 54) and are also an indication of personal interest and history. It is interesting, therefore, that Sizwe chose to write his article on 'Price determination in the Gold Industry'. Of the six topics students could select from, this one was most closely linked to the economics content they had been studying. Many of the students, who are successful in economics and enjoying it, selected this topic because it allowed them to demonstrate their knowledge of economics.

Sizwe has produced a text, which draws on a variety of discourses. This may be because he has researched his topic well and used four different and very complex websites. The tutor's biggest criticism of his text was that it lacked coherence and, when I questioned Sizwe about this, he indicated he had struggled to condense and link the vast amount of information he had found on the Web.

Students were not required to reference because they were writing newspaper articles, however, they were asked to provide a list of sources at the end of the assignment. Intertextuality, though not signalled, is quite clear in Sizwe's text, and it is possible to identify some of the different websites Sizwe has drawn from,

> In 1998 the four firm concentration ratio has shown that the largest four firms produce about 53.6% of the total production in Johannesburg Stock Exchange.

This sentence comes from the Chamber of Mines Website, but mostly, where he has integrated information from the websites, he has summarized and paraphrased it in his own words.

What is particularly striking about Sizwe's article is the way he links the information he finds on the website to the economic theory he has learnt. Repeatedly through the text there is evidence that Sizwe is trying to use the academic discourse of economics (textbook discourse) in an attempt to position himself as a member of that community.

Existence of a small number of big firms with sufficient essential resources in this industry makes it difficult for new firms to enter into this industry.

We recognize this sentence and the ones below as economic discourse because he uses economics terms such as 'resources', 'firms', 'demand', 'determinant of price' 'supply', 'luxury goods', 'economic downturn'. The sentence is typical of academic discourse in that it starts with a long nominal group of 14 words, while the phrase 'difficult for new firms to enter into this industry' is drawn from another economic theory, the theory of the firm.

After a discussion of the background (history) to the gold industry, Sizwe begins his discussion of price theory and puts together quite a clear explanation of how price is determined in the gold industry.

Demand and supply are the most obvious determining factors of gold price. Most products made out of gold are luxury goods and during the economic downturn, their demand decreases and therefore their prices. On the 26th December 1996 gold price reached $369.20 as a result of increased demand for jewellery (graph).

Although political instability may be seen as a different determinant of price from supply and demand, they are related to supply in that they affect the supply of gold. Recent Zimbabwean and Russian political crisis had a negative effect on gold supply and therefore increased price.

These paragraphs draw intertextually on economic theory. Economists have to simplify the world in order to develop 'scientific' theories and mathematical models so as to be able to make precise predictions but often students have difficulty applying these theories to the real world (Dudley Evans and Henderson 1990). Sizwe is applying the theory of demand and supply to the gold industry. But what I find most interesting is that he is doing more than simply reproducing the discourse. He has transformed this understanding and made it his own so that in the final paragraph he is able to apply what he knows about price to a new context i.e. political instability and to come to the conclusion that instability must be another determinant of price. This is not something that he would have found in the textbook; it is a very clear example of his own reasoning. He deduces that the increase in the gold price in politically unstable times is due to a fall in production.

For the project, Sizwe went to great lengths to research his article and to use the newspaper genre appropriately (a number of students did not bother to do this). He formatted his assignment as a newspaper article and included a graph of the gold price, an indication that he recognizes graphs as part of the multimodal discourse of economics. Students were also told that the headline of a newspaper article was usually 'catchy' and Sizwe identifies himself as a successful rhetorician with the dramatic metaphor he uses as the title for his article *'A substantial decline of gold price impale most gold producers'*. He follows through with this theme in the extended metaphor he uses for his first paragraph:

> Like a spear, hardly thrown into the animals' skin by a bushman, accompanied by a moan, so does the substantial decline of gold price to gold producers leaving them bankrupt.

Here Sizwe has combined two discourses. The discourse of hunting is likely to be a home-based discourse in the rural Eastern Cape, but he links it to his newly acquired economics discourse. In using this metaphor, Sizwe is drawing interdiscursively on the newspaper genre. To introduce students to the genre of the feature article, we gave them a model of a feature article in a newspaper and they had identified metaphors as one of the typical characteristics of feature articles. However, only a mere handful of students were poetic and creative in this way.

Writer's authorial voice or sense of authority

The metaphor in the first paragraph of Sizwe's assignment is an indication of how he is establishing his identity. Ivanic says:

> ...learner writers are not so much learning to be creative, as learning to use discourses which already exist – creatively. ... On the other hand, a writer's identity is determined not completely by other discourses, but rather by the unique way in which she draws on and combines them. (1997: p. 86)

After reading the first paragraph, one expects that the author will establish his authorial voice quite strongly in the text but he doesn't do this. I think this is partly because he fails to develop a main argument and partly because he does not yet have the confidence to do this. Sizwe is one of the students whose access to English and the discourse of economics has been more limited than for many others. Therefore he is still struggling to express himself and has not yet developed the skill in writing in English to put into words what he wants to say and present a more authoritative position.

There do seem to be further glimmers of the writer's 'voice' (his own beliefs) such as in the paragraph below.

> The now large firms have... treated labourers, the variable cost of production, with indignity that most of the workers lost their jobs.

By means of the phrase 'treated with indignity' he seems to be showing his disapproval of job losses on the mines which may be affecting people from his own community.

I would argue that, at times, 'form' or ability to use the syntax and vocabulary of English interferes with this writer's attempts to incorporate his understandings of economics into his writing. For instance it is quite tempting to comment that the last phrase in the sentence below does not make sense / is a non-sequitur, unless one is aware that second language speakers often have difficulty with connectors and linking words and the sentence would be perfectly clear if he had introduced it with the word 'although':

A use of gold in dentistry, electronics and the aerospace industry may have increased the demand for gold, the gold price decrease unstoppably.

Daniel

The writing of the second student I have chosen as a case study contrasts quite dramatically with that of Sizwe's. Daniel is a more mature student as he has been out of school for two years and he is from a very different socio-economic stratum. He is white, a mother tongue speaker of English and he went through private school education in the Western Cape. As such he has had very privileged access to educational resources such as good teaching, books, computers and the more academic discourses. Daniel makes a statement about himself when he walks into a room because he has developed a very particular identity in the way he dresses. He is tall with long black hair to his shoulders and dresses mostly in black with heavy studded belt, chains hanging from the belt and high cut boots, indicating that his Discourse (capital D) is 'Gothic', a style associated with Gothic music and games like Dungeons and Dragons. Unfortunately I have not had an opportunity to interview him since he wrote this assignment, but informal discussions with him and with his tutors indicate that this is just one of Daniel's multiple identities. His tutor verifies that he is very concerned, almost passionate, about environmental issues, that he showed a keen interest in political matters and 'seemed aware that the issues we dealt with in tutorials were somehow all related on a bigger scale' (tutor D).

Daniel has indicated that he is not particularly interested in Economics and prefers the course he is doing in Political Studies. The marks he has achieved in the two courses confirm this. He did well in Political Studies but had to write a supplementary exam for economics and collapsed completely in that exam, only scoring 30 per cent. The lecturer commented that he had seemed keen initially but had gone 'off the boil'. This would indicate that Daniel had lost interest in the course as it moved from the more descriptive socio-political economics, to the models and mathematics of analytical economics i.e. price theory and theory of the firm. First year economics and particularly economics textbooks have been criticized because they tend to be organized around mainstream viewpoints and try to promote a consensual view of the world and yet economics is a discipline of multiple and contesting perspectives.

> Overwhelmingly students in the US are learning basic concepts from the neo-classical paradigm as a catechism.... They do not give students experience in model building analysis and evaluation of controversy in order to extend abstract reasoning powers and their moral judgements. (Helburn 1986: p. 29)

The ECO110h course uses an American textbook which presents a further problem for South African students as all the examples are American e.g. College bowl games, the Dow Jones etc.

The Industry Research Project however caught Daniel's interest and he seemed to invest in both the online writing process and in the final group oral presentation. He scored 79 per cent for the assignment. For the project assignment, he has written a very critical and reflective piece, which demonstrates his skill as an articulate and persuasive writer. His selection of topic positions him as an environmentalist from the start. He chooses to write on *'Past present and future impact of the gold industry on you, your family and your community'* and focuses on the impact the gold industry has had on the environment and the people in it. This topic allowed for more flexibility than most and did not confine students to discussing economics content.

Discoursal Self

As Ivanic (1997) points out, the conventions writers draw on depend partly on their life histories, educational backgrounds, affiliations to different groups etc. and this means they often draw on a hybridity of discourses, presenting multiple, shifting and possibly contradictory impressions of themselves. Daniel draws on a variety of discourse practices in this assignment, partly because of the issues that interest him and partly because of the course he is writing it for. However, his avoidance of the use of economics discourse, may be an indication of his resistance to it.

At times his writing is very typical of academic discourse as shown in the extract below, but it is academic discourse linked to ecology or environmental geography.

> Listed among the problems caused by large-scale mining is environmental destruction, deforestation and the severe nature of the damage done to pastures and farmlands due to leakages and fallout from large-scale mining accidents.

This is shown in the 35 word sentence above, where he uses a 24 word nominal group with extensive nominalization of verbs and adjectives e.g. *'Destruction', 'deforestation', 'damages', 'leakages'* and *'fallout'*. He uses the present tense *'is'* as is often done in academic discourse to express timeless truths and he quotes from sources and acknowledges them appropriately. There is evidence of the ease with which he uses academic language in his entries in the online discussion forum.

At other times in the final assignment, he switches to newspaper discourse.

> Governments across the world are surely, but slowly waking up to the fact that large multinationals should and must be held responsible for irresponsible and dangerous practices in their mining areas. The bottom line? It is not only politically correct to be ecologically aware as a company, it is becoming more cost effective to be so.

The strong modals he uses such as *'should and must be held responsible'* indicate that he holds very definite opinions on these issues and is not afraid to express them. This language differs from the more neutral academic language above. He uses stylistic techniques for persuading the reader with the catchy question and answer *'The bottom line? It is not only politically correct to be ecologically aware as a company, it is becoming more cost effective to be so'*. This last sentence is clearly appealing to an audience of economists. His language is at times metaphoric as he evokes the picture of governments *'across the world'* *'surely but slowly waking up to the fact'*. This use of evocative metaphors runs throughout the piece. In his opening paragraph he paints a picture of the landscapes of the future as *'cyanide gravescapes'* and places the responsibility and ownership of these problems on all our shoulders by using the first person plural.

> As the need for mineral resources across the world continues to grow, our greed could soon turn the land we hold so dear into the cyanide gravescapes of the future.

This is also a very effective use of the genre of a newspaper feature article where the first paragraph usually sums up the article in a dramatic and often metaphoric sentence. This sentence also serves to position him from the start, as resistant to the dominant 'winner take all' beliefs and values of free market capitalism.

Then there is a sudden switch to a rather different discourse – the 'safety discourse' from the mining industry itself. He refers to the recent Mine Health and Safety Act and reports that the Act has been successful in reducing workplace fatalities and quotes the Chamber of Mines safety advisor, from the Chamber of Mines Website:

> Dr Mike Gouws ... has stated that 1997 and 1998 were 'record breaking years' and the long term efforts of the mining industries commitment to reducing accidents and fatalities were continuing to bear fruit.

This seems to contrast quite notably with the outspoken criticism of the mining companies that follows and is quoted below.

> However, mining companies still continue to gouge steaming wounds into the ground with destructive materials and destroy the land with chemical anathema to both human and animal life. You ask what economic concern is this to us all?

He then points to the financial cost of pollution by noting the clean up costs of a recent mining accident which released 2.5 million tons of cyanide sludge and buried a gold mining village and killed 17 people and concludes:

> Our Government is still paying to clean it up, which means we are still paying for it. All because of shoddy workmanship and unsafe materials. The question on everybody's minds is; how much is life worth in gold bullion?

This dramatic and fiery conclusion to the article seems to provide a clear enough indication that he does not see himself as an 'insider' to Chamber of Mines 'safety speak'. The reference to the Chamber of Mines Website may be a brief attempt to conform to the project requirement that the newspaper article should be 'well researched' and that students should provide a list of the references they had used.

Authorial self

By now it will be clear that just as Daniel establishes a presence when he walks into a room, he also establishes a presence within his writing and exerts control over it. He feels he has the authority to be quite outspoken about environmental issues which are so important to him. He fits the role of the white middle class male who is likely to have a greater sense of authority than students from the black working class.

This is probably best illustrated in the excerpts from his final few paragraphs, which are quoted above. Although Daniel never uses the first person singular we are left in no doubt as to what his opinion is, because of the certainty with which he writes and the way he positions himself in terms of other authorities.

Daniel's choice of topic and theme indicates he is probably not interested in writing about economic issues; unlike Sizwe he has no wish to display his knowledge of the new concepts he should have been acquiring. For him, 'taking on' economic discourse meant aligning himself with economic ideas and values which he disapproved of. However, he does show some understanding of economics in the way he builds his argument that destruction of the environment will ultimately impact on the economy and on human life – 'The Price of Life in Gold Bullion'. For instance he indicates that multinationals must be held responsible for *'dangerous practices in their mining areas'* because *'it is not only politically correct to be ecologically aware, it is becoming more cost effective to be so'.* His text shows he has quite a thorough knowledge of ecological issues and is clearly positioning himself on the side of ecological epistemologies rather than those of economics.

Daniel is a good example of a student who is refusing to reproduce the social relations of mainstream economics and he appears to be challenging the dominant discourse. The quality of his assignment and his presentation were indications that he had the ability to acquire and control the discourse of economics but that he chose not to. This led ultimately to his failing the economics course.

For students like Daniel, the acquisition of mainstream discourses is facilitated by the fact that their primary discourses have adopted features of the dominant discourse and they get constant support in these discourses at home (Gee 1996:158). This is certainly true in Daniel's case and is illustrated by the ease with which he masters academic discourse. However, when students feel conflict or tension between two or more of their discourses, this can deter acquisition of the conflicting discourse. Although Daniel is articulate and performed well on the project, he avoided linking the project to his economics course and we may well speculate that many of the economics concepts he should have been learning conflicted with his own values and beliefs.

Conclusion

In this chapter I have shown how identity is a useful framing concept for examining the intersection of student voices and curriculum and I have argued that Ivanic's framework can be applied to a rather different writing and learning context from those she has explored in her work with adult learners. I have used it to look at the relationship between identity and meaning making in the context of second language writers learning first year economics.

In concluding I would like to review some of the points that emerge from this analysis. It would seem from the two studies that access to the discourse of economics may be linked to the way students construct their identities as writers and students of economics.

Sizwe is a successful student of economics who seems to invest relatively sincerely in the role of apprentice economist as it is constructed for him by the Industry Research Project. He is also beginning in somewhat tentative ways to show his creativity and develop a distinctive identity in his writing, which blends his prior history with the new target discourse. At times, difficulties with form seem to get in the way of Sizwe making his understandings clear, but typically, these difficulties will disappear over time.

Daniel on the other hand, 'chooses' to contest the identity of an 'economics student' and to develop a different and almost oppositional identity for himself. He is articulate and authoritative enough in his writing to be able to do this, but it seems that this assumed identity of his may stand in the way of his assimilating the disciplinary knowledge into his personal repertoire and succeeding at economics.

So, a conclusion is that it is not only considerations of ability and levels of home literacy that influence academic success but also that the roles and identities that are negotiated in learning contexts construct the personal agency of learners. It seems that the curriculum can extend or constrain possible identity positions and that the ideologies embedded (often tacitly) in curriculum are an important factor in this. In a sense the Industry Research Project, with 18 different assignment options, allowed a diversity of students to find an issue that interested them. This gave Daniel the opportunity to negotiate a place for himself within this component of the economics curriculum and for his identity to emerge quite forcefully, whereas elsewhere in the curriculum he seems to have chosen not to invest himself.

I have already mentioned that the Convenor of the first year Economics course felt that the Industry Research Project should be discontinued in 2001 because it had not been linked closely enough to the dominant neo-classical mainstream of the economics curriculum and had distracted students from the focus of first year microeconomics. This raises a further question about access i.e. does wholesale immersion in a single dominant discourse allow better access than the multiple forms of engagement provided by this project? Would contrasting the neo-classical tradition of economics with other intellectual traditions better enable access for diverse student cohorts or simply distract them from in-depth engagement?

The theme of this chapter has been that universities like other institutions are sites for the inscription of powerful discourses in the talk of those who take up the subject positions available. Therefore the withdrawal of the Industry Research

Project from the economics curriculum represents a significant delegitimation of the flexible discursive positions the project made available to students. The discipline of economics has the power to set boundaries by only making available sites that maintain the coherency and rigour of the discourse and withdrawing those that allow the discourse to be fractured and challenged and dispersed.[9]

References

Bakhtin, M. M. (1981), 'Discourse in the Novel' (First Published in 1929) in M. Holquist (ed.), *The Dialogic Imagination*, Trans. By C. Emerson and M. Holquist. Austin: University of Texas Press.

Blommaert, J. (2001), 'Context is/as Critique', *Critique of Anthropology*, vol. 21(1), pp. 13-32.

Cazden, C. (1992), *Whole Language Plus: Essays on Literacy in the United States and New Zealand*, New York: Teachers College Press.

Clark, R. and R. Ivanic (1998), *The Politics of Writing*, London: Routledge.

Dudley-Evans, T. and W. Henderson (eds), (1990), *The Language of Economics: The analysis of economics discourse*, London: Modern English Publications and the British Council.

Fairclough, N. (1989), *Language and Power*, London: Longman.

Fairclough, N. (1990), *Discourse and Social Change*, Cambridge: Polity Press.

Fairclough, N. (1992), *Discourse and Social Change*, Cambridge: Polity Press.

Gee, J. (1996), *Social Linguistics and Literacies: Ideology in Discourse* (2nd edition). Basingstoke: Falmer Press.

Halliday, M. A. K. (1978), *Language as a Social Semiotic: The social interpretation of language and meaning*, London: Edward Arnold.

Heath, S. B. (1983), *Ways with Words: Language, Life and Work in Communities and Classrooms*, Cambridge: Cambridge University Press.

Hill Duin, A. and Hansen, C. 'Reading and Writing on Computer Networks as Social Construction and Social Interaction', in C. Selfe and S. Hilligoss (eds), *Literacy and Computers: The Complications of Teaching and Learning with Technology*, pp. 89-112.

Ivanic, R. (1997), *Writing and Identity: The Discoursal Construction of Identity in Academic Writing*, Amsterdam/Philadelphia: John Benjamins.

Piaget, J. (1954), *The Construction of Reality in the Child*, New York: Basic Books.

Recchio, T. (1991), 'A Bakhtinian Reading of Student Writing', *College Composition and Communication*, vol. 42, pp. 446-454.

---

[9] This chapter describes only two of the texts that I have analyzed, but I am in the process of looking at a wider range and going into more depth and this study is beginning to give me a sense of the interesting patterns that will emerge from this kind of text analysis. The study has also provided opportunities to reflect on research methods particularly methods of interviewing. Thesen (1997) points to the importance of students identifying which discourses *they* perceive themselves to be operating in and I think this is a useful idea for this research.

Scollon, R. and Scollon, S.W. (1981), *Narrative, Literacy and Face in Interethnic Communication*, Norwood, N. J.: Ablex.

Snyder, I (1998), 'Beyond the hype: reassessing hypertext' in I. Snyder (ed.), *Page to Screen*, pp. 125-143.

Thesen (1997), Voices, Discourse and Transition: In Search of New Categories in EAP, *TESOL Quarterly*, vol. 31(3), pp. 487- 511.

Vygotsky, L. (1978), *Mind in Society*, Harvard University Press, Cambridge MA.

Warschauer, M. (1997), 'Computer-Mediated Collaborative Learning: Theory and Practice' *The Modern Language Journal*, vol. 81(iv), pp. 470 – 481.

Wells, G. (1992), 'The Centrality of Talk in Education' in K. Norman (ed.), *Thinking Voices: The Work of the National Oracy Project*, Hodder and Stoughton, London.

Wells, G. (1999), *Dialogic Inquiry: Towards a Sociocultural Practice and Theory of Education*, Cambridge University Press, Cambridge.

Wertsch, (1991), *Voices of the Mind*, Harvard University Press, Cambridge MA.

Chapter 3

Pay as You Learn: The Effects of Part-time Paid Employment On Academic Performance

Catherine Watts

Reflection on Method: Recruiting Subjects

One of the main concerns I had with conducting this study was the recruitment of the student participants. The problems started during the pilot stage. I decided to target the same degree programme as I was planning to use in the main study (the BA in Business Studies) using similar recruitment procedures to enable me to evaluate their effectiveness and to gauge the likely response rate. Thus, I wrote individual letters and addressed lectures on two occasions to target a total of fifty-eight selected students during May 1999 to take part in the pilot study.

The response rate from those students willing to take part in the pilot study was, however, disappointingly low with only nine students saying they undertook part-time paid employment during term-time and were willing to be interviewed. No students without part-time term jobs responded. This poor response made me stop and think hard before conducting the main study. My recruitment procedures, if they remained unaltered, would obviously not enable me to carry out the full enquiry I had planned: I needed a reasonable number of 'non-working' participants to allow me to compare their marks with those of the 'working' students.

On reflection I decided that May was not the best time of the academic year in which to target student participants due to examination demands in June. It would appear that trying to recruit students in the context of higher education to take part in studies after mid-April is just not viable and I organized the interviews in the main study during March 2000 as a result.

A further consideration was that, as many of my colleagues pointed out, many students were reluctant to participate in research studies without an incentive of some sort. Indeed, 'Body Shop' vouchers, books and chocolates have been offered by both undergraduate and post-graduate students to potential recruits to various studies in my institution recently and it would appear that the offer of such incentives is increasingly becoming accepted practice.

I was, and remain, uneasy about doing this myself for a number of reasons. First, I feel that as students are studying in higher education institutions there should be a degree of reciprocity within educational studies. I am concerned that if students will only co-operate for (financial) incentives, the nature of participation in educational research will change and place further demands on those students who are already facing financial difficulties funding their studies.

Second, I was worried about creating a precedent for the educational research community which could mean that the cost of participation incentives would have to be included in any bids for future research funding however small.

However, my research colleagues endorsed my idea of raising a £30 cash-prize draw as an inducement to encourage participation in the main study and a 33 per cent response rate was eventually achieved with a balance between 'working' and 'non-working' students.

Introduction

This study was triggered by my increasing concern at the numbers of undergraduates whom I teach at the University of Brighton who frequently request me to end lectures early in order to accommodate the demands of their part-time employment. On exploring the issue further with the students concerned on an informal basis it became apparent that some of them were working well over thirty-five hours per week during term-time in low-skilled, poorly-paid 'McJobs' (Guardian Higher 26/5/1998) and were, as a result, having difficulties coping with their academic work. Although full-time students who undertake part-time paid employment during term-time are not a new phenomenon, it seems that the many changes regarding the student funding mechanism which have taken place over the past decade in particular have contributed to the increasing numbers of students who are in this situation (Pilkington, 1994; NUS, 1996).

This has implications first for the students themselves in terms of the effects their paid employment has on their studies. Second, there are implications for the educational institutions regarding policy decisions that may need to be made to support those students concerned. Third, those who teach in the post-compulsory sectors need to be aware of the changing financial circumstances of the students they teach and respond appropriately as, lastly, do the employers of the student workforce themselves.

The study presented in this chapter explores some of the implications surrounding these issues and thereby seeks to contribute further to the emerging academic debate surrounding the effects of undergraduate employment (defined as any paid work) on academic performance.

Background and Rationale

Many academics today work in an environment which is fundamentally different to the one they themselves experienced as students. It is worthwhile briefly exploring some of the recent key changes to the student funding mechanism to contextualize the study and to provide a background to the later discussion.

Following the recommendations of the Anderson Committee, the student grants system was introduced in 1962 which entitled all university entrants to mandatory awards for fees and maintenance, the latter being subject to parental means-testing. Undergraduate numbers rose steadily over the next twenty years until the mid-1980s when the numbers of undergraduates were allowed to double in size again to over one and a half million to encourage greater participation in higher education. This second major expansion in student numbers was, however, accompanied by a series of measures, introduced between 1980 and 1992, designed to reduce public expenditure and included the freezing of the student maintenance grant in nominal terms, the introduction of a student loans system and the withdrawal of the right of most students to claim housing and unemployment benefit and income support during vacations. The continued expansion of student numbers in higher education, together with increasing pressures on scarce public resources throughout the 1990s, culminated in the recommendation made by the Dearing Committee to introduce tuition fees on all full-time undergraduate courses. This recommendation was followed by a government decision to convert all maintenance grants into loans as well, thus effectively ending the universal entitlement of students in higher education to state funding. This study is therefore timely as it coincides with the first two years of the introduction of tuition fees on all full-time undergraduate courses.

These key changes in government policy have contributed to the growing financial hardship amongst students in full-time higher education (Cremieux & Johnes, 1993 and Ford *et al*, 1995). It is surprising that there have been relatively few studies to explore specifically the impact of the changes in undergraduate funding on the lives of students in higher education although several studies have been conducted into the general nature of undergraduate finances (for example, Cremieux & Johnes, 1993; McCarthy & Humphrey, 1995; Hakim, 1996). This may be because student status lasts only a few years and financial stringencies faced by individuals are consequently temporary in nature (Cremieux & Johnes, 1993) or it may be that researchers feel they are faced with a constantly shifting field in which findings very quickly become out of date.

The issue concerning whether or not the term-time employment of undergraduates affects academic performance is relatively under-researched although one 'in-house' study conducted at Oxford Brookes University (Lindsay & Paton-Saltzberg, 1993) examined the impact of paid work upon academic performance and was particularly relevant to this study at the University of Brighton. The Oxford Brookes study found that 57 per cent of the sample worked during term time and concluded that: 'Students who work in term time get marks which are demonstrably poorer as a result; many probably get poorer degrees' (Lindsay & Paton-Saltzberg, 1993).

However, whilst some studies have documented negative academic consequences of part-time, term-time employment ranging from missed lectures and tutorials to reduced time for academic study and fatigue (for example, Leonard, 1995; NUS, 1996), others have highlighted various benefits. Winn & Stevenson (1993), for example, noted that some students felt that if their paid employment was related in some ways to their main degree it could have a beneficial effect on their academic studies, whilst Harvey *et al* (1998) suggest that part-time, term-time employment enables students to develop employability skills which they can use to good effect in job interviews.

There is therefore a need, also identified by Ford *et al* (1995), to move beyond the currently available data to a more detailed documentation and understanding of the implications of increasing numbers of undergraduates who are undertaking part-time paid employment during term-time to finance their studies and this was the global aim of my study. Full-time students only are the subject of this study, although I am aware that part-time students may experience similar effects, albeit in slightly different circumstances.

This study therefore aimed to build on the findings of other relevant studies and to contribute further to the academic debates surrounding the effects of undergraduate term-time employment on academic performance. The main research question underpinning the study was: *to what extent is the academic performance of first-year, full-time 'traditional' undergraduates affected by the undertaking of part-time paid employment during term-time?* The study sought to address the following four sub-questions using primarily qualitative research methods:

a)   is the part-time work related to the degree course being studied;
b)   what effects do those students believe their employment has on their academic performance;
c)   does objective evidence support the beliefs expressed in b);
d)   is there any significant difference between the end-of-year marks of the 'non-working' and the 'working' students?

Methodology

Students were recruited from the BA in Business Studies degree programme at the University of Brighton in March 2000. The respondents were first-year, full-time, home entrants aged under twenty-one with a minimum of eighteen 'A' level points. Letters (and then follow-up reminder letters) were sent to individual students who fitted the pre-defined criteria and lectures were addressed on two occasions in an attempt to encourage a good response. All students who participated in the study were also entered into a £30 cash-prize draw to maximize participation. A total of ninety-three students were targeted in this way but the response rate was still disappointingly low at 33 per cent. The sample eventually comprised thirty-one respondents with nineteen students saying they did *not* work part-time during term-time but who were willing to take part in the study. These students played no further active role in the research, but their final end-of-year marks were used as a basis for comparison with the final end-of-year marks of those twelve students who *did* work part-time during term-time.

Individual interviews were held with the twelve respondents in April and May 2000. An interview schedule (see Appendix) was developed and the interview data were transcribed. The data were subsequently coded and analyzed using descriptive methods involving the 'constant comparison' method of qualitative analysis (Glaser & Strauss, 1967).

Findings

Ten of the twelve respondents interviewed had one part-time job during term-time whilst one person had two and another three. Half of the interviewees worked between ten and fourteen hours per week with four students working more hours and two working fewer. Only one person interviewed was employed for more than twenty hours per week.

Although the study conducted at Oxford Brookes University by Lindsay & Paton-Saltzberg (1993) found that 'all students who reported working part-time during term-time claimed to do so for ten hours or more per week', more recent studies have found that students were working slightly longer hours at their paid employment during term-time. In the most recent study conducted by the NUS (1999) for example, students were employed for an average of 13.3 hours per week whilst Kular & Winn (1998) reported that 39% of their sample at the University of Brighton worked for more than fifteen hours per week. Curtis (2000) found the average number of hours worked per week by undergraduates at Manchester Metropolitan University was sixteen. Further discussion of the implications of the number of hours worked by the University of Brighton sample reported here are included later in this chapter.

The majority of respondents worked in the retail industry whilst three people were employed in hotels or pubs and one in an office. Two students' employment fell into the category defined as 'other' and included a restaurant waiter and waitress and a kitchen assistant in a nursing home. Table 3.1 shows a full breakdown of the types of employment the respondents are involved in and it should be remembered that two students had more than one job.

Table 3.1 Type of employment undertaken

Employment type	Number of respondents
retail	7
hotel/pubs	3
cleaning	0
office	2
building	0
other	3

These findings are reflected in the studies by Leonard *et al* (1995) and Kular & Winn (1998) who noted that increasing numbers of students are employed in the retail industry rather than in the catering industries. In other recent studies the catering industry and the retail industry were also found to be the most common employers of the student workforce (NUS, 1999; Curtis, 2000).

No one interviewed said that their part-time job was definitely related to the content of their degree course and five respondents said their part-time job had no relation at all. The most recent NUS survey (1999) also found that the vast majority of students interviewed (91 per cent) were not employed in work which was related to their chosen careers. However, the remaining seven students interviewed in the study reported here said their job was related in part.

Two of these seven respondents saw only loose connections between their part-time employment and their studies but others mentioned the fact that what they had experienced in practice at work related to their studies in a more meaningful way. S10 for example said the Information Technology component of his course had explored the use of computers in the retail industry and, as he was familiar with aspects such as stock control and waste management from his workplace experience, he found his work quite useful in terms of his academic studies.

Two other students said that as they worked in customer services they had direct experience of aspects of their management course. Another respondent did 'all the paperwork' and had experience of the 'financial side of things' as well as working in the head office of the company. She could see the relation between her work experience and the finance and marketing aspects of her course. S8 worked in a bank and said she needed to understand processes at work so there were loose connections between what she had to do at work and what she had learnt at university. Another student said that he hoped that his part-time job at Asda would provide him with course-related opportunities in the future as he wanted to spend his placement year in America. Walmart had just bought Asda and as he was working in Asda's head office he hoped he would be able to tie in his work experience with his placement year later in the course. This same student was able to use his work experience to feed into his current coursework as well as can be seen from the following comment:

> it's had some good effects because I can use the information I've got from work ... in doing certain projects so ... I'm doing pest analysis of ... Sainsbury's at the moment and obviously they're a supermarket so I can use my knowledge of Asda to ... compare it. I can get information quite easily as well. (S1)

Comments from these students who said they felt their jobs were in part related to the content of their degree course therefore support the arguments in favour of student term-time employment outlined previously as they are able to feed aspects of their workplace experience into their academic studies.

Table 3.2 represents the responses to question eight on the interview schedule (see Appendix) which asked the respondents to indicate what effect they thought their paid employment was having on their academic work. There are thirteen responses in total as one respondent thought it had had both a good and a bad effect on his academic work. Without the money he earned he would not be able to come to university at all but, at the same time, he thought his paid employment had a detrimental effect on his studies.

Table 3.2 Respondent perceptions of the effect of their paid employment on their academic studies

---

Section A Responses to the statement: 'My paid employment has had no effect on my academic work'.

	Number of respondents
Agree	4
Disagree	0

Section B Responses to the statement: 'My paid employment has had a good effect on my academic work'.

	Number of respondents
Agree	5
Disagree	0

Section C Responses to the statement: 'My paid employment has had a bad effect on my academic work'.

	Number of respondents
Agree	4
Disagree	0

One of the respondents in Section A was employed for more than fourteen hours a week with three working between ten and fourteen hours and one working between five and nine hours. As S5 remarked, her job 'doesn't really take up a lot of my time' and she, like the other respondents in this category, said she was able to cope with the demands of both her job and her academic work.

One of these respondents in Section B was S10 who needed the money he earned to enable him to study at university in the first place as previously indicated. The other four respondents gave a variety of reasons for their reply. S6 worked on-site in the Student Union office and found working in the university environment a positive experience as she was forced to be more organized to accommodate the demands of both her job and her studies. S2 also commented that she needed to be well-organized to enable her to combine her academic work, her job and her social life and that her part-time job 'gives me like a break to do something completely different' which she found motivating. S12 remarked that his job 'keeps me busy and it keeps me sort of moving and slightly focused'. He felt that having a part-time job was a more positive use of his time than not working as 'all my other friends just spend the time I work sitting around and not really doing anything'.

S12 said that although he had less time for revision towards examination time he did not think his academic performance had really suffered. S11 listed several reasons to explain why she thought her part-time job had a good effect on her academic work as can be seen from the following comment:

> well although it's not actually connected to my degree it's given me an insight ... like working with employees and working around other people's needs and that ... I want to go into human resource management for my degree when I've finished it and it's given me some insight on like how employees affect you in the workplace and how you need to maintain the motivation levels ... and it's also taught me to balance my time between my studies as well. (S11)

The respondents in Section B worked a variety of hours. S10, who said his job had both good but essentially bad effects, worked between fifteen and nineteen hours per week whilst S12 worked between twenty and twenty-four hours per week which are the longest hours worked of anyone interviewed in this study. S6 and S11 were each employed for between ten and fourteen hours per week whilst S2 worked for between five and nine hours per week. Although other studies, for example Kular & Winn (1998), found that there was an association between the number of hours worked and whether or not individuals thought this had a positive or negative effect on their academic performance, this is not reflected in the study reported here. Kular & Winn (1998) noted that the fewer hours worked, i.e. under ten per week, the more likely students were to say that their academic work benefited from their employment and *vice versa*. Whilst all the respondents in the study presented in this chapter who reported no effects on their academic work from their paid employment worked fewer than fourteen hours per week, those who reported positive effects worked up to between twenty and twenty-four hours per week. It may be that a larger sample than that obtained here would in fact support the findings of other studies on this issue. A quantitative analysis of student perceptions and actual marks achieved is presented briefly at the end of this section.

S10 responded to Section C as well as to Section B for reasons already outlined. He thought the main negative effect his part-time job was having on his academic work was that he had little time to do much extra reading around subjects and, because he chose to do a lot of overtime at work, he did not have much free time in which to study. The three other students in this category also mentioned the fact that, as their paid employment prevented them from spending as much time on their academic work as they would like, they thought their academic performance had suffered. Three students said they had missed lectures due to their work commitments and this is illustrated by the following comment from S3:

> basically I'm working very long hours during the evening and ... I'm sometimes not getting home until about two o'clock because by the time the pub's shut you clear up it's tiring so I'm often not going in to morning lectures which of course puts me behind and also I'm finding I've got no time really to do any work outside of university basically and I haven't got no spare time any more. (S3)

One of these three students had only missed lectures when they were re-arranged due to bank holidays, but another said he had missed lectures because he was working overtime in his job. S8 said she only managed to read the set text books rather than doing any other background reading because of her work commitments and was unable to use the library for the same reason. She also said she constantly felt guilty because she knew she should be doing more academic work.

None of the students in Section C had ever asked for an extension to a deadline or handed in coursework late. Three of the four respondents were employed for between fifteen and nineteen hours per week whilst one student worked for between ten and fourteen hours per week.

Findings from other relevant studies which explore the perceived negative effects on academic work of part-time, term-time student employment are not consistent. Fifteen per cent of participants in the NUS study (NUS, 1999) said that their studies had been badly or very badly affected by being employed whilst studying, but nearly a quarter of respondents reported that their paid work had had no effect on their studies and 58 per cent said their studies were only slightly affected. Kular & Winn (1998) found that 59 per cent of their sample believed their paid employment had adversely affected their academic work, whilst in the study undertaken by Leonard *et al* (1995), 63 per cent of employed students felt that working during term time had had a detrimental effect on their studies.

The findings presented in this chapter however do not support those of other studies as the number of hours worked are not consistent with student negative perceptions concerning the effect of their employment on their academic performance. In fact one student, who believed her employment had negative consequences for her academic work, worked the same number of hours as two students who both reported beneficial effects for their studies. Again a larger sample than that obtained here may provide a different picture.

Only one student interviewed said he had talked to members of the academic staff about the effects he felt his part-time job was having on his studies. This student mentioned the lack of access to his personal tutor and said it had been much easier to talk to his tutor at sixth-form college whom he saw every day. Another respondent said she too had discussed the issue of student employment with her tutors at sixth-form college but not at university because she hadn't been asked. Only two other students could give a reason why they did not talk to the academic staff at university about the effects of their employment on their academic studies whether positive or negative. S8 said she had 'never really considered it. I just get on with what I'm doing' and S10 said she didn't think anyone was interested. In their recent study in the sixth-form context, Hodgson & Spours (2000) found that students 'overwhelmingly see school and part-time work to be separate' and this is reflected in the university setting by the study reported here.

Only one student therefore was asked to comment on question eleven on the interview schedule (see Appendix) regarding the attitude of the academic staff towards the demands made on students by their part-time jobs. S1 thought the academic staff were not particularly sympathetic towards students with part-time employment although they realized students had to 'get money from somewhere'. He reported the academic staff as saying 'in an ideal world we don't want you to work because university is full-time'. Perhaps this reflects the comment made by Harvey *et al* (1998) in their study of undergraduate work experience who concluded that:

> Staff in higher education institutions are often unaware of the numbers of students working during term-time, the hours spent on part-time work, the nature of that work, the students' reasons for doing it and, thus, the extent to which it impacts on the total student experience.

Respondents were then asked whether they thought there was anything the university or the academic staff could do to help those students whose academic progress was being adversely affected. As far as the university as a body is concerned there was little the respondents thought it could do. One respondent thought the university could establish greater links with the National Union of Students in their protests for more student funding.

Were the university to issue guidelines regarding limits to the number of hours students undertook to work outside their studies most respondents thought this would have little influence. As S10 said 'people do what they want to do'. Both S2 and S3 thought it was a matter of individual choice for students to prioritize different aspects of student life. These comments about individual choice are reflected in the findings of the study by Hodgson & Spours (2000) where 'post-sixteen students maintained that there is no fixed threshold of hours at which part-time work becomes a problem for achievement and that it depends on individual choice'.

Although the University of Brighton encourages students not to undertake more than twelve hours per week of paid employment, S9 said she had never heard of any such guidelines although her sixth-form college had recommended a maximum of twelve hours employment per week. S9 said 'at the end of the day if you want more money to go out and spend then you aren't going to listen to the guidelines'. S5 thought that twelve hours employment per week was sensible whilst S1 said that a weekly maximum of sixteen hours would be reasonable but admitted that he exceeded this figure himself. As S4 pointed out 'at the end of the day people aren't working for the enjoyment. If you can't afford not to work then unfortunately you've got to work ... to stay here' and this sentiment was echoed by S12.

S7 called on the university to play a more prominent role in advertising jobs available locally and, in particular, those within the university itself. He said that jobs such as part-time library staff or bar staff or shop staff within the university were hard to find out about and he would welcome more help from the university as a whole and not just the Student Union in facilitating access to these jobs.

There were calls too for greater understanding on the part of the academic staff towards the student situation regarding part-time employment during term-time. As S8 commented 'they don't consider that you do work. They just assume that you're a student and that's what you do'. Greater understanding could manifest itself in not re-arranging timetabled lectures (S8) and allowances being made for the late submission of coursework (S5, S7, S9 and S10). However, S9 and S12 thought such concessions were unfair on other students.

Several respondents wanted extra support for their studies from the academic staff. This could take the form of extra tuition offered as drop-in sessions and small work groups (S1) as well as an appointment system for discussing academic work on an individual basis outside timetabled lectures and tutorial slots (S4). S5 also wanted extra classes to be offered at different times for example later in the afternoon or earlier in the morning to accommodate the employment hours of working students. There were calls too for greater communication between academic staff and students. S6 said she didn't know who her personal tutor was and added that she would like to be monitored on a regular basis at least once a term to look at issues such as balancing the demands of part-time employment and academic workloads.

A final issue concerned the widespread nature of the timetables with one student saying he would like them to be more compacted. This comment is also reflected in the study by Kular & Winn (1998) in which 45 per cent of the sample thought that courses should adapt the timetable to make it easier for students to work part-time.

Respondents were asked to comment on how they spend the money they earned from their part-time employment. Five of the twelve interviewees said they owned a car which they described as essential. If car ownership is accepted as essential, and this is discussed later in the context of public transport, a total of ten respondents said they spent the money they earned on a mixture of basic living costs/essentials and non-essentials/luxuries. One student said she used her earnings purely to fund her luxuries and not her basic living costs at all, whilst the complete opposite was true for another respondent.

The most commonly mentioned essentials were food (seven students), books (four students) and car-running costs whilst going-out was mentioned most frequently in the non-essential category (seven students). Other non-essential expenditure included: buying clothes, cigarettes and presents; going to the cinema; paying mobile telephone bills; buying football season tickets and paying for Sky television.

In the 'essential' category the following additional items of expenditure were mentioned by three respondents: university fees and accommodation costs; photocopying cards; computer print-out cards; credit card bills. These comments reflect the findings of other recent studies too. The NUS survey (1999) found that 'students work overwhelmingly to pay for their basic living and study costs and to have some money for a social life as well as to pay off debts such as credit agreements incurred before they started their courses'.

The issue of car ownership, which was also raised in the studies by Hodgson & Spours (2000) in the sixth-form context and by Kular & Winn (1998) at the University of Brighton, is worth considering in more detail. All five of the car-owners in this study described their car as 'essential' and defended their opinion when probed by analyzing their individual situations in the context of public transport in the area. Three of the five car-owners lived more than ten miles away from the site where they studied. These three respondents said that the public transport possibilities for coming to college were expensive, unreliable and inconvenient. S8, who spent fifteen pounds a week on petrol to run her car, said it

following headings: issues for the students; issues for the academic staff; issues for employers; issues for the institution.

Issues for the students

Although the issues of compacting timetables and more individual contact and support from tutors raised by several students in this study are largely issues for the individual institution and the academic staff to address, it is pertinent for students themselves to recognize that full-time education requires full-time commitment, particularly during term-time, above and beyond that of timetabled lectures and tutorials. Other studies (for example, Curtis, 2000) have found that many students do not consider university to be a full-time occupation and that when not in class they are available to work. This attitude can have a detrimental effect on the cohesion of group work performed outside class and can eat into time available for extra reading around subjects. This in turn can lead to a climate of individuals straddling their academic work and the labour market and not being fully committed to the cultures of either (Hodgson & Spours, 2000).

A further issue for students to consider which emerged from this study is that of the expense of being a full-time student. Several students appeared to be surprised by extra and unanticipated course costs and car-ownership put added financial pressure on individuals. Whilst those who study in Brighton and live further away are frequently affected by the nature of an inadequate public transport system and may feel they really need a car, it may also be that individuals should think more carefully about accepting jobs involving unsocial hours which can not be serviced by public transport. This would enable individuals to avoid car-running costs and ease the financial burden to some extent.

It appears from the findings in this study that were the university to strictly stipulate and enforce the number of hours deemed appropriate for students to undertake part-time employment during term-time it would have little effect. The prevailing student culture to emerge in this respect from this study seems to be that of freedom of choice with students saying that it is up to the individual to balance the demands of combining academic study with paid employment. If this is the case, the onus is on individual students to achieve this balance and serious consideration must be given to how such a balance can best be achieved.

Issues for the academic staff

Several students in this study mentioned the widespread nature of the timetables and said they would welcome extra study support groups. There are of course financial and organizational constraints on providing the latter whilst the practicalities of compacting timetables is complicated given the undergraduate numbers on many courses and the variety of pathways through degree programmes being offered. However, as Kular & Winn (1998) in their study within the same institution also found, many students thought that staff should adapt the timetable to make it easier for students to take paid work in term-time. It may be that academic staff need to at least consider this possibility in more detail.

Several students also reported a lack of communication between the academic staff and students in relation to the demands placed on students outside lectures and this was interpreted by several respondents as a lack of interest in the student situation on the part of the academic staff. This apparent lack of interest is not borne out by my informal conversations with colleagues but perhaps a more prominent voice needs to be heard by the students in this area. Hodgson & Spours (2000) noted in their study that there is a growing consensus that we need to accept part-time work as a reality of student life and that the positive features of student employment need to be harnessed. Harvey *et al* (1998) concluded that many academic staff ignore term-time, part-time work altogether and regard it as an unfortunate part of student survival rather than as part of the student learning experience. Perhaps it is pertinent to suggest that more effective use could be made in academic studies of the student part-time employment experience which would, in turn, lead to greater communication between the academic staff and the students themselves.

Several interviewees contrasted the support received from tutors in their sixth-form college with that received from their tutors at university. The latter was deemed insufficient by several students and it may well be the case that the jump from sixth-form college to university requires greater recognition in the form of student support by the academic staff at university than is currently offered.

Issues for employers

Other studies (for example, Hodgson & Spours, 2000) have noted the apparent lack of awareness on the part of employers concerning the effect their employment practices may be having on the students who work for them. Only 32 per cent of respondents in the study by Curtis (2000) said their employers allowed them to work fewer hours around examination time and these findings were reflected in the comments made by students in the study presented here. It would appear that student employers generally need to be more aware of the periods of high pressure for students in order not to add to it by unexpected calls for overtime and additional hours of work.

Issues for the institution

Many respondents in this study appeared to be financially naive about the costs of student life. Indeed Kular & Winn (1998) found consistently that 70 per cent of respondents thought students should be provided with financial guidance. With recent press reports (for example, *Times Higher Educational Supplement*, 21/8/1998) indicating that sixth-formers anticipate paying £87 less per month than the average amount actually spent by students, it may be appropriate for the institution to consider introducing financial management as part of personal development studies in the future in an effort to raise awareness of this issue.

Some students in this study also felt it would be helpful if the institution could encourage students to undertake employment within the institution itself. This would allow individuals to remain in the university culture and would mean that appropriate jobs could be found in terms of hours, conditions, pay and skills. Many universities have established Job Shops to meet this demand for institution-based employment with a degree of success according to recent press reports (for example, *Guardian Education*, 20/10/2000) and it would appear that it is relatively simple for institutions to facilitate such opportunities.

The implications of the Excellence Challenge Package are also pertinent to the findings of this study in the institutional context. One of the aims of this package is to encourage universities to recruit and retain students from deprived backgrounds. Whilst funding to support such students is proposed, in the light of the changes to the student funding mechanism that have taken place over the past few years as outlined in the background to this study, it seems reasonable to suggest that future students from poorer backgrounds will also have to undertake paid employment to sustain their studies. Whilst this study did not find that objective evidence supported the hypothesis that part-time, term-time paid employment has a detrimental effect on academic performance, it did find that 'working' students encounter problems which institutions may need to address. If universities are to recruit an increased number of students from deprived backgrounds who also have to work whilst undertaking their studies, it suggests that the number of students encountering the kinds of difficulties outlined above will increase and the need for universities to resolve these difficulties will be that much the greater.

Limitations of the methodology

Any conclusions drawn from this study can be but tentative as they are limited by the nature of the sample which was taken from one degree programme at one university with data being collected over a period of two months. The sample itself was relatively small and self-selecting and it is therefore not possible to claim that the findings are representative of all undergraduates who work part-time during term-time.

The findings from this study indicate that the issue of whether the part-time, term-time employment of traditional undergraduates affects their academic performance is complex. It appears that the effects exist in a complex relationship with a number of key personal and contextual factors which can not be treated in isolation and it may well be that other factors play a role in poor examination performance as well as employment demands.

A further consideration is that no one interviewed in this study worked over twenty hours per week. It is possible that had those students who do work longer hours been willing to participate, greater depth would have been added to the findings of the study.

Conclusion

With regard to the four research questions underpinning the study the following conclusions can be drawn. Firstly, five of the twelve students interviewed said their paid employment was not related at all to the degree course studied whilst the remaining seven interviewees said their employment was in part related.

Secondly, those interviewed said their part-time, term-time employment had various effects on their academic performance. These have been explored in the data analysis section.

Thirdly, objective evidence did not fully support the students' perceptions concerning the effects of their paid employment on their academic performance.

Fourthly, there was found to be no significant difference between the end-of-year marks of the 'working' and the 'non-working' students.

I hope that the findings from this study will contribute to the debates in the wider academic community surrounding the issues of undergraduate part-time, term-time employment. It would appear that the student body has changed over the years and reflects the increasingly complex nature of higher education today, whilst most academics now working in higher education operate within a system which is fundamentally different to the one they themselves experienced as students. As Barnett (2000) notes, higher education has become a world of 'supercomplexity' and rapid change. It is, he argues, a world of uncertainty, unpredictability, challengeability and contestability in which our frameworks for understanding ourselves and the circumstances in which we live and work are increasingly complex. I hope that the study presented in this chapter has gone some way to penetrating this complexity to a limited extent.

Appendix: The Main Interview Schedule

Q1. What is your name? _____

Q2. Are you under the age of 21?   *Response:*   *YES*   *NO*

Code: 1   2

Q3. Do you have at least one part-time job during term time for which you are paid?   *Response:*   *YES*   *NO*

Code: 1   2

Q4. How many part-time jobs do you have at the moment?

Prompts:	*One*	*Two*	*Three*	*Four*		*Other*.........
Code:	1	2	3	4		5

Q5. What is the average total number of hours you work per week on your term time job(s)?

Prompts:	*0-4*	*5-9*	*10-14*		*15-19*		*20-24*
Code:	1	2	3		4		5
Prompts:	*25-29*	*30-34*	*35-39*	*40-44*	*45-49*		
Code:	6	7	8	9	10		

Q6. What kind of work does your term-time employment involve?

Prompts: retail   hotels/pubs   cleaning   office
Code: 1   2   3   4
        building   *other..*
Code: 5   6

Q7. Is your part-time job related in any way to the content of your degree course?
Prompts: *YES   NO   IN PART   NOT SURE*
Code: 1   2   3   4
Comments?

Q8. Which of the following comments applies to you? *(SHOW CARD)*
My paid employment has had *no* effect on my academic work
Prompt: Agree   Disagree
Code: 1   2
My paid employment has had a *good* effect on my academic work
Prompt: *YES   NO*
Code: 3   4
My paid employment has had a *bad* effect on my academic work
Prompt: *YES   NO*
Code: 5   6

Q9. If your employment has had an effect (good or bad) on your academic work, could you describe how it has affected your work and to what extent?
Prompts (-)   *Prompts (+)*
• missed/cancelled lectures/tutorials   • improved time management
• extensions to deadlines requested   skills
• change of class/lecture time   • better understanding of
• reduced use made of library facilities coursework content
• late submission of coursework   • opportunity to discuss course-
• failure to complete assignments   related issues at work
• missed/cancelled group meetings with peers   •
• failure to do background reading adequately
Comments:

Q10. Have you ever discussed the effects you feel your part-time job is having on your academic work with a member of the academic staff at the university?
Prompt: *YES (ask for comments - go to Q11)*
Code: 1
Prompt: *NO (ask for comments - go to Q12)*
Code: 2

Q11. How would you describe the attitude of the academic staff at the university towards the demands made on you by your part-time job(s)?
Prompts: • tolerant towards non-attendance/cancelled appointments
                     • flexible regarding deadlines
                     • generally concerned and helpful

• intolerant of late submissions of coursework
• not prepared to accommodate employment demands
Comments:

Q12. Is there anything you think the university or the academic staff could do to help those students whose academic progress *is* being affected by their part-time employment?
Comments?

Q13. On what do you spend the money you earn from your part-time employment?
Prompts: • basic living costs / essentials
• 'luxuries' e.g. social life / running a car - (*probe* re. car + distance lived from university)
Comments?

• Is there anything else you would like to say about these issues that we haven't discussed?

References

Barnett, R. (2000), *Realizing the University in an age of supercomplexity*, Buckingham: SRHE & Open University Press.

Berkeley, J. (1997), Keynote presentation at the Association of Graduate Recruiters' Annual Conference, Warwick University, 7-9 July.

Cremieux, F. & Johnes, G. (1993), 'Student poverty in the UK: some new evidence', *International Journal of Educational Management*, vol. 7(4), pp. 27-32.

Curtis, S. (2000), Undergraduates are now filling the McJobs, *Professional Manager*, May 2000, pp. 44-46.

Curtis, S. (2001), 'A coincidence of needs? Employers and full-time students', *Employee Relations*, vol. 23(1), pp. 38-54.

Ford, J., Bosworth, D. & Wilson, R. (1995), 'Part-time Work and Full-time Higher Education', *Studies in Higher Education*, vol. 20(2), pp. 187-202.

Further Education Development Agency (FEDA) (1999), *Learning and Earning: pilot survey*, London: FEDA.

Glaser, B. & Strauss, A. (1967), *The Discovery of grounded Theory*, Chicago: Aldine.

Hakim, C. (1996), *Working students. Students in full-time education with full-time and part-time jobs*, London: Department of Sociology, LSE.

Harvey, L., Geall, V. and Moon, S. with Aston, J., Bowes, L. and Blackwell, A. (1998), *Work Experience: expanding opportunities for undergraduates*, Birmingham: Centre for Research into Quality, The University of Central England.

Hodgson, A. & Spours, K. (2000), *Earning and Learning: a local study of part-time paid work among 14-19 year olds*, London: Lifelong Learning Group, Institution of Education.

Kular, R. & Winn, S. (1998), *The financial situation of students at the University of Brighton: the seventh report, 1997/98*, Brighton: Health and Social Policy Research Centre, University of Brighton.

Leonard, M. (1995), 'Labouring to Learn: Students' Debt and Term Time Employment in Belfast', *Higher Education Quarterly*, vol. 49(3), pp. 229-247.

Lindsay, R.O. & Paton-Saltzberg, R. (1993), *The effects of Paid Employment on the Academic Performance of Full-Time Students in a British 'new' university*, (Report of a study commissioned by the Academic Standards Committee of Oxford Brookes University).

McCarthy, P. & Humphrey, R. (1995), 'Debt: the reality of student life', *Higher Education Quarterly*, vol. 49(1), pp. 78-86.

NUS (1996), *Students at Work*, London: National Union of Students/GMB.

NUS (1999), *NUS Students at Work Survey*, London: National Union of Students.

Pilkington, P. (1994), 'Student Financial Support', In S. Haselgrove (ed.), *The Student Experience*, Buckingham: SRHE and Open University Press. pp. 55-71.

Winn, S. & Stevenson, R. (1993), *A Study of the Financial Situation of Students at the University of Brighton*, Brighton: University of Brighton.

Chapter 4

University, Employability and Employment

Josep M. Masjuan
Helena Troiano

Reflection of Method: Focus Groups

As a general rule, academics who study universities rarely stand back from their research. Perhaps the problems and concerns associated with university life, and how they cope with them, are experienced differently. But to a large extent beliefs, visions, assumptions, and interrelations – in short, identity keys, – are shared with other academics.

When the research methodology employed is aimed at some kind of intervention this problem becomes more acute. The focus group technique used here is halfway between group interview and group intervention and puts the focus on the practical implications from research. And of course this impinges on aspects of university life to which researchers belong as teaching staff and as researchers.

In much research, part of the subjectivity of the people who belong to the object of study is denied them when the categories for analysis are imposed from the outside. To involve peers in research poses the problem that such an imposition of meanings makes this group feel treated as inferiors, and this may provoke a revolt. This is especially the case where we are dealing with expert academics in social science research.

In a focus group, the asymmetry between the leaders and the people invited is not as high as is the case with other techniques. Here the imposition of meanings is restricted to the selection of some generic subjects on which to focus the discussion. Thus, the session is planned as an exercise in reflection with open questions where the participants have the possibility to let their discourse flow from one subject to another, as well as to incorporate new subjects into the debate. In this sense, there is no radical imposition from an a priori external expert knowledge. But of course pressures will nonetheless exist due to the very way in which the discussion sessions are organized.

The imposition of viewpoints is inherent in the way focus groups are organized. Firstly, the structure of the discussion in this particular case stems from the issues that appeared as being important from the preliminary survey research. This disempowers participants, who have limited control over the agenda.

Secondly, the selection of people to participate in the focus group creates a specific social situation with implicit connotations. The social context, including both university 'insiders' and 'outsiders', is set up by the researchers themselves.

The underlying intention beneath this rather contrived social situation is not that academics fully accept the requirements that are made from outside the institution, but that they critically reflect on the new demands, the changing context and the mission of the university in this new context. For academics themselves, however, their impression may be that they are placed in a situation where the need to listen to contributions and external demands is unavoidable.

The reactions of the different academic groups to this situation are diverse. We have to say, however, that the presence of external participants encouraged every internal participant to make much more explicit the premises and the taken-for-granted knowledge which their everyday practices in the university are built upon.

Introduction

Generally, modern universities, and the Universitat Autònoma de Barcelona (UAB) among them, are striving to take a position sensitive to the needs and expectations of the outside world. Actions to achieve this tend to be multiple, take place in different areas, and have variable outcomes. However, in all cases, there is a strong belief in the need to establish a dialogue and reach mutual understanding with the relevant agents involved. It was within this context, of need for new mechanisms of information and dialogue, that the UAB authorities set up the *Graduates Observatory*. Responsible to the Vice-chancellor for Quality Assurance, the Observatory had financial and organizational support from the University's Social Council as well as scientific support of the Institute of Educational Science.

The research reported in this chapter is of a broader investigation that combines a telephone interview of graduates and focus groups involving representatives of the academic community and external professionals. The purpose of the focus group was for the participants to discuss different points of view and to generate solutions to the problems that emerged in the survey. There were seven focus groups in all. Two research team members and two university representatives were present at all of them. The rest of the participants included:

- Psychology: 5 external representatives and 6 academics.
- Pedagogy and Teaching: 6 external representatives and 9 academics.
- Geography, Politics and Sociology: 10 external representatives and 5 academics.
- Degree in Economics and Business Administration: 6 external representatives and 3 academics.
- Diploma in Business Administration: 4 external representatives and 4 academics.
- Maths and Physics: 10 external representatives and 5 academics.
- Geology, Chemistry, Biochemistry: 10 external representatives and 5 academics.

This chapter briefly presents the results of the quantitative research and, in accordance with the subject of this book, focuses more extensively on the analysis of the focus groups. Finally, a critical review of the research results and the methodology is given.

Theoretical background and research objectives

Existing theories that relate the educational system and the labour market may be classified and described in a very simplified way into three different groups:

The functionalist model This corresponds to the theory of human capital (Becker, 1964) and to the first functionalist theories of social stratification. Technological change generates a need for new skills in the work force in order to put in motion new technological instruments and to move to new organizational forms. This phenomenon increases the demand for people with these new skills. The increase in demand for trained people is what provokes the extension of the educational system, and therefore, of university training, which results in a change in the number and the features of the professions. The system is regulated through supply and demand mechanisms.

The credentialist model (Collins, 1979; Boudon, 1973). Here occupational groups are seen as competing for professional promotion in the economic sphere and new generations try to improve their training in order to place themselves in a better position when looking for a job and their subsequent promotion. This process increases the demand for training and therefore produces growth in the educational system in general and specifically in higher education as an inflationary process. Middle classes, which are better placed in this competition, try to monopolize higher jobs.

The reproduction model (Bowles & Gintis, 1981; Bourdieu & Passeron, 1970; Bernstein, 1996). The contribution of this model mostly revolves around the mechanisms that favour success for some social classes or categories over others in the education system and in the labour market. The model emphasizes the correspondence between the cultural requirements underpinning schooling which favour middle class culture, to the detriment of the manual labour working classes, and of men to the detriment of women. In this same context the contributions made by theoreticians regarding the segmentation of the labour market is also of relevance.

Our point of view is that these models are not absolutely incompatible and, therefore, it is better to study the different explanatory mechanisms within a specific context in this case the relationships between the educational and the productive systems. This approach has been extensively developed in other work (Masjuan, Troiano & Vivas, 2002) and due to reasons of space we only offer here a short illustrative list of the factors that have been taken into consideration.

Several sets of mechanisms that closely interact have been identified; each one fits in more coherently with the explanation derived from one of the three aforementioned models.

Firstly, we find that the global volume of students and their distribution among the different disciplines (and the higher or lesser importance of the social variables of origin) depends on, among other things: size of the cohort, expectations, information about the labour market, assessment of costs and risks, and personal preferences.

Secondly, the variable 'offer of jobs' to holders of different qualifications depends on, among other things: planning of training needs and allocation of resources, institutional policies of organizational expansion, restriction of admissions, and inertia.

Thirdly, the demand in the labour market for graduate students happens according to the following variables: situation of the economy; availability of people with a university degree and technological development (despite the fact that this does not always imply an increase in the required competencies).

Fourth, the specific dynamics of the labour market may have an effect on the opportunities in the first jobs due to: regulation of the labour market, individual positioning in the market; characteristics of the candidates, selection systems, and work expectations. This framework provides a multiple approach to the problem of the relationship between higher education and the labour market that underpins this research.

The research meanwhile aims to contribute to informed decision-making by the university via the Graduate Observatory. The *general objective* of the Graduates Observatory is to gather information and knowledge about what happens to university graduates in the 'outside world' (especially with those of the UAB), in order to reflect on the achievement of objectives and to improve the transition from higher education to the world of work.

The transition processes from the university to the labour market that we analyze in this chapter took place in the 1990s when the Spanish job market was in the process of recovery. However, there remained a deep and basic structural change in the development process of Spanish capitalism. This presented difficulties for the professional placement of students with a university degree. Joaquim Casal (1999) explains it as follows:

> The 90s were characterized by prefiguring a new form of capitalist development. It is not so much a discourse on the old crisis anymore, but the consideration of the birth of a new social configuration that has received a large number of epithets by its authors and which, provisionally, we identify as *informational capitalism,* already incipient in the 60s. It is not a change faced with a recessive conjuncture; it is a much deeper change on a structural level: the irruption of a new societal model. The changes are not merely circumstantial, but we are witnessing the birth of a new social model defined by an irreversible tendency towards 'global economy', the informational character of production and the distribution of goods, flexible production as regards demand, substantial change in the job structure and the organization of work, etc. A new *technological paradigm* that ultimately appears to be very aggressive, very excluding

and which very much creates a duality as regards the labour market since it produces a surplus of labour force in the central countries.... (pp. 161-162)

Therefore, generally speaking, the quantitative adjustment between the supply of people with university degrees and the demands of the economy has been – up to the turn of the century – clearly inflationary (Planas & Beduwe, 2002).[10] Yet this is a context where there are difficulties in absorbing graduates into the labour market. The survey results in the study reported below largely support this account. Graduates tend to follow longer and more complex placement routes. These have been defined as 'successive approaches' for they imply precarious work situations, combining training and work, a time lag, badly-qualified jobs etc., until a sustainable job is attained (Casal, 1999).

The identification and characterization of this insertion route becomes, thus, the *first specific aim* of our research. This was: to gain knowledge about the UAB graduates process leading to employment four years after graduation and to understand their assessment of the training received at university after their employment experience.

In order to explore this 'insertion route' we begin by discussing changes in the skills required by the market. Various authors in the field of economics and sociology have debated the changes in the production model as a result of the transition from the so-called 'fordist' to 'post-fordist' organization. This has been triggered and amplified by multiple factors such as new information technologies (Castells, 1996; Casal, 1999; Young, 1998; Barnett, 2001; Brown & Scase, 1994).

A useful model to summarize these changes is provided by Brown & Scase (1994). Particularly they describe change in the organizational paradigm as organizations evolve from bureaucratic organizations towards adaptive organizations. (Table 4.1)

---

[10] This citation refers to a large piece of research into the relationship between production of diplomas and the demands of the labour market in the European context in which the authors of this chapter have participated.

Table 4.1 Changes in the organizational paradigm (Brown & Scarse, 1994)

Adaptive Organization	Bureaucratic	Organization
Selection	Depersonalized individual attributes	Personal qualities, personality characteristics
Socialization	Compartmentalized, Inter-positional, Following rules	Global, Interpersonal, Breaking codes, Building up rules
Cognitive style	Bureaucratic personality	Charismatic personality
Symbolic social control	Impersonal, Explicit rules	Personalized, Implicit rules
Promotion/Success	Explicit fulfilment Criteria based on a bureaucratic work programme	Implicit fulfilment. Criteria based on interpersonal compatibility and performance
Corporate Culture	Weak	Strong

Investigating the perceptions of some of those involved in the context in which the professional placement processes take place allowed us to explore this model from an empirical point of view.

In the first place we were interested in knowing how the 'outside world' perceived the employment difficulties of the majority of graduates, and to what extent they were attributed to a lack of the competencies required, that is to lack of employability. Secondly, we examined the extent to which the world of work was making explicit demands on higher education institutions, according to the adaptive model. We were also interested in how academics reacted to this new situation. Altogether, it is included in the second specific aim which, once more, contains an aspect of action.

Second specific aim: To know the views of different social agents – private companies, public services, professional bodies, recruitment agencies, unions, students – regarding the training of UAB graduates, the situation of the labour market, the evolution of their own professions and the competencies necessary for their practice. This included gathering suggestions about possible modes of cooperation between the university and the outside world and the exchange of different views between the academics responsible for each discipline, the university authorities and representatives of the world of work.

We have to this point been focusing on the changes outside the university. We also sought to understand change with the university. One of the factors that has most transformed the university in our country has been the increase in the number of students over the last three decades. Not only has this increase brought more students to university, it has also, brought a broader range of students with more diverse social characteristics.

If we want to capture the future transformation of the university as regards these factors, we also have to explore the extent to which academics are aware of the increase in diversity among the student population as a result of the growth in the number of students. And we need to know how far they are prepared to deal with this by using new teaching approaches. This is especially important if high rates of failure and drop out are to be avoided.

There exists a potentially conflictual situation in which the presence of a more diverse student body is combined with new external training requirements centred around the development of broader range of skills. Here Brown and Scase's thesis appears relevant (1994). They argue that curricular forms emphasizing transferable abilities and new competencies favour the middle classes as they already possess the cultural capital coherent with these forms.

In this tension between efficiency and social equity, the third aim of the Graduate Observatory's is to contribute to the development of a quality system that takes into consideration the contradictions which are inherent in today's university.

Specifically this involved the analysis and comparison of data in order to obtain relevant information so that it can be used in processes of evaluation and decision-making intending to improve the quality of the training at the UAB.

The multiple aims of this research, together with the diversity of the data to be collected, suggested the adoption of a combined strategy of methods. On the one hand, the study of professional placement routes (first specific aim) must provide an overview of the placement process. Here we explored responses from an entire graduate year of individuals. (See appendices for graphical representation of placement route for all graduates.) As far as possible, we have attempted to record the greatest possible diversity of routes in a specific time frame. As regards the other aims, it is useful to collect interpretations of the situation, new definitions of the professional reality, creative solutions, and justified demands within their context. Here, a qualitative approach is used (focus groups) which allows us to capture the nuances and the depth of the discourse. The remainder of this chapter reports the findings from this part of our work.

Focus Groups

As noted the focus group method was chosen in order to address several aims. They allow a certain depth in the interpretation of the results, references to new contexts of professional development, clarification of the demand for new skills and so on. Turning 'inward' they also allow us to explore the transformation of the university. As noted academics have been subject to a range of pressures including increased student numbers.

Group interview: data collection and interpretation

The technique of the focus group is oriented towards the *group interview* in which the aim is to expose the existing discourses. Experts on a subject are gathered who embrace a wide range of viewpoints. Here the differences and similarities between different participants, as well as the dynamics between the perspectives of a problem, become available. In this process we expect the articulation (of equivalence, nuance, extension, opposition, etc.) among the existing discourses to become evident (Steyaert & Bowen, 1994; Valles, 1997).

Group intervention: exchange of ideas and reflection

However if we take into account how focus groups function within the framework of the Observatory, we may also consider that they are a form of *group intervention*. This is due to the fact that the interpretation of the data, and the assessment of the situation carried out in the focus group pushes the university members who participate in these to reflect on the following questions: 'Who are we?', 'What do we want to change?', 'Which problems do we have?', 'How are we to solve them?'. We could say that focus groups also have implications for action at a socio-relational level (Steyaert & Bowen, 1994).

This emphasis on self-reflection and the will to carry out organizational changes is what characterizes the orientation of the *group intervention*. In this case, we can consider this emphasis as proper to the focus groups of the Observatory. We understand it as an exercise in external collaboration, where an organization is open to its environment. The aim of this intervention is to foster change in the way of thinking and acting.

Methodology

Drawing on the results obtained in the graduates' survey, an outline identifying a group of relevant topics related to professional employment in the discipline studied was produced. Essentially, an assessment of the current situation, employability conditions, convenience of changes in the university, and suggestions for ways of improvement were requested. The outline was sent to the participants prior to the meeting of the focus groups together with a brief report on the most significant data from the quantitative survey, so that participants could reflect upon the different subjects before their contribution to the discussion.

Participants from the University were academics with a position of responsibility in the Faculties or Departments involved in the discipline studied, as well as representatives of the University's governing bodies. The choice of participants from the wider society was conditioned by the results obtained in the survey which identified the most frequent types of employment among the different groups of graduates. The participants were from industry, public services, unions, recruitment agencies, professional bodies, and chambers of commerce.

In certain cases it was necessary to put together participants from more than one discipline to carry out a focus group. The criteria used stems from the combination of different elements: affinity of the programmes of study; career opportunities in similar areas and/or employment with contractual conditions in similar proportion.

The group discussion was conducted during a session that lasted approximately three hours. A member of the research team acted as a moderator and opened the session by presenting the main results of the quantitative research.

After that, the moderator introduced the main topics for discussion encouraging the participation of the external professional first, and the academics afterwards. The group discussion was conducted in a semi-directive manner that attempted to establish dialogue between the different participants about the relevant topics. Another member of the research team attended the focus group adopting a role of non-active participation with the task of registering the contributions and observations, and monitoring the recording of the session. The analysis involved:

- Classification of the participants' contributions in generic topics and specific sub-topics.
- Identification of different lines of discourse regarding each topic and sub-topic, and of possible partition axes.
- Analysis of the relationship between different types of discourse and the participants producing them, taking into account that they belong to a particular group.

The data from the groups was classified by themes, taking into account who the speaker was (as a member of a particular group), and bearing in mind the context in which the discourse takes place. First, an initial thematic reduction was carried out for each focus group, which tried to retain all the relevant information in terms of contents, context, and expressiveness. This first report was sent to the authorities of the University and to the academics responsible for each discipline studied. Secondly, a thematic summary maintaining the core aspects was prepared and attached to the first report.

Results of the focus groups

The tables below summarize the content of the discourse produced in the different focus groups. The content of the boxes is illustrated with some verbatim comments by those involved.

Table 4.2 Perception of employment difficulties

	Psychology	Pedagogy	Teaching
Difficulties	Difficulties in placement of graduates.	Difficulties in placement of graduates.	Difficulties in placement of graduates. Demand to increase in the future.
Number of university graduates	Surplus of psychologists.		
Profiles	Vague profile and overlapping with	Vague profile and overlapping with other	

		university degrees	
	other university degrees.	Lack of specific employment sectors. Poor knowledge of these professions in the market.	
Public/private market			Segmentation of the sector in public/private.
Other specific characteristics of the diploma		Poor status.	Poor status.

	Geography, Politics, Sociology	Degree in Economics and Business Administration	Diploma in Business Administration
Difficulties	Difficulties in placement of graduates.	Relatively easy placement of graduates.	Good employment, although slightly underemployment.
Number of university graduates	Excess of supply.		
Profiles	Competition between different disciplines. The labour market is poorly informed about these graduates' profiles. Some disciplines are relatively new and need further specialization.	At the moment the labour market does not differentiate between the two profiles (B.A. and Economics). Even recruitment does not differentiate between Engineering, Mathematics or Law for jobs related to Economics.	Versatility and continuous modification of studies. Participation of external professionals in teaching.
Employment conditions	Insecure employment conditions. Some types of self-employment are a cover up for precariousness.		Poor capacity for creating companies due to social origin (working class).
Public/private market	Obstacles to access the public administration compared with other disciplines.		Difficulties in the public sector.
Other specific characteristics of the diploma		Firms employ university graduates to do jobs previously performed by less qualified personnel. This may be due to the excess of supply, or to the	

		slow maturation of current graduates.	

	Maths and Physics	**Biology, Geology, Chemistry, Biochemistry**
Difficulties	Despite having experienced some difficulties in placement of graduates, the prospects are good.	Chemistry: Difficulties of placement of graduates during that period. Geology: Difficulties of placement of graduates.
Number of university graduates		Geology: Graduates supply is higher than demand.
Profiles		
Employment conditions		Contractual flexibility.
Other specific characteristics of the diploma	An academic noted that these degrees are not particularly attractive today, except for the labour market.	Chemistry: Serious difficulties during that period due to a huge process of restructuring of the chemical industry. Competition between universities has led to the creation of unnecessary degree courses.

In terms of perception of employment difficulty it is not possible to talk about a uniform discourse as each profession has a different situation. Historically, sciences and technical disciplines have experienced fewer difficulties, but when they occur they are attributed to the current situation. For instance:

The period we are studying is one of the most difficult periods in the history of the Catalan industry, particularly for the chemical sector. (Chemistry. External. Professional)

Problems related to the Humanities and Social Science disciplines are attributed to excess of supply and competition problems between poorly defined profiles:

There is an oversupply of psychology graduates and I understand very well why psychologists work in other fields, because society does not absorb them. (Psychology. Academic)

There are lots of professionals from other fields doing educational tasks and they have more career opportunities than [teachers] themselves. (Pedagogy. External Professional)

Table 4.3 Relationship with the labour market

	Psychology	Pedagogy	Teaching
New areas	Several beyond the clinical: human resources, hospitals, personnel, management, education.	Not restricted to formal teaching, but to all areas of training. (vocational, continuous, etc.) Planning. Organization.	Multidisciplinary services for children. Adult Education. Abroad.
Market control		Need for Professional Bodies.	Need for Professional Bodies.

	Geography, Politics, Sociology	Degree in Economics and Business Administration	Diploma in Business Administration
New areas	Pol. and Soc.: Very versatile professionals and therefore: managers, marketing, public managers, consultants, etc. Health, Education, Social Services. Geo.: Information, Tourist Guides, cartography, publishers.	Current employment mostly in Marketing, Accountancy and General Management. New areas: International commerce. Logistics. International Organizations.	
Market control	Importance of social networks.	Social network is important for employment, therefore the University should generate networks with the world of work.	
Univ./environment relations	Increased contact of University departments with external professionals in the research field. Combined research.	Positive appraisal of the University's effort to link with the industry.	University needs to further improve the cooperation with world of work.
Difficulties and university action	The University needs to promote these professionals, provide orientation, cooperation with external professionals, involvement of external professionals	Difficulties of producing a good curriculum internally. Need for external contribution. It is necessary to maintain the effort to improve the	Limitations (for creating companies) in type of degree and characteristics of students, linked to small business or working class.

	on an applied programme of study. Academics emphasize that the plans of study are significantly improving in that respect.	university's teaching methodology.	
Other possibilities	Self-employment.		Creation of new business. To promote new ideas in existing business.

	Maths and Physics	**Biology, Geology, Chemistry, Biochemistry**
New areas	Phy.: Material Science. Telecommunications and Computer Science in combination with others. Maths: Mathematics applied to finance. Phy. and Maths: Artificial Intelligence, Areas related to the Internet, Publicity, Holography. An academic noted that things are rapidly changing and there is a need to change the image of mathematics as academic only. Need to open up to the professional world.	Commercial, Health and Safety, Environmental Management, Occupational Health (Hygiene, Ergonomics, Psycho-sociology).
Market control	Lack of Professional Associations.	
Univ./environment relations	Active position of the University in relation to its graduates by setting up innovative businesses, halfway structures (spin off) to facilitate the university-business dialogue. To continue having a role in secondary education by improving teaching methods. Dialogue difficulties from both academics and the world of work.	Very positive assessment of the links between University-Business Sector, and need to increase them. Also links with the Local Authorities.
Difficulties and university action	Difficult to make changes from inside. Inertia among academics. Need to recruit lecturers from outside. The University cannot do everything.	The academics point out that this relationship (University-Business Sector) is very positive, there is no tradition and they are working on it. Rigidity of the academic world. Determinants of material and human resources.

The pressure for new organizational forms linking the university and the world of work is obvious. This takes the shape of suggestions regarding new labour areas and also regarding the need to establish stronger links between the university and the professional sphere: to reinforce the functions of the professional associations or to create new forms of collaboration. Sometimes this last system impinges on the modification of the most traditional teaching methodologies:

> If we think about what could be done to improve employment prospects for these graduates, we could look at what works in the USA and Europe and it could easily be implemented at the UAB. It's about developing specialized experiential courses where problems from the real world are brought up. Students have freedom, guided or non-guided, and are given a real problem to which they have to find a solution during that term. They are given the tools and help needed, but they are responsible for designing a group dynamics and talking to the firm who will then manage what they can do. (Maths and Physics. External Professional)

Academics recognize both the need to change the orientation of the university and the impossibility of carrying it out without the collaboration of external agents.

Table 4.4 Study plans and postgraduate studies: curricular changes

	Psychology	Pedagogy	Teaching
New contents	Usefulness of having a good clinical training.	Languages.	Training about families, social context, etc. Languages.
Orientation of the studies	The new curriculum has a strong professional focus.	Better defined professional profiles.	Widen curriculum with a broader base, without such early specializations as we have today.
Postgraduate courses	Need to have a more practical and specialist approach, if possible, after having acquired some work experience. Sometimes, they function as waiting rooms before finding a job.		

	Geography, Politics, Sociology	Degree in Economics and Business Administration	Diploma in Business Administration
New contents	Computer programming.	An academic suggests that Strategic Management and Human Resources should have more weight. With regards to small	Advanced Computer Science.

		businesses knowledge is important when postgraduate training is not possible.	
Orientation of the studies	Application of statistics to problem solving.	There are no problems. Versatility.	
Postgraduate Studies	No agreement on whether the curriculum should have a more specialist or generalist approach. Academics tend to prefer a more generalist orientation in the degrees and specialization in postgraduate courses. Advantage of linking with external professionals for Postgraduate Courses.		Practically orientated. There is no agreement on the subject Specialist/Generalist. Management of small businesses. Sometimes, they function as waiting rooms before finding a job.

	Maths and Physics	**Biology, Geology, Chemistry, Biochemistry**
New contents	Academic knowledge is not the problem.	Lack of additional knowledge: budgeting, marketing, languages, management, logistics, health and safety, quality assurance, environmental issues.
Orientation of the studies	Learn to translate technologies in terms of costs. Learn the value of time in a company. Business culture.	Problems are not derived from disciplinary knowledge. To maintain a generalist training, leaving specialization to postgraduate courses.

Postgraduate Studies	Suitability of specialized postgraduate courses with participation of external professionals. Firms are interested in PhD graduates because they bring scientific rigour and critical thinking, but they are not indispensable.	There is no agreement on the importance of doctorates for firms. Postgraduate specialization courses will be implemented in the future.

The discussion shows there to be some agreement on the need to incorporate a greater volume of vocationally-relevant knowledge. No lack of specific disciplinary knowledge was identified, rather there is an expressed need for the type of competencies required by the world of work.

It is also necessary to reinforce the capacity to apply knowledge acquired to new work contexts:

> I agree, and I also have experience of arguing to get things done on time, but this is more of an academic general problem.... In the University you can choose a research question with no limits of time and resources, and if you cannot solve it you go and publish six papers saying that it was a very interesting question but you have been unable to find an answer.... I am not criticizing that, its what the university should do. The world of industry is radically different, is 'Darwinian', companies simply survive [or die].... if you do not finish a contract on time you will not be able to pay your employees and will face extinction ... . (Physics and Maths. External Professional)

But the suitability of modifying the balance of the curriculum in either a more generalist or a more specialized nature is not unanimous. Thus, Physics and Maths academics, who have traditionally been more distant from this tendency, now appear more willing to accept the challenge of changing orientation while academics in Psychology and teacher education tend to want to retain subject-specific knowledge. Business Administration feels that versatility is necessary as a guarantee for employment, whilst economists would like to differentiate more clearly between Business Administration and Economics.

There is no agreement about the orientation to be given to postgraduate studies. It appears that the majority favours a tendency towards a generalist training at degree level oriented to professional practice, leaving specialization to postgraduate training. The function of postgraduate degrees remains diverse and sometimes contentious. For example such degrees were regarded as initial specialized training, a waiting room while postgraduates find a satisfactory job, and continuing professional development.

Table 4.5 New requirements: skills and attitudes

	Psychology	Pedagogy	Teaching
Abilities	Need for report writing skills.		

	Geography, Politics, Sociology	Degree in Economics and Business Administration	Diploma in Business Administration
Abilities	Ability to start own business. Ability to sell one's abilities in the labour market. Communication skills. Ability to move in the new market context. Good writing skills. Ability to speak in public. Negotiation skills. Geogr.: To promote generic competencies in relation to the field.	Ability to work in a team, to know where to obtain information. Decision making skills. Communication and presentation skills. Leadership and negotiation techniques.	Knowledge of new markets. Approach new businesses. Mobility in the global market.
Attitudes	To improve self-concept. Not possible to focus on research only.	Cooperation attitudes sometime clash with the competitiveness of the work environment. An academic pointed out the importance of changing teaching methods.	Open-mindedness. Versatility, practicality. In front of under-employment, need to lower horizons and adapt.
	Maths and Physics		**Biology, Geology, Chemistry, Biochemistry**
Abilities	Ability to cope with uncertainties in the work environment. Interdisciplinary work. Critical thinking in relation to models. To increase the applicability of the curricula.		Communication and commercial skills, group work, problem solving, interdepartmental work. Ability to reflect.
Attitudes	Interest in the external world. Positive attitudes towards the business world. Academics pointed out that to make changes in this area is not an easy task, but it is necessary to change aspects of the curricula and teaching, and evaluation methods as well.		Learn to sell their skills and knowledge. Ability to sell their expertise. Worldly-wise, open-mindedness, adaptability to business culture. Adaptability in general.

The discussion highlighted demand for attitudes and abilities more coherent with the dominant discourse on transferable skills, and the requirements of the new organizational forms. These include, a demand for social skills that contribute to improvement in relations with the public, clients, workmates, employers. Good oral and written communication skills are also required.

> There is a growing globalization (...). Globalization makes interaction detached from physical reality, therefore knowledge about the global market, foreign languages, and social interaction ability should be encouraged. (Business Administration. External Professional)

There is also a broader demand for cognitive skills, such as creativity, a 'critical spirit' and independence:

> How to look for information, how to present it, how to [predict and] respond to demands.... [new recruits] feel lost and initially find it difficult to respond. They feel like orphans. (Economics. External Professional)

The ability to meet these demands is perceived as linked to the capacity to change the culture of university professors and teaching methodologies:

> There is a barrier between the excessively academic orientation of the university lecturers and the way students work. What I mean is that the academic component may be useful to foster abstraction ability, but to develop these other competencies that are so important in the world of work, the teaching methods and academics' way of thinking represent an obstacle to the process. It is a very difficult problem to solve from a (university) Department.... Traditional lectures where the student spends seven hours taking notes, are not useful for some things. If someone from outside does not change it we are not going to, it requires too much effort. We try, we experiment but it is really very difficult. There is a barrier, an inability to make this necessary change, maybe it should be instigated in a different way. This is the issue I'm more concerned about. (Physics and Maths. Academic)

But, more than anything else, aspects related to the students' change of attitude are highlighted:

> ...the discussion is not so much about one more competency, which is what you were counting, but about a kind of feeling, a question of sensibility. (...) a model of behavior that would take into account that in management you are also dealing with people, and this is becoming more important. (...) not to explain how it should be, but how we experience it and how we feel about it. (Economics. External Professional)

> Rather than experience, what is expected from a fresh graduate is energy, enthusiasm, and to be free of old working habits that sometimes can be an obstacle. Usually, recent graduates have no ties, are more mobile and open-minded. (Chemistry. External Professional)

We have to pay attention to the fact that, in some cases, this implies a change in the job expectations of university graduates (Mathematics, Physics, Political Science,

Sociology and Geography, not in research) or, even, a lowering of these expectations (degree in B.A.).

Table 4.6 Training practice in external institutions

	Psychology	Pedagogy	Teaching
Placements	Placements take place in external centres and are very diverse.	Problems with fragmentation and short experience of most centres.	Poor involvement of the Administration. Teachers without experience acting as tutors.

	Geography, Politics, Sociology	Degree in Economics and Business Administration	Diploma in Business Administration
Placements	Need to improve professional work experience. Difficulty in finding suitable placements in the industry.	Work experience with firms represents a different learning environment and a very important one.	Now compulsory. There is a need for further improvement of the relationship with the business world. International programmes.

	Maths and Physics	Biology, Geology, Chemistry, Biochemistry
Placements	The new plans of study have started contacts with firms, external work experience, involvement of external professionals. Need to motivate students.	Need to continue with external professional placements, increasing control and quality.

Academics and external professionals of all disciplines make a positive assessment of the relevance of work placements in firms and institutions during the course of study. This was being implemented following the recent curricula reform.

> By spending time there (work experience in a firm) you are providing the student with an opportunity to learn what the world of work is like. So at the end of the experience he knows how to introduce himself, how to give a presentation, how to look for information, etc. and will be able to start more rapidly. (Economics. External Professional)

Even academics from disciplines far removed from the world of work talked about measures to improve cooperation between the world of business and higher education. The general feeling was that tighter links had to be drawn with the outside world.

Discussion of the results

Higher education and labour market

In the arguments used by participants in focus groups concerning the professional placement of graduates we can identify elements of both the functionalist and the credentialist models.

With regard to the credentialist model, we have referred to problems linked to the inflation of some specific diplomas. Spanish higher education has grown spectacularly in the last thirty years. The move from an elite system to a mass one has produced a generalized democratization of access to university. However, the growth process has in various ways impinged on the different academic areas. It has dramatically increased the size of Humanities and Social Sciences, particularly. Some fields, e.g. Health Science, experimental Science, and technological areas have only adopted open access.

Therefore, it is not unexpected to find in areas that have undergone growth voices asserting that more individuals with qualifications are being produced than the market can absorb.

But the inflationary argument does not annul the interpretations which are linked to the needs and the evolution of the market. These fit the functionalist perspective better. In effect, the argument that there are labour sectors which generate new productive needs is used to explain the need for people with Chemistry and Business Administration diplomas (even though these sectors may undergo periods of recession).

For instance, in the public sector the need for people with a university degree may change over time. Teachers and other public administration fields, which has undergone a strong expansion with the administrative restructuring of the Spanish State, are nowadays graduate professions. However, while some statements in the focus groups suggest that some jobs could be covered by people with different university degrees, the regulations restrict these to certain type of subjects studied e.g. public administration.

Perhaps a less obvious characteristic of diploma inflation is the specialization which these diplomas undergo. This, ultimately, gives way to the emergence of new diplomas. In Spain, this phenomenon has been much more acute in the areas of Humanities and Social Sciences than in the scientific and technological areas (Carabaña, 1991). One consequence is that the profiles of university degrees overlap, and lose their distinctiveness.

The difficulties of finding professional jobs not only appear in situations of unemployment and inactivity but come in various guises. On the one hand, situations of underemployment have been mentioned. On the other, precarious contract situations are widespread. The process of making the contracts in the labour market more flexible is partly responsible for this. But what is also important is the evidence of some falsity in self-employed labour situations. This hides the difficulties of placement. While short contracts are part of a shift in the nature of the labour market these also 'hide' the difficulties of finding jobs.

Course Content

In general, the contents of university curricula are considered appropriate. Only in some cases do external participants in the focus groups make clear the need for changes to the studies for a more generalist or specialized orientation.

However, in the area of postgraduate studies there are clear shifts underway. On the one hand it is clear that students are using postgraduate study differently. One of the uses is as a form of self-defence from the labour market, and as a 'waiting room'. This links to the inflationary phenomenon of diplomas. Thus, we understand that some academics highlight the versatility of their diplomas as a strength conferred on their students, while others advocate for the increase in the specialization in their study plans.

On the other hand, there is a clear tendency towards professional application, in other words, towards the application of knowledge to the demands of the economy. The participant academics are in general not opposed to that tendency. However, at times different principles are at work underpinning this apparent consensus. The most superficial version is that academics have incorporated training practice periods in companies and institutions into such courses. This creates links with external agents and reflects the pressures that the university has experienced in this direction.

But this demand from the 'outside world' goes a step further to the need to develop social skills, wider cognitive competencies, and attitudes regarding work. Professors have been involved in changes in the orientation of the curricula that incorporate change in the attitudes and values of students toward the work sphere. In short, we are talking of a change in the 'culture', and the adoption of the work principles of labour sphere possibly to the detriment of academic principles.

Faced with these deeper requirements, the reaction of academics tends to take two paths. On the one hand there are serious difficulties involved in carrying out this transformation: organizational inertia and regulations and the structure of the organization limit the capacity to meet these needs. On the other hand some basic reactions take place which obstruct the development of alternatives: in some focus groups a vague uneasiness is experienced which expresses itself in some personal attacks or in generalized complaints.

It seems clear that these reactions only make evident the fact that the educational and productive systems follow different logics. In other words, what is suggested is a shift towards what individuals can do, rather than to what they know:

> The dominant change in higher education is an orientation towards the world of work. Accordingly, change at the macro level will be particularly evident in the direction of projection. (Barnett, 2000)

However, it is worth observing that this acceptance, at least apparently, implicitly assumes the classic contrast between theory and practice, ignoring a third important component of the traditional curriculum in many universities, that is qualifications which Barnett calls (2001) 'self' or identity development.

This assumption of a contrast may explain why, the topic did not attract much debate in the focus groups. This indicates the influence of the context and the strength of dominant ideas. In our view, the university should review its policies and attempt in some way to reach a consensus regarding the role of higher education in today's society.

In a similar way, the discourse is taken for granted when the subject of the new competencies is approached. According to Brown & Scase's (1994) theoretical model, which follows Bernstein, external pressures about certain competencies, together with a lack of critical consciousness among the academics, is likely to have selective class repercussions. Specifically, the competencies required from students – ability to communicate orally, problem solving skills, ability to negotiate, to guide, etc. – often refer to non-scholarly abilities based on early experiences related to social class and other primary socialization contexts. These will translate to inequalities of opportunity with regards to employment. Generally, neither the external or internal participants in the focus groups expressed any criticism regarding the inequalities of opportunity. Surprisingly even the sociologists involved did not react. In this sense, the results obtained are perfectly consistent with Hesketh's (2001) view that:

> The policy discourse of employability consecrates privilege on the minority by ignoring inequalities, glossing over them by treating everybody as if they were the same when in fact everybody begins the race for employability with different handicaps based in cultural currency or cultural capital. For some, attempting to enter the world of work with the values and symbolism that careers seem to require is a constant effort. For others equipped with the dominant ideology and skills a middle class career represents their legitimate heritage. (2001: 18)

Teaching methodologies

Continuing this discussion of new competencies, we have to remind ourselves here that one of the major changes the university has undergone in recent times is the increase in the diversity of sex and social origin of its students. This exacerbates the problem of the unequal distribution of social competencies.

Nevertheless, if we stop to analyze the kinds of new competencies required by the market, we see that some belong to what traditionally have been considered properly academic competencies such as written language or a critical spirit. Some academics taking part in the focus groups refer to them by mentioning the new difficulties in acquiring these competencies within the context of overcrowded lecture rooms. This issue suggests the need for good pedagogical research on the acquisition of these competencies through new or changed teaching methods in the new 'mass' higher education context.

However, new classroom methodologies may allow students to acquire new ways of working that seem to be required by the new 'adaptive organization' model. An external professional in the Business Administration area indicated that while the studying experience tended to be individualist and competitive, the capacity for working cooperatively is increasingly valued in the workplace.

The need to change a large part of the teaching methods used in degree studies, and a willingness to do so, was evident in most focus groups. However, analyzing the context of the production of this discourse, we have to firstly ask ourselves whether the discourse of the participants may have been conditioned by the context. In other words, the same individuals could react differently in a context of academics only. Focus groups involving both internal and external participants provide a context in which people tend to be more formal and less free to express their opinions. There is also the question of whether the desire to change may be extended to other teaching staff. The participating academics are responsible for the University's basic units (Faculties, Departments) and provide limited information on the reactions and perceptions of the rest of the academic community, and the extent to which they are likely to change.

Conclusions

Here we will conduct a brief review of the specific aims that we had for this research.

Firstly, after obtaining a general view of the professional placement of university graduates, we wanted to collect data on the interpretations of these from representatives of the work and academic spheres. We wanted to take into account how they argued in favour of one or another theoretical model of the relationship between the labour market and higher education. We have seen that there is a multiplicity of interpretations and they belong to more than just one model. Although the placement difficulties of graduates may be somehow related to credential inflation (as in the credentialist model), it is also true that they are also related to the evolution of productive needs (as in the functionalist model).

Secondly, we have to consider the possibility that new work skills are being asked of graduates, skills derived from the new forms of labour organization. We have been able to verify that these demands exist and are related to the competencies required by what Brown and Scase identify as the 'adaptive organization' (1994).

Thirdly, we intended focus groups to be constituted a space where it would be possible to gather new ideas on the possibilities of cooperation among the external agents and internal university agents. At the same time we wanted to create a space for the exchange of viewpoints between different actors. We found ourselves working with two groups of people each demonstrating a receptive attitude. In general the academic representatives evinced a desire for change, and this bodes well for future transformation plans at UAB.

Fourthly, the possibility that the focus group method would help to foster reflection and the improvement in university quality was foreseen. This action-orientation is the one that presents more fissures between discussants, and shows the weakness and limits of specific actions. On the one hand, external participants did not question other social institutions (including their own). They tend to assume that the university should passively adjust. There is also a certain pessimism regarding the labour market situation. In relation to academics it is important to note that the academics' discourse is not uniform and therefore no consensus emerged, except for a (sometimes reluctant) acceptance of the need for change. We also found limited awareness of the relationship between the new social competencies required by the market and the unequal distribution of these competencies in the different social categories (sex, social class, ethnic group, etc.). While this was expressed it did not become part of the challenge to the prevalent discourse around the demands of the economy. Sadly there was no challenge to this discourse. In our view universities also have a role in questioning and challenging this self-perpetuating discourse of social reproduction. They have a role in contributing to actions that not only legitimizes existing social arrangements but also develops forms of action that challenges their arrangements.

Appendix: Graduate employment: 1999 cohort

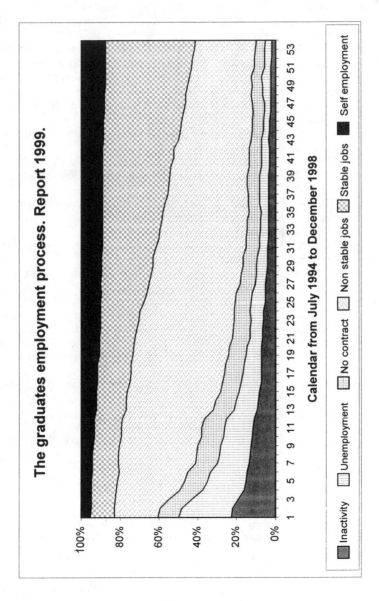

The graduates employment process. Report 1999.

References

Barnett, R. (2000), 'Supercomplexity and the Curriculum', *Studies in Higher Education*, vol. 25(3), pp. 255-265.

Barnett, R. (2001), *Los límites de la competencia. Conocimiento, educación superior y sociedad*, Gedisa, Barcelona.

Becker, G. (1983) [1964], *El capital humano*, Alianza, Madrid.

Beduwé, C. & Planas, J. (2001), *Hausse d'éducation et marché du travail. Final Report. 4art PCRD*. (in preparation).

Bernstein, B. (1996), *Pedagogía, control simbólico e identidad*, Morata, Madrid.

Boudon, R. (1973), *La desigualdad de Oportunidades*, Laia, Barcelona.

Bourdieu, P. & Passeron, J.C. (1970), *La reproduction. Éléments pour une théorie du système d'enseignement*, Minuit, París.

Bowles, H. & Gintis, H. (1981), *La instrucción escolar en la América capitalista*, Siglo XXI, Madrid.

Brown, P. & Scase, R. (1994), *Higher Education and Corporate Realities. Class, Culture and Decline of Graduate Careers*, UCL Press, London.

Carabaña, J. (1991), 'Por una evaluación sistemática de los planes de estudio' in *III Jornadas Nacionales de Didáctica Universitaria*, Universidad de Las Palmas, Las Palmas de Gran Canaria.

Casal, J. (1999), 'Modalidades de transición profesional y precarización del empleo' in Lorenzo Cachón (ed.), *Juventudes, Mercados de Trabajo y Políticas de Empleo*, 7 i mig, Benicull de Xucar.

Castells, M. (1996), *La era de la información: economía, sociedad y cultura.* vol. 1. *La sociedad red*, Alianza, Madrid.

Collins, R. (1979), *La sociedad credencialista: sociología histórica de la educación y de la estratificación*, Akal, Madrid.

Díez Gutiérrez, E. (1999), *La estrategia del caracol*, Oikos-Tau, Barcelona.

Hesketh, A.J. (2001), 'I Say Tomato, You Say Tamato: A Realist Critique of the Role of Employability and Skills in the Labour Exchange Process' in J. Cruickshank (ed.), *Critical Realism: What Difference Does it make?*, Routledge, London. (forthcoming)

Kivinen, O. & Ahola, S. (1999), 'Higher Education as Human Risk Capital', *Higher Education*, vol. 38, pp. 191-208.

Masjuan, J.M., Troiano, H. & Vivas, J. (2002), *I després de la universitat, què?*, ICE-UAB, Barcelona. (forthcoming).

Platt, J. (1981), On Interviewing One's Peers, *British Journal of Sociology*, vol. 32(1), pp. 75-91.

Spenner, K.I. (1985), 'The Upgrading and Downgrading of Occupations: Issues, Evidence, and Implications for Education', *Review of Educational Research*, vol. 55(2), pp. 155-200.

Steyaert, C. & Bouwen, R. (1994), 'Group Methods of Organizational Analysis' in C. Cassell & G. Symon, *Qualitative Methods in Organizational Research. A practical Guide*, SAGE, London.

Valles, M.S. (1997), *Técnicas Cualitativas de Investigación Social*, Síntesis, Madrid.

Young, M.F.D. (1998), *The Curriculum of the Future*, Falmer Press, London.

PART II
TEACHING PRACTICES IN HIGHER EDUCATION

Chapter 5

Expressive Practices in the Higher Education Classroom

Tom Phillips

Reflection on Method: Ethnography

If, as Lincoln and Denzin (1994) suggest, qualitative research has an, 'avowed humanistic commitment to the study of the social world from the perspective of the interacting individual', then ethnography is its most paradigmatic method. In this chapter, a teacher utilizes *practitioner ethnography*, in an attempt to make explicit an area of HE teaching experience he regards as significant in classroom work. As most ethnographic studies readily generate post hoc insights, those offered here will help explain why this approach needs to invoke a *stand alone epistemology* to explicate any claims made. These will also show how choosing the methodology helped solve some practical problems.

Firstly, a method was needed to place centre stage a teacher's experience, and perhaps allow its voice, as a qualitative one, to take its place among the many others in the pantheon of educational research. Calling it practitioner ethnography serves to point up its exclusive use of one person's speaking from within their practice.

Secondly, how should accounts produced in this way be understood, and how might any claims made contribute to extant educational ideas. Following Denzin (1997) in his delineation of the evolution of ethnography in terms of moments, he sees its sixth moment as defined by:

> a proliferation of interpretive epistemologies grounded in the lived experiences of previously excluded groups in the global, post-modern world.

While feminist and anti-racist studies best exploit this dispensation of standpoint epistemology, could such an explicative rationale also be applied to the major issue of expressive issues in teaching. It was felt that it could since, like such studies, this one was attempting to recover a range of experiences not usually featured in HE classroom studies. This teacher is very clear that, in contrast to the instrumental, expressive cultures within higher education have a subjugated status.

Thirdly, there was a need to be clear about the kind of text that would emerge, with Denzin helpful in suggesting the following as identifying characteristics:

1. there would be a *starting point in the ethnographer's own experience* which are the regularities of practice introduced as 'Points of departure' in the study.
2. a *non essentialising stance* would be taken, which is reflected in choosing practice as the key analytic category to present the expressive in.
3. the discourse has a *starting point in an autobiography* which may be readily seen in how the study is introduced.
4. a need to have a *subjugated expressive self asserted* as valid and legitimate in the context of practice.

This notion of what can constitute an expressive text may help clarify how the understanding of this is quite distinct from the instrumental and its basis in prescriptions for good practice resting on quantitative research. Is it too much to hope that some time in the future, educational studies will comprise instructional research in the various forms of scientifically based reports and expressive studies as distinct emancipatory texts?

Finally there is the wider question of a characteristic expressive discourse which such texts might illustrate. This is the most interesting consideration of all since there is, and has been for 300 years, an expressive discourse in English literature; Charles Taylor has partly vivified this in seeking to clarify modern identities. The emergence of a vigorous expressive discourse among HE teachers might connect these.

> My claim is that the idea of nature as an intrinsic source goes along with an expressive view of human life. Fulfilling my nature means espousing the inner élan, the voice or impulse. And this makes what was hidden manifest for both myself and others. But this manifestation also helps to define what is to be realized. (Taylor 1989)

Introduction

In their final semesters I often notice students beginning to apprehend the consequences of having specialist knowledge in Community Studies. I follow them resigned to passing into achieved worlds. As I pick up the tensions around individuals, I become aware of my own modelling of elements of this vocation and of seeking opportunities to open out such moments for reflection. In this way my attention gets drawn to what, after Harre (1993), can only be defined as expressive aspects of this classroom work:

> a public showing of skills, attitudes, emotions, feelings and so on, providing, some times consciously, the evidence upon which our friends, colleagues, neighbours, rivals and enemies are to draw conclusions as to the kind of person we are. (p. 26)

Although different in kind from the direct work of instruction, such features are important in how I have come to see and value my overall work as a teacher in Higher Education. For any quality inspectors, trainees and peer observers who observe me over sessions the main concern is with instruction. But is there something odd here; 'yes'; they seem to be saying, 'we look at the instrumental and that is sufficient for our purposes, thank you very much': and yet distinctions between the expressive and the instrumental is one of advanced learning's oldest debates (Berlin 1997). Is it not now time for education studies to give due attention to expressive type practices and arrive at more inclusive notions of work in the HE classroom?

In what follows, a set of practices will be identified which help me open out moments over a course to complement what is achieved in the more predictable and closed moments that characterize instruction. There will be nothing unfamiliar about these since they have been absorbed from the life around me. In these the teacher as researcher is featured, qualitative data is generated and exploration across a whole course is needed. As a research topic they inevitably challenge those orthodoxies of educational studies which feature the researcher as third party in the classroom, and data that is quantitative. For them, exploration across a whole course is demanded, the teacher as researcher is featured and qualitative data is generated.

Methodology

Five descriptions of regularities in my work as these become manifest across a whole course will be presented and reflected upon. Each will be characterized as a 'Point of Departure' to underline its emergent status. Each reflection will attempt to articulate and clarify a distinct area of expressive practice using selected interpretive frameworks. Finally, the place of these practices in my work will be summarized within an explicatory framework to which, hopefully, other practitioners can respond. In attempting this, which is not unlike working with ill-structured problems, implicit use will be made of Toulmin's model of jurisprudential argument (Voss 1988; Toulmin 1958). A description of this will help set the scene.

Most legal arguments consist of a series of elements which lead to a person making a claim to, or about, something and which another may dispute. To identify such elements Toulmin has developed the model shown in Fig. 5.1. At its centre is one or more *claims* (C) whose merits are based on a series of facts or *data* (D). In making or defending any claim further grounds may be invoked in the form of propositions, to support links between D and C, and which *warrant* (W) the claim being made. While there may be direct links between D, C and W, support may also be invoked from anything that supports the warrant or gives it *backing* (B). Finally, claims can be subject to *qualification* (Q) in various ways; and can also give rise to counter claims as *rebuttals* (R).

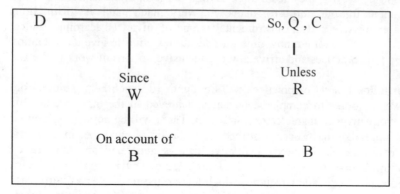

Figure 5.1 Toulmin's model of jurisprudential argument

In this study, the presenting data will consist of practice regularities, about which claims will be made, subject to the qualification that they occur outside of instructional activities. These claims in turn are warranted by the whole course reflection that makes their emergence here possible. Finally the claims and the warrant they rest on are backed by the assumption that we have a need to employ expressive practices in how we can seek to influence learning and development in others. Two of the five reflections will be summarized in terms of the argument structure to illustrate how claims are made about specific expressive practices.

This way of presenting practices grounded in lived whole course experience, can be regarded as resembling what Hammersley (1992) understands as practitioner ethnography. The explication of the practices will be generally consistent with Denzin's (1997) notion of standpoint epistemology. The writer's background in educational psychology (teacher training) may show at times. This work follows a previous paper clarifying whole course work within my higher education teaching (Phillips 1999). The teaching contexts are those of undergraduate Community Studies.

Five Regularities of Practice with Reflections

Point of Departure 1

At the start of each session most students and myself arrive in the classroom together and for five minutes busy ourselves in our places. Then I take the register, around which notices are given out. If there is anything I particularly need to draw their attention to, I do it now. This is me/us at home base where, we relate in ordinary social ways and from which position (P1) I can launch into either of two other ways of relating. In one I adopt a position (P2) where I am intent on the required and formal content of the curriculum, and where I act as instructor and through teacher talk, address and seek contact with the student's knowledge representations; seeking after Rumelhart and Norman (1969), to restructure, fine tune and elaborate these as appropriate. In the other way of relating, which is much less common and which I attempt as opportunities arise, I adopt a position (P3) where I am more intent on making explicit, many of my own experiences of the vocational in this subject matter, and of drawing the students and their bourgeoning experiences into this as a way of opening a dialogue between us.

Reflection

This is teacher thinking like a drama director while availing of *positioning as* an expressive practice (Harre & van Langenhove 1999). Using a notional mise-en-scene three positions are identified as loci for specific classroom realities, with movement between as necessary to engage in different activities. While P2 is central to instruction and each session's main teaching activities, P3 allows a different kind of work to be engaged with. This need not interfere with what is currently running at P2, except to consolidate it. Some theoretical perspectives help elaborate how this happens.

While teacher talk is the main driver of movements between positions and the activities taking place at these, some explanations are first needed on how these emerge as work sites. From Berger and Luckman (1966), relative notions of social realities and locations can be gained through describing how exchanges of everyday knowledge are explicated within social constructions:

> Compared to the reality of everyday life, other realities appear as finite provinces of meaning, enclaves within the paramount reality marked by circumscribed meanings and modes of experience. The paramount reality envelops them on all sides, as it were, and consciousness always returns to the paramount as if from an excursion. (Berger and Luckman 1967, p. 39)

This maps quite neatly onto the three positions, with ordinary social relating in the classroom equated to paramount reality and engaged with at P1. The other two become enclaves within this. To indicate how a course's main action can unfold within these local terms use will next be made of Goffman's ideas on framing.

A feature of classroom work is that teacher and students project selves, mainly through their talk, in ways compatible with whatever reality they are jointly engaged with. Goffman generically elaborates on this as 'footing', an essential construct to explain how changes in the form of talk can re-define any immediate social reality being engaged with:

> A change in footing implies a change in the alignment we take up to ourselves and the others present as expressed in the way we manage the production or reception of an utterance. A change in our footing is another way of talking about a change in our frame for events. (Goffman, 1981, p. 128)

So how might a change of footing explain moves between P1, P2 and P3 where each has a different participation framework? At P1, when engaging, say, in social niceties prior to, after, and in between activities at P2 and P3, a teacher's utterances may be characterized, after Goffman, as coming from an individual, 'active in a *particular* social capacity, the words taking their authority from this capacity' (p.147). If teacher talk breaks off from this to embrace the subject matter, that is to move from P1 to P2, it is usually to invite and assume a participation framework involving them as givers and leaders and the students as receivers and questioners. Typically this production format allows teacher's talk to take any of three relatively constrained modes, from accessing memories, (reading from notes) (aloud reading) to spontaneous talk ostensibly reflecting on-going mindfulness of the topic (fresh talk). To move to P3, and give the teacher scope for relating to the wider subject world, a more dramatic change of footing is called for and one that allows utterances to be constructed with less constraint, where:

> as speaker, we represent ourselves through the offices of a personal pronoun, typically 'I,' and it is thus a *figure* – a figure in a statement – that serves as agent, a protagonist in a *described* scene, a 'character' in an anecdote, someone after all, who belongs to the world spoken about, not the world in which the speaking occurs. And once this format is employed, an astonishing flexibility is created. (Goffman, 1981, p. 147)

Clearly, the teacher's immediate convictions about what is being pursued, their skill in timing, the choice of words and phrases used will all determine how successful each attempted move will be. Only with time and across a developing course can a teacher's ability to work up to such positioning manoeuvres become understood and accepted. Plainly there is a kind of art at work here where the content of instruction is being enriched by some momentary moves putting it in more interpersonal terms.

In the regularities of practice (D) described, (Figure 5.1) *positioning* is explicated and claimed as an expressive practice, 'C', warranted on what whole course reflection can reveal 'W', and backed by this teacher's need to employ such expressive means to influence student learning and development, 'B'.

Point of Departure 2

The focus of my whole course work at P2 is leading students through a sequence of knowledge representations and ensuring these are adequately covered within the time allocated. I think of this as a movements of minds through structures to be apprehended. When I break out of P2 to move to P3, it is to help them through my experiences of living in this world. Here I work more with truths, part truths and contested truths, as a dramatist might, where my convictions are part of the appeal I make. What is covered is always a sampling from my experiences, wrapped up in stories and vignettes and where the students can be left to fill in gaps in what is presented, in ways similar to how some novelists may work with their readers. Through the work at both sites I seek to make the students aware of the fuller world of the subject and to bring them nearer to it, so they can begin to construct their own versions.

Reflection

This is teacher engaging in *world making* as an expressive practice, attempting a synthesis greater than the sum of what can be achieved separately at P2 and P3. This term, world making, serves to pick out any area of circumscribed thinking and knowing that rest on an explicable and generative symbolic framework, and has a sustaining community and culture that reproduce it (Goodman 1978). Hence in becoming a subject expert, the student is attempting to take a place within a constructed world which has to be understood objectively through its publicly verifiable concepts and subjectively through direct or vicarious experience of this world.

As the extract implies, to understand a tutor's world making practices both aspects need explicating. The first aspect can and will be specified, in the course's aims and objectives and constitutes the main tasks of learning. The second aspect is more associated with the expressive, through which the student can be made more aware of a subject's community, the role of collaboration, honest debate and the openness that beckons for students to become involved. One theorist offering ideas that may be applied is the cultural psychologist Bruner (1986). He proposes two fundamental modes of thinking all humans use in relating to the world around them.

The first of these is called the 'paradigmatic' and equates to logico-scientific thinking as based on:

> ...categorization or conceptualization and the operations by which categories are established, instantiated, idealized, and related one to the other to form a system. Its language is regulated by requirements of consistency and non-contradiction. Its domain is defined not only by observables to which its basic statements relate, but also by the set of possible worlds that can be logically generated and tested against observables, that is, it is driven by principled hypothesis. (Bruner 1986, p. 12)

While germane to empirically based subjects, forms of this thinking are commonly applied to teaching other subjects whose epistemologies are not strictly those of the natural sciences. For areas of social science teaching, this is not inappropriate, since concepts here are typically built up through patterns of data and social constructions with competing claims at truth and validity presented and resolved in valid ways. Engaging with such processes of clarification also help the teacher show, how the making of a subject world is a natural consequence of this. Most of the work at P2 features this kind of thinking.

The second mode Bruner derives from our very different human capacities to entertain and learn in and through narrations resting on processes of infusing individual experiences with meaning. Typically the creation of narratives illustrate this which he describes after Ricoeur (1983) as, 'models for the re-description of the world':

> The imaginative application of the narrative mode leads instead to good stories, gripping drama, believable historical accounts. It deals in human or human-like intention and action and the vicissitudes and consequences that mark their course. ...It

operates by constructing two landscapes simultaneously. One is the landscape of action, where the constituents are the arguments of action: agent, intention or goal, situation, instrument. Its other landscape is consciousness: what those involved in the action know, think, or feel. ... Narrative is concerned with the explication of human intention in the context of action. (Bruner 1986 p. 13)

While literary novelists best exemplify this mode, it is also engaged in by most people on a daily basis and is the form most activity can take at P3. Within stories, vignettes, jokes and quips of various sorts, a teacher has the flexibility to hint at and indicate the world of their living subject. Using either landscape of action they can share with their students the experiences of living their subject as part of a community of discourse centering on what Bourdieu (1971) has described as, an intellectual force field whose patterns of oppositions and combinations make up its 'structure at any given moment in time' (p. 161).

Within the paradigmatic at P2, this teacher's dominant experience is that of being busy with direct lecturing and getting through required content in the time available. Each passing moment seems to precede what follows, in a rigid sequence dictated by session objectives and where the student's experience is of passing through many such foreclosed moments. One good way of understanding this is to see it as similar to how Morson (1994) characterizes a novel reader's experiences of foreshadowing, as when they have a sense of where the author is taking them. At P3 a very different dynamic is possible where more open moments can be experienced. In breaking off from an instructional sequence at P2, this teacher works to open out a moment at P3 where succeeding ones may not be so apparent and where direction is much determined by the sudden and often short narrative developed. In referring to the vocational self in a less than definite way, these students can often be drawn into projecting future selves onto this situation as if responding to a Rorschach Ink Blot Test (Gregory 1987). In such moments the student may experience a shadow falling from their future lives in sidewise fashion reflecting their future vocational selves; what in reading Morson calls, *sideshadowing*. As Bakhtin (1984) has so powerfully illustrated, this is often how reading... Dostoevsky can be experienced by the reader. Through such moments at P3 students can begin to sense their role and responsibility in living in a subject world and be encouraged in their own self construction endeavours.

Specimen Summary in Toulmin Terms

In the regularities of practice 'D' described, *world making* is explicated and claimed as an expressive practice, 'C', warranted on what whole course reflection can reveal 'W', and backed by this teacher's need to employ such expressive means to influence student learning and development, 'B'.

Point of Departure 3

Once I feel rapport with a class group, moves from P2 to P3 can reflect subconscious impulses associated with the instructional topic and lead me into essentially narrative activity. Once at P3, I usually seek to articulate through 'fresh talk', whatever has declared itself in this way. The narrative is often a reliving of some excitements whose articulation is also helping me understand it through either of Bruner's landscapes; what I have done or what I am conscious of. These narratives also vary with perceived maturity of audience. I tend to treat final year students increasingly as specialist colleagues with whom I share some common understanding of the wider historical and social context of the subject. Trusting to the many resources of narrative helps me in having these perceptions and moments. Bourdieu's (1971) notion of a force field also helps, as I feel I am speaking from within this at P3. The powers of narrative are important here and can leave their own mark on how the experiences are understood and represented to others and myself, though narratives of course also come into work at P2.

Reflection

For one person to influence another about a cherished world narratives about lived experiences are always relevant. This is teacher using *narrativising of subject adventures* as an expressive practice at P3, particularly to underline their active involvement in the subject world. Of course narratives also come into work at P2, though more as segments in building up a subject's historical background or reporting on past or present research endeavours and outcomes. Narratives often offer the only way to explore, say, leading edge developments.

At P3 narrative can have a dramatic presence as entertainment, where some wider expressive takes become possible on the subject. One common source here involves representing the subject as a continually growing body of knowledge in an ever changing world. Teachers can easily present adventures depicting themselves as partisans engaged in an active struggle to maintain some cherished paradigm or tradition. Using a suitable idiom and language a narrator can, as Polkinghorne (1988) suggests, 'configure these givens into a narrative form in which desires and aspirations are used to transform the passing of life into an adventure of significance and drama'. One useful way of understanding how this can happen is to look at the work of the stand up comic Eddie Izzard:

And sometimes you want to buy a tea towel.
So you nip down your local supermarket. which are as big these days as a village...
and they have grecian columns outside, they're the new religious palaces I think,
they have huge congregations...
you have rich people...low income people, high income people, trendies, straight
people.
Everyone is there pushing trolleys along.....
youghourt....do we...I eat yoghourt?
No... lets not eat yoghourt I can't even spell it...
cos yoghourt spells the same as it sounds going down your throat...yooog huurt
So you go in the supermarket
soon as your in you've got stress...you've got basket or trolley stress
basket...................trolley
the basket has arms that go, 'take me, take me'

whereas the trolley is going,
'no we're chained, no you cannot have us, we're chained...
you give us money ..cross our handlebar with gold'....
But its great..... as soon as you're inside the shop you can leave your shopping and go,
I am bored with the shopping, i'm going to start again'
Because you haven't bought it, you've just moved it!
Till you leave that shop you're not buying anything, you're just moving it around,
you can fill 6 trolleys worth, piled high, look all shifty go up to where the doors are,
and just leave it and run,
that's legal, that's just moving it!
(Eddie Izzard Definite article)[11]

While teachers' narratives are seldom as daring or as entertaining as this, there are features at work here which explains how such spontaneity can reap rich entertaining and educational dividends and be seductive to a teacher. Firstly, spontaneity with an audience suggests self expressiveness at work in the teller of tales and an invitation to be interested in them. Secondly, offering a display through language like this of one person's experience of shopping in a supermarket, is less a telling and more a showing (Booth 1991) of personal experiences and subconsciously inviting audience members to compare their experiences to these. Thirdly, such an act's impetus often comes from the performer's fully articulated experiences, leading an audience of lesser articulated experiences into an ever greater awareness of the existential contingencies these open up. For many who hear Eddie Izzard, the experience of shopping will never be quite the same again. Fourthly, there is the use, after Langer (1957), of many non-discursive devices to represent a topic as a cultural reality as is done with this supermarket trip. Hence fairy tales, myths, superstitions, legends, dreams, fantasies, music, are all put to good use in the performance. They also help him objectify many experiences shared with individuals in that audience. Operating with such aids contrasts strongly with the more discourse based work of literal understandings being attempted at P2, as can be explicated through Bruner's paradigmatic logico-scientific thinking.

Outside of such improvisatory short sequences narratives can also be of a serial nature as when a teacher over weeks builds up a story line featuring them as a kind of putative author. Within these, more fundamental effects can be created in how the realities represented in the serial can in turn be construed by the receivers of the tales. One pertinent literary theorist here is Northrop Frye (1958) who, in accounting for different literary genres, identified the stance an author can adopt to their characters and the situation they are in, as determining how readers or listeners may experience a story. In all, he identified five kinds of story from myth making, tragedy, naturalism to comedy and irony; each offering the resourceful teacher a rather neat way of making comments that they might not want to make directly. In drawing the students into tales from the subject world and its

[11] Permission to quote this granted by Laughing Stock Productions, London.

applications, the tutor/narrator can set the terms within which this is done, just as an author can, in writing a novel. Where a tutor comes over as greatly in awe of say research and its applications, they will construct a reality tending towards myth or legend and which can all too readily take in the naïve student. If developments and applications are presented as the work of peers then comedy and naturalism is more usually construed, particularly if a work based dimension is present in the student's programme. A more common position is for academics to feel inferior to their subject's wider world using irony to come to terms with it. In fact the stating of formulaic ironies is a stock in trade of many academics. What is undeniable is that much HE teaching is of an interesting and often exciting nature and amenable to extended narrativising at P3; the real challenge for the teacher is to make this fresh and entertaining while also reflecting the world making aspect.

Point of Departure 4

It is through laughter that I tune into much of the emotional and intellectual excitement that unfolds across a course. A difficulty with early eruptions is that they can extend across all three realities. Hence I work to attenuate these laughters until they are particular to each reality: what arises at P1 need be no different to how laughter occurs in any other social relating where I can entertain or be entertained. At P2 as a formal working through required content, there can be many dramatic moments of exposition, imaginative leaps, surprise outcomes, often resulting in laughter. Such laughter follows from the instruction and to contrive this risks confusion with being at P1. At P3, it is usually my excitements, with a quick change of footing, that lead into this reality, manifest as spontaneous laughter arising from some revealing experience or stance on subject topic of that moment.

Reflection

Wherever and whenever advanced teaching takes place, the potential for laughter of many different kinds is always high. This is teacher valuing laughter and engaging in, what only can be called, *excitement management* as an expressive practice. While switching between the positions makes much possible here, having some background on how laughter and advanced learning can variously relate also helps. While it is a delight to be caught up in the excitement of students' minds working with advanced knowledge and of advanced knowledge working with students' minds, it is easy to get confused about how this relates to the instructional work at P2 and P3 and where the expressive comes in.

Firstly, for any teacher there are always temptations to arouse laughter, interact with it, play off it, induce as a blandishment: how good to have faces wreathed in smiles emerging from your classroom! If used insensitively narratives can be sharpened and amplified by the many projections their laughter lends itself to: sadistic, nervous, crude, teasing, taunting, cynical, bitter, morbid, liberating, triumphalist, hysterical and ecstatic. If used appropriately it greatly helps to open up the wider world of the subject. Secondly, there is predictable resistance laughter at the start of some instructional sequences as tedious, but required, content ahead is anticipated. This is often how opposition and resistance to prevailing orthodoxies as stock responses can come to light, reflecting the sober truth behind the assertion of Bourdieu and Passeron (1990), that:

> all pedagogic action is, objectively, symbolic violence insofar as it is the imposition of a cultural arbitrary by an arbitrary power. (Bourdieu & Passeron 1971, p. 5)

The fuller significance of this laughter can be gained from historical studies. Before the emergence of the modern world, Keith Thomas points to changing beliefs in Tudor and Stuart England indicating that:

> to study the laughter of our ancestors, to go on reading until we can hear the people not just talking but also laughing, is to gain some insight into changing human sensibilities. (Thomas 1978)

Likewise, Stallybrass & White (1986) point to how laughter was seen as a social transgression in seventeenth century England when directed to its gentility codes. In medieval Europe and later, Bremmer & Roodenburg (1997) use resistance to changing sensibilities to explain a good deal about its jest books, comic painting, classical rhetoric and even the parliamentary archives of the first French constitutional assembly. If ones teaching today has any historical significance, it is sure to be best revealed in a class' laughter. Thirdly, there is laughter as set piece responses to specific stimuli as when within instruction at P2 excitement often emerges in the analyzing and synthesizing of intuitive and counter-intuitive phenomena. Here connections are made between objects, events and living things in ways that amuse and can set off involuntary feelings of relief from some dogged mind set. Such familiar laughter has various explanations: from a fundamentalist kind by Ribot (1896) or Freud (1905), to the empirical of McGhee (1978), to the specialist of a Koestler (1961) within a theory of creativity. These laughters are then of an immediate kind, involve technique, and are most likely to arise at P2.

In contrast laughter at P3 is to be taken less as an entertaining interlude and more as serving to bring out some aspect of the learning experience not easy to deal with in any other way. Part of *this* excitement is finding temporary relief from P2 and what can be its remorseless affirming of a subject's power to explain, control and define human progress. This can often arise within insights of an inexplicable or paradoxical nature and declare itself at the outset within the spontaneous laughter of the tutor. But laughter here may be less an end than a beginning, of some deeper appreciation of a subject matter:

> One of the functions of the comic is to call attention to the element of ambiguity in all things, an ambiguity which admits of different interpretations and perceptions, none of which should be absolutised or taken with absolute seriousness. (Hyers 1973; p. 94)

In such ways a comic spirit can enter into the course serving to round out a fuller learning experience than can be achieved by instruction alone and where the idiosyncrasies of a subject's wider culture start to announce themselves. Teachers of course take risks when projecting a persona to facilitate this:

> For the comic jest or jester does not simply profane Beauty, Truth, Goodness and Holiness, but rather muddies them, places their purity and preciseness somewhat in doubt, and calls them to a vague, chartless no-mans land between competing categories and forces. This ambiguity heralds that wondrous playfulness that moves within all phenomena, disturbing all the labeled drawers of the mind, emptying them and sporting with their contents, returning both form and contents to the inexhaustible sources of their being. (Hyers, 1973, p. 89)

An added significance of this laughter is how it provides students with a fuller picture of their teacher as a contemporary and a fellow learner having to cope with the seriousness of the subject and of living within its immediate force field.

Point of Departure 5

Over the last quarter of a course, I place increasing emphasis on instruction using the specialist vocabulary of terms, the acquisition and extension of core concepts as well as the issues and controversies which have given rise to these concepts. In following the progress of learning in the group, I often sense that usage of terms can run ahead of conceptual understanding, as if some students have learned how to play with the discourse while still struggling to understand what it conveys. As terms are used and ideas tried out, many individuals discover gaps in understanding and some overlooked learning tasks. My own performance will also seek to promote this, showing how specialist terms uniquely extend my ability to articulate parts of reality in an engaging way or how specialist concepts can take the burden for carrying areas of meaning with a certain, 'lightness of touch'. I also work at P3 to help students discover how the discourse can relate to vocational identities.

Reflection

This is teacher acknowledging the centrality of discourse in HE learning and engaging with *discourse modelling* as an expressive practice. The idea that discourse exploration can propel learning needs to be clarified in respect of how this may be happening within instruction and within the less formal encounters at P3.

In instruction, much core knowledge is acquired through recapitulating historical argument. This draws attention to the discourse as it has evolved over generations of users and of the central importance of epistemological scruple in resolving debates and allowing a distinct foundational knowledge to emerge. Such formations will make their own appeal to a student's credibility and their need to become mindful users of the discourse resulting in a wariness about what loyalty to epistemological underpinnings can commit them to. Such scruples will also inform the concepts, taxonomy of terms, principles of association, historical patterns of empirical speculation, error correction and clarifications through which characteristic knowledge structures emerge. In acquiring the planned knowledge in these ways, the student is also learning how the discourse constructs objects with epistemological statuses to win the confidence of the wider world and to there serve public purposes. Hence classroom instruction helps the student to know a discourse as something that can be applied to events, objects or living things in ways illuminating them in definitive ways. This is how discourse is largely encountered at P2, pointing towards the epistemology it rests upon and reflects. At P3 however other discoveries are possible.

As a tutor engages with expressive features of living a subject, it is likely that in the eyes of the learners, they are also reflecting how this discourse informs their way of being in the world:

> Discoursing or talking is the way in which we articulate 'significantly' the intelligibility of Being-in-the-world. (Heidegger 1962)

Using a discourse draw a user's attention to how it can enhance or empower *their* ways of being in the world and raise ontological issues that will run on well beyond the course (Parker 1992). Often in making a vocational choice, students are disposing their *selves* to becoming articulated in the specialist subject world they are in the process of giving prime personal loyalty to. For many HE teachers, involvement in a subject is their most demonstrable way of existing in the world. This may interest students who foresee a similar scenario opening up for them. Hannah Arendt (1959) is insightful here in how she provides a context to see this issue in a fuller developmental perspective. In exploring the human condition she identified three activities of labour, work and action as corresponding to 'the basic conditions under which life on earth has been given to man'. Of these, the first two need not detain us: 'labour' is the biological process of the human body, *animal laborans*; 'work', is the work of hands, *homo faber*, which, 'fabricates the sheer unending variety of things whose sum total constitutes the human artifice'. It is her 'action' as, 'the only activity that goes on directly between men without the intermediary of things or matter and corresponds to the human condition of plurality' that is of relevance here:

> With word and deed we insert ourselves into the human world, and this insertion is like a second birth, in which we confirm and take upon ourselves the naked fact of our original physical appearance. This insertion is not forced upon us by necessity, like labour, and it is not prompted by utility, like work. It may be stimulated by the presence of others whose company we wish to join, but is never conditioned by them; its impulse springs from the beginning which came into the world when we were born and to which we respond by beginning something new on our own initiative. (Arendt 1959, p. 157)

In this we see the person valued as agent who when ready will make their own approach to the world they want to join. It shows how significant a teacher's work at P3 can be, where the student as agent can relate to the tutor as agent within a world circumscribed by subject discourse and where the epistemological and the ontological can be separated.

Summary of the Reflections

As Toulmin indicates, it is sometimes necessary in argument to forego criticisms of details to allow the larger picture to emerge as is shown in Figure 5.1 and which may be summarized as shown in Figure 5.2.

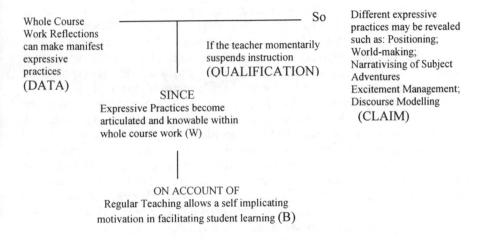

Figure 5.2 Utilizing Toulmin's model for claiming expressive practices within higher education teaching

Certainly there will be points of detail that specialists will correct me on. Nonetheless it is hoped that the explications show how claims can be made for these five distinct practices based on the regularities presented as data and warranted by taking a whole course context. A surprising outcome, partly occasioned by the Toulmin model, is the likelihood of some kind of self-implicating motivation giving ultimate backing to these expressive practices.

Conclusions

This study began with a teacher seeking to show how sharing the experience of living with advanced knowledge can be used to enhance student learning and inform their teaching. If the expressive is to develop as a research topic in educational studies it challenges both the scope of qualitative methodology and theories about HE classroom work.

Methodologically, any study of the expressive will emphasize the subjective over the objective, the practitioner over any other presence in the classroom, the whole course experience over the session, the qualitative over the quantitative and the small budget over the large. (This may be somewhat novel for education studies.) If understood as ethnography it is less unusual and could claim affinity with recent work by Woods (1996) and earlier writings by Highet (1963). While neither is mindful of the expressive, they are impressively eclectic in their interpretive frameworks. By stating the expressive as a presence in the general terms of Figure 5.2, it is to be hoped that other practitioners may see possibilities to apply this to their work. It is hoped the Toulmin model might be retained as a productive but also neutral kind of enquiry and argument structure. The reflexive sociology started by the late Pierre Bourdieu might also inform methodology here.

Theoretically, expressive issues are perhaps best understood historically after Taylor (1989) as, deriving from the 'romantic' with its emphasis on the rights of the individual, the imagination, and opposed to the 'classical' with its emphasis on rationalism, tradition and formal harmony. (The contrast of mirror and lamp made by Abrams (1999) offers one vivid contrast of these.) Next, they need to be considered as issues arising within critical education perspectives, in reaction to our present evaluative practices and their inordinate emphasis on rationality and instrumental approaches. More specifically the expressive needs to be traced back to sources within the practitioner, whose articulation as practices will help them recognize and clarify their own inner voice and impulses. The five reflections hopefully show this practitioner discovering and working with their expressive impulses and through this and how instrumentalities of instruction no longer adequately represent what they are doing with students.

References

Abrams, M.H. (1999), *A Glossary of Literary Terms*, Seventh Edition. Fort Worth: Harcourt Brace.
Arendt, H. (1959), *The Human Condition*, New York: Doubleday.
Bakhtin, M. (1984), *Problem's of Dostoevsky's Poetics*, Minneapolis, Minnesota: University of Minnesota Press.
Berger, P.L. and Luckman, S. (1969), *The Social Construction of Reality*, London: Penguin.
Berlin I. (1997), *The Proper Study of Mankind: an anthology of essays*, edited by H. Hardy and R. Hausheer. London: Chatto and Windus.
Booth, W. (1983), *The Rhetoric of Fiction*, London: Penguin.
Bourdieu, P. (1971), Intellectual Field and Creative Project, in: M.F.D. Young (ed.), *Knowledge and Control*, London, Collier and Macmillan.
Bourdieu, P. and Passeron, J.C. (1990), *Reproduction in Education, Society and Culture*, Second Edition. London: Sage.
Bremmer, J. and Roodenburg, H. (1997), *A Cultural History of Humour*, London: Polity.
Bruner, J. S. (1986), *Actual Minds, Possible Worlds*, London: Harvard University Press.
Denzin, N. K. (1997), *Interpretive Ethnography*, London: Sage.
Freud, S. (1905), *Jokes and their Relation to the Unconscious*, London: Hogarth Press.
Frye, N. (1957), *Anatomy of Criticism: Four Essays*, Princeton: Princeton University Press.
Goffman, E. (1981), *Forms of Talk*, Oxford: Blackwells.

Goodman, N. (1978), *Ways of Worldmaking*, Hassocks, Sussex: Harvester Press.

Gregory, R. (ed.), (1987), *The Mind*, Oxford: Oxford University Press.

Hamarsley, M. (1992), *What's Wrong with Ethnography?* London: Routledge.

Harre, R. (1993), *Social Being*, London: Blackwells.

Harre, R. and van Langenhove, L. (1999), *Positioning Theory*, London: Blackwells.

Heidegger, M. (1962), *Being and Time*, Oxford: Blackwells.

Highet, G. (1963), *The Art of Teaching*, London: Methuen.

Hyers, C. (1973), *Zen and the Comic Spirit*, London: Rider and Company.

Izzard, Eddie (1996), *Definite Article*, (London, Laughing Stock Productions, Audio Cassette).

Koestler, A. (1961), *The Act of Creation*, London, Pan.

Langer, S. (1957), *Philosophy in a New Key*, London: Harvard University Press.

Lincoln, Y.S and Denzin, N.K. (1994), 'The fifth moment', In N.K. Denzin and Y.S. Lincoln (eds), *The Handbook of Qualitative Research*, Thousand Oaks, CA: Sage.

McGhee, P.E. (1979), *Humour: its Origins and its Development*, San Francisco: Freeman.

Morson, G. (1994), *Narrative and Freedom*, London: Yale University Press.

Parker, I. (1992), *Discourse Dynamics*, London: Routledge.

Phillips, T. (1999), 'Whole Course Work in Higher Education Teaching', *Teaching in Higher Education*. vol. 4(2).

Polkinghorne, D. (1988), *Narrative, Knowing and the Human Sciences*, New York: State University of New York Press.

Ribot, T. A. (1896), *Psychologies des Sentiments*, Paris: F Alcan.

Ricoeur, P. (1983), *Time and the Narrative*, Chicago: University of Chicago Press.

Rumelhart, D. E. and Norman, D.A. (1971), Accretion, Tuning and Re-Structuring: Three modes of learning, in: J. W. Cotton and R. Klatzky (eds), *Semantic Factors in Cognition*, Hillsdale: N.J, LEA.

Stallybrass, P. and White, A. (1986), *The Politics and Poetics of Transgression*, New York: Cornell University Press.

Taylor, C. (1989), *Sources of the Self*, Cambridge: Cambridge University Press.

Thomas, K (1977), The Place of Laughter in Tudor and Stuart England, *Times Literary Supplement*, 21 January, pp. 77-81.

Toulmin, S. E. (1958), *The Uses of Argument*, Cambridge: Cambridge University Press.

Voss, J. F. (1988), Problem Solving and Reasoning in Ill-Structured Domains, in C. Antaki (ed.), *Analyzing Everyday Explanation*, (London, Sage).

Woods, P. (1996), *Researching the Art of Teaching*, London: Routledge.

Chapter 6

The Marriage Analogy: Personal and Positional Relationships in PhD Supervision

Sara Delamont

Reflections on Method: Access

The access negotiations were, in general, easier in geography, town planning and the interdisciplinary areas than in anthropology. The access negotiations to anthropology were mainly conducted by Paul Atkinson (my co-grantholder) and Odette Parry (the research associate who did the bulk of the data collection). We have discussed them in Delamont, Atkinson & Parry (2000). I have drawn out three aspects of them here: personal networks, interdisciplinary stereotyping, and the image of the PhD process itself. Two of these were problems to be surmounted, the other an advantage we exploited.

We got access at all the departments we approached, but sometimes the processes were stressful. In all the departments we emphasized that we were not evaluators, and that we were not going to tell the ESRC what academics were doing. We made the usual points about anonymity and confidentiality, but they were doubly important in this project. The academic profession in Britain is small and close-knit, and prone to gossip. We have tried very hard to deliver anonymity and confidentiality. We have given pseudonyms to the universities, and where we actually sampled two departments in the same university we have given them different pseudonyms (so if we had been to Trinity Dublin to research biochemistry and physical geography, we would have given TCD two pseudonyms, and subsequently written of 'Foxhampton' and 'Badgerville').

The access processes revealed stereotyping across disciplines. In the science departments, the commonest questions concerned the unscientific nature of our research methods: how could interviews produce reliable and valid data. In the social sciences the anthropologists stood out from the other disciplines. Academics in human geography and town planning were not suspicious of sociologists, or of interviewing as a method. The negotiations with anthropologists, however revealed a stereotype. We found that anthropologists in Britain believed that sociology used questionnaires, and worked in a positivist paradigm. Our statements that we had applied for ESRC money to do an ethnography, and were only doing interviews because the director of the programme would only recommend funding for an interview study, and our stated plans to do ethnographic interviews, were met with disbelief. The anthropologists were, overall, most hostile to the ESRC's changes, and most dubious about our credibility. In some departments Paul and Odette were faced with academically testing questions: the most taxing being 'Where do you stand on Riceourian inscription?'

Those access negotiations foreshadowed one of the major findings about the ways in which different disciplines understood the PhD-getting process itself. The less comfortable the discipline was with the idea of a PhD as an apprenticeship, or a formal training, the more sceptical they were about our research.

In this summary of our sampling of three social science disciplines, the use of personal contacts, and the use of public roles in social science is laid bare. We used the same strategies to gain access in biochemistry, physical geography and AI.

For AI we gained access to Yowford, an urban university; and Illington, a famous research university. For biochemistry we chose Forthampstead, a sixties campus university; Ribblethorpe, a famous research university; and Baynesholme, a typical redbrick university. For physical geography and environmental sciences we worked at Ottercombe, a sixties campus; and revisited Hernchester and Tolleshurst.

To protect the students we chose pseudonyms that sounded American, and therefore 'unlikely' (such as Beulah Wyston and Joe Attschuler). For the staff we chose surnames from detective stories of the 1930s, giving them a rather upper class and other-worldly air. A decade after our first publications, few informants have recognized themselves, and a couple of anthropologists have suggested they can recognize one of their contemporaries. We, of course, have totally refused to comment on any claims of recognition.

Introduction

Using data on science and social science PhD students and their supervisors, gathered by ethnographic interview and observation, this chapter explores the 'marriage analogy'. Many commentators use the analogy of a marriage to describe the privacy, uniqueness, and developmental cycle of the PhD supervision relationship. The differences between science and social science disciplinary cultures, however, mean there are different types of marriage, many varieties of family life. Drawing on the theoretical ideas of Bernstein, especially his contrast between personal and positional families, the everyday lives of doctoral students and their supervisors will be illuminated. The theoretical stance of the chapter is unashamedly Bernsteinian. As the most innovative and challenging theorist in the sociology of education this is entirely appropriate. It seems likely that after a period of neglect (Delamont 2000) his work will be reassessed and re-fashioned in the next few years.

In *Implicit Meanings* Mary Douglas reflected on Basil Bernstein's position in sociology, arguing that he was 'neither fish, flesh nor fowl' and commenting: 'In sociology Bernstein is to some a fearsome scaly monster, cutting across all the tidy categories' (Douglas, 1975: p. 174). In this section a brief discussion of Bernstein as an example of an uncomfortable thorn in the flesh of sociology leads on to four other examples of ways in which mainstream sociology has treated the subspecialism of education, for most of the last fifty years – the BSA's history – sociology of education has been an uncomfortable sub-specialism, regarded with considerable ambivalence. Bernstein is anomalous in British sociology for a variety of reasons, including adopting a post-Durkheimian structuralism in a Parsonian era.

The death of Basil Bernstein in Sept 2000 produced a series of memorial events, and will produce a second round of commemorative and tribute volumes to follow the *Festschriften* that marked his retirement (Atkinson *et al.*, 1995; Sadovnik, 1995). In this chapter one of his central oppositionary pairs, personal versus positional, is used to theorize about the role and status of doctoral students. The data come from two ESRC-funded projects conducted in the 1990s, in which ethnographic interviews were carried out on 286 students, supervisors and department heads, in twenty academic departments in three of the four nations of the UK. The full report of the whole programme can be found in Delamont *et al.* (2000).

The chapter is in five sections. First, the research context and process are described. Then Bernstein's concepts are explained. Next, two 'ideal types' of PhD work are contrasted. In the fourth section, the Bernsteinian concepts are used to illuminate the roles of doctoral students. Finally, a research agenda is set out.

The title of the chapter evokes one of the analogies frequently used by supervisors to describe the relationship between doctoral students and supervisors: that of marriage. Like marriages and/or families, the supervisory relationship is *private*, intense, central to a happy life, and hard to study. However just as social science research on marriage has revealed that there are differences in ways that marriages can function, so too there are differences in supervisory patterns. It is to illuminate those differences that the chapter uses Bernstein's oppositional binary.

The Research Context

The years between 1979 and 1997 were hard for social scientists in Britain. The New Right ideologies which informed social policies and the general hostility to the higher education and research communities provided a backcloth against which a variety of specific attacks took place. The main channel for government money into 'pure', or 'blue skies' social science research in the UK, the Social Science Research Council (SSRC) had been created by Harold Wilson a Labour Prime Minister in the 1960s. The Conservatives began to attack it soon after 1979. The conservative minister, Sir Keith Joseph, insisted that the SSRC change its name to the Economic and Social Research Council (ESRC) to emphasize its economic importance, and remove the claim to 'science'. During the 1980s the senior executive of ESRC allowed the ESRC to be vulnerable to an attack over the way public money was being wasted: always a good basis for criticism in the Thatcher years. The ESRC was, critics said, giving studentships to PhD students most of whom did not submit their theses. At the same time, many social scientists apparently lacked skills in research methods, and there was an ageing labour force which needed replacement. These accusations were superficially plausible, and social science PhD students did appear to be far less likely to submit their theses than those funded in science and engineering. In fact, the statistics were not gathered in the same way: students who withdrew during their first year in science and engineering, or were recommended or required to terminate their candidatures, in their first year, were not included in the statistics. In social science, the statistics included such people.

There was a moral panic, and ESRC acted to save itself, and to safeguard PhD studentships. ESRC introduced sanctions against departments and universities with poor completion rates and only gave studentships to recognized outlets. To be a recognized outlet a university department had to have a decent completion rate, and introduce compulsory training in a variety of research methods. These policies were enshrined in *The Winfield Report* (1987). Britain's social scientists were suddenly required to change the ways in which PhD students were taught, and to engage in surveillance of them.

The research described in this chapter took place in two phases: the first on social sciences, the second on sciences. The political attacks on the ESRC and on social science involved a rhetorical contrast between 'good' sciences whose students completed on schedule and 'bad' social sciences whose students were 'non-competitors'. After we had finished our research on social scientists we conducted a study on biochemists, physical geographers, environmental scientists and practitioners of artificial intelligence. The access negotiations to the social scientists were more problematic and are discussed in more detail. The social science research was conducted in this politically charged context. Some famous and high status universities had been sanctioned, and were not getting any ESRC students for the first time in twenty years. In others, there were departments who wanted to resist the new training, and arguments between departments with good completion records sanctioned because colleagues in other subjects had bad ones.

The ESRC's graduate training is run by the Training Board, and three years after the policy changes, they funded a research programme. I was part of a team which obtained one the grants. We were then faced with the problem of gaining access to our peers – fellow social scientists in UK universities and polytechnics – for research on a contentious issue funded by the very organization that had made the issue contentious. The various teams that had received grants to study students and supervisors divided the main disciplines up between them. We agreed to study anthropology and human geography as pure disciplines, town planning as an applied discipline, and urban studies, area studies and development studies as interdisciplinary domains allied to our three disciplines. The two parallel projects took education and psychology (Bristol) and sociology, economics, and business and management studies (Warwick).

The Research Process: Sampling and Access

The access negotiations were inextricably linked to sampling issues. The PhD project needed a principled sampling technique to ensure that key variables were covered. There were four teams involved in the programme, so each group had to find sites where the other three were not already working, or planning to investigate. The Cardiff team needed to find two or three places to study anthropology, two or three to study geography, and one or two for each of town planning, urban studies, development studies and area (e.g. Slavonic and East European) studies. The departments/higher education institutions needed to vary (Oxbridge, Redbrick, Plateglass, Ex-Cats, Polys., etc.), the status in their subject needed to vary (i.e. small and/or not known for research excellence versus large and/or famous), and ideally the organizational arrangements and the 'ethos' of the places had to be different too. There were many different ways to proceed – but we started with personal contacts, and places we felt we would get cooperation. It is an excellent idea to use contacts to get started on access negotiations. Therefore we approached for social anthropology the following departments:

1. Southersham: a Redbrick, Northern University, where the professor and head of department (Professor Tenderton) had taught both Atkinson and Delamont when they were students and had employed Atkinson on a research project.
2. Kingford: a high status urban department, where the professor and head of department (Professor Dimsdale) was a member of the ESRC committee that was funding the research. He was a stranger to us, but would find it hard to refuse a piece of research set up and funded by a committee on which he served.
3. Masonbridge: a Plateglass campus university where the Dean had been at school with one of us and at university with both, and whose most recent edited collection had been suggested to the publishers by one of us.

For human geography we approached the following departments:

1. Tolleshurst: a high status department where one of the professors (not the head of department) knew one of us from a committee.
2. Hernchester: a Redbrick department where one of the professors was a major figure in the politics of social science, knew one of us slightly from committees, and knew colleagues of ours well.
3. Boarbridge: a small department in a provincial town pursuing innovative PhD training funded by ESRC, so again unlikely to refuse us access.
4. Eastchester: a sixties university with a small staff, where there were no full time students left after funding cuts so only staff could be interviewed. They felt very strongly about their funding, and were keen to express their views to researchers.

For town planning we approached:

1. Chelmsworth: then a Polytechnic which prided itself publicly on high quality provision for PhD students, so could hardly refuse us access.
2. Portminster: a centre of research excellence where several of the professors were friends of ours and would give us access.

3. Wellferry: a small department in a former CAT, where one of us was a visiting professor and so able to 'cash in' on our 'guest' status to do some interviews.

Those departments were likely to treat our access request seriously because of personal contacts or the politics of social science, and they generated a range of high and low status, urban and rural, northern and southern, large and small sites.

Bernstein's Concepts

Bernstein (1977) contrasted two modes of Socialization: personal and positional. He applied it to families, as contrasting ideal types. Each type provides its members with their sources of identity. The two modes of Socialization derive from the classic sociological distinction between ascribed and achieved statuses. In the positional family, social roles are primarily ascribed. Each family member has an identity which is fixed, closed, and explicit. Ascribed roles and statuses, such as age, sex, and position (e.g. oldest daughter, unmarried son), determine identity. The family has strong boundaries separating it from other units, and clear demarcations within it. It has a clear, explicit hierarchy, and the generations are distinct.

The contrasting ideal type is the personal family, where relationships are more open and fluid. Here achieved identities are more important, and may even be more salient for family members than ascribed ones. Boundaries around the family are more fluid, and relationships more open-ended, inside and outside the family. So the decision about software for the computer can be made by a child who is skilled in computing, the car chosen by a woman, a man may cook the meals. *Personal* qualities are important, not formal roles. Identities are negotiated, not based on *one* hierarchy. Gender and generation are less important than personal qualities.

In the positional family the lines of social control are clear. Age, sex, and position define the lines of authority which are explicit. In a personal family there is social control, but it is implicit and grounded in negotiation and persuasion. Families of the two different types are located in all social classes, although positional families are commoner in the working class, the upper class, and characterize the *old* middle class. Personal families are typical of the new middle class, and of the intelligentsia. (Delamont, 1989). Children reared in the two types respond differently to education; women's roles are very different, especially in their role as mothers. Families of the two types want contrasting types of pedagogic regime. One type is not superior to the other: they are designed to reproduce different sectors of the labour market.

Ideal Types of PhD Work

Bourdieu's (1988, 1996) work has reminded us that in all academic disciplines and departments, control is exercised by the established staff over their successors. However the nature of the authority, and the ways in which it is exercised are different in science and engineering on the one hand, and in arts and social science on the other. Disciplines are themselves cultural creations. The methodological and aesthetic devices that are used to understand cultural processes and cultural differences are, reflexively, part of the domain of culture. Academic cultures are no more 'given' than any others, whether they be academic disciplines or particular theoretical and methodological traditions. In the science and engineering disciplines control is clearly hierarchical, and the structure is overt. In humanities and social sciences, the system of control is implicit and even covert. Authority is more negotiable, grounded in personal qualities rather than seniority or formal leadership roles.

This is not a novel point about science and engineering. The explicit, personal control often irks those who dislike the way science and engineering are taught. This is clear from Tobias (1990), Downey and Lucena (1997) and Seymour and Howitt (1997). It is central to the mechanics of pedagogic continuity (see Delamont *et al.*, 1997a, 1997b). The replication of science in the undergraduate years constructs a domain of relative stability. Indeed, the pedagogic practices of undergraduate science are in themselves potent devices for the mobilization of students' trust in the methods and outcomes of scientific investigation.

The academic and scientific enculturation of scientists through doctoral research training has received little explicit attention in the research literature of the sociology and anthropology of science and technology, the sociology of the professions and the sociology of education (Delamont 1987, 1989, Delamont *et al.*, 2000). It is dealt with implicitly in more general studies of the social organization of scientific work and culture of science settings (e.g. Charlesworth *et al.*, 1989; Traweek, 1993). The relative neglect of science education in universities generally, and the neglect of doctoral research in particular, may reflect the fact that it is largely conducted under conditions of routine laboratory work, with relatively little opportunity for innovation or controversy. On the other hand it is a context in which can be explored issues of enculturation, competence and expertise. Science PhD students are socialized in a research group, with a clearly defined role for them. There is a division of labour in the research group, and equally visible boundaries between one research group and the next. Students are incorporated into the group, and should be loyal to it. Kevles' (1998) account of *The Baltimore Case* demonstrates the importance of such loyalties.

Kevles provides a detail account of a scientific and political row which broke out in the USA over a paper published in 1986 in *Cell*, a biomedical journal. David Baltimore, who had won a Nobel Prize in 1975, was the senior author of the paper, and that is why the row is called *The Baltimore Case*. The disputes lasted for a decade, and included a congressional inquiry. At the centre of the Baltimore case were issues about roles and responsibilities in a research group. Briefly, a junior scientist accused her line manager, Thereza Imanishi-Kari, of having published fraudulent data in the paper jointly authored with Baltimore and four others in *Cell*. Baltimore himself stood behind Imanishi-Kari, arguing that she had not cheated: because he was the head of the research group he took responsibility for the quality of the work done by it, and contributed 100,000 dollars to her defence costs.

The key figures apart from Baltimore and Imanishi-Kari were Margot O'Toole, a postdoctoral fellow and Charles Maplethorpe a graduate student in his final stages. Margot O'Toole was supposed to consolidate the results in the *Cell* paper and then build on them. She could not consolidate or replicate Imanishi-Kari's results, and therefore accused her of fraud. There were disputes in all the various laboratories in which both O'Toole and Maplethorpe had worked during their careers, over sexual relations between their line managers and other junior colleagues, over O'Toole's and Maplethorpe's bench skills, and over names on publications. They both found it impossible to work for Imanishi-Kari, while she felt both wasted time on personality disputes and politics rather than doing basic bench science.

Reading the Kevles account, it is clear that both O'Toole and Maplethorpe refused, or were unable, to behave 'properly' in the roles they occupied: they did not like the authority of their line managers, regularly 'saw' irregularities and complained about others they believed were being given more favourable treatment. Both left science for other fields. Those they left behind in the various labs where they had worked query their lack of loyalty to their research groups. Neither felt comfortable in a strongly positional system.

If the science PhD student is a member of a positional 'family' the social scientist experiences Socialization as a scholar in a personal 'family'. This is best described by drawing comparisons with the scientist's experience. The social science PhD student is an isolated individual (Deem & Brehony, 2000). They do not experience other social scientists doing research alongside them: they do not see social science being *done*. There is no tradition of the research group socializing together regularly. The group does not publish jointly as a team with all the names on the products. Teams do not go to conferences together, have regular colloquia, share the same equipment. However, the social science PhD is freer to negotiate an identity. The expectation is that she is an autonomous scholar who will soon be an intellectual equal. Students choose their own topic, theory, method and fieldsite. The project is individualized: if a student withdraws that research will simply never happen. The supervisor may be controlling the topic and its execution *in practice*, but if so, the control is exercised by persuasion, negotiation and suggestions. The personal style of the student, issues such as the extent to which they are 'cue-deaf' (Delamont *et al.*, 1997c), and other individual qualities, skills and interactions determine their role and status in the department.

In the next section this distinction is elaborated and exemplified using the data.

The Roles of Doctoral Students

The occupational Socialization of the doctoral student in science occurs in an hierarchical research group, in which the positional logic rules. When postgraduate students meet the unpredictable, real world, of their doctoral research, they find themselves alternatively elated and required to grit their teeth and carry on trying (Delamont & Atkinson, 2001). They account for their ability to carry on with the work by virtue of their engagement in a supportive social context: the research group with its teamwork and its pedagogic continuity. This pedagogic continuity is a fundamental element in the lives of doctoral students of science which enables them to come to terms with the vagaries of experimental research without abandoning the notion that science is for the most part a very stable and highly convergent activity. Most science is not in fact revolutionary. On the contrary much of science concentrates on addressing problems which arise out of, and are solvable within, the existing framework of research. Despite enthusiasm for refutation and revolution, most science activity leads to a large amount of permanent knowledge, devices and practice. One explanation for this and which lends support to the proposition that science stands apart from the real world, is that science is a 'self vindicating' activity. Hacking has described how this stability arises and is maintained because scientific practice is like a rope with many strands. Even if one of the strands is severed, the others persevere. In other words science encompasses several traditions, including theoretical, experimental and instrumental, and a break in one tradition is not necessarily fatal for the others. The structure of PhD science research functioned to maintain stability through continuity and mutual dependence: two elements highly visible in research at doctoral level. Using Hacking's (1992) analogy of a rope we can see how the interests of group members are mutually intertwined in a linear process through which the work of individuals is shaped and developed. The research group provides both intellectual continuity, and pedagogic continuity because new entrants are taught by the more established members.

Earth science, physical geography and biochemistry PhD students continue to expect, and indeed do, produce results from their experiments and from their fieldwork. Furthermore on the basis of these results they expect to, and a large percentage do, successfully complete PhDs. This raises the following question. How, when scientific work is apparently so capricious in nature and unpredictable in outcome, can doctoral candidates predict the successful outcome of their labours? One answer is that research groups provide intellectual and practical environments in which manageable projects are constructed.

The construction of a PhD project involves the identification of realistic goals. Furthermore these goals are intended to be realizable within the allotted period of time for study. The doctoral candidates whom we interviewed were not responsible for identifying their initial research topics nor the outline structure of their intended study. This task had been accomplished by the supervisor who assumed full responsibility for the identification of projects and attracting necessary funding. Thus the assignment of thesis topics to students is part of their experience of pedagogic continuity. Many of the students' accounts of their work in the laboratory sciences are couched in terms of problems and projects being determined for them. They construct research problems that arise from the research programmes of the laboratory, the research group or the group leader. They are not necessarily derived initially from a personal commitment or personal relationship with the topic of their research. For example, Antonia Viera at Forthamstead said of the topic given to her, 'It was a definite topic. The research project was fairly set out when I arrived and it had an outline to it and how it was theoretically supposed to go'. Her project had not proceeded according to plan, however, partly Antonia suggested because, 'I'd come from America and had very little lab experience'. A Baynesholme student, Karl Gunderson, told us, 'Professor Gantry tells me what experiments to do, and other people in the lab show me how to do them'. Karl went on to say that when he was offered his PhD topic, 'It wasn't an area I was interested in before but I'm very interested in it now'. The students expect the supervisor to choose a manageable project, and to alert them if it is going seriously wrong and needs to be changed. For example Alma Strottle, at Ribblethorpe, said:

> It's a very new technology, very new technology, its been done by one other lab. I'm taking it and using it for something quite big really, and they've been using it on a very small scale. So whether I can get the technology to work is another matter. I'm aware that it is going to be difficult. Dr Dewry is aware that it's going to be difficult, and he's got a kind of thing up his sleeve if, in a year's time, I'm still not getting anywhere. So at the end of the day I kind of know I'm going to get a PhD even if it's not exactly what it should be on.

Similarly Elissa Tyrone at Baynesholme believed: 'If things go really wrong, keep going wrong, then your supervisor should make you change what you're doing'.

These women are biochemists, but the physical geographers and earth sciences students spoke the same way:

> But at the time I applied for Ottercombe there were actual research objectives written by the two supervisors. So it was all more or less set up...it was a very interesting project actually, the more I got into it the more I found out how really interesting it is and the potential it has within its own subject is quite large. (Leo Gilligan, Earth Sciences, Ottercombe)

> It's been drummed into you that its interesting so you believe its interesting. I need pushing in some direction because I'm not the best judge, at this stage, which direction I should go in...they'll tell me if its practical or not. (Ben Safford, Geography, Tolleshurst)

> You've got to be a very exceptional person to come up with your own project. Normally the idea is the supervisor's which he knows is feasible – he knows it has the potential to be a PhD. I feel that X supervises very well because he always knows if it's on the rails. (Jim Vorhees of Tolleshurst)

Research students thus expressed their commitment to a particular research topic as something that was derived from external sources, rather than in terms of a personal choice or commitment. One can characterize their academic identities, loyalties and commitments in terms of ascribed positions, in contrast to the more personalized identities of research students in the social sciences. The research students undoubtedly found personal commitment and identity out of the work that had been allocated to them, but the initial source of such identification was externally derived.

Doctoral students in the social sciences have experienced a different enculturation at undergraduate level, and come to doctoral level with a contrasting position. Independent thought, and criticism of the dominant scholars in the field has been rewarded throughout the first degree. The PhD student in social science has to take personal responsibility for his or her own work. This implies a more intellectually equal relationship with the supervisor, which causes uncertainties and isolations. There is a fine line between independence, isolation and disorientation for the student. The following two supervisors are extreme examples of the style:

> I don't feel that one should be poking one's nose into a student's fieldwork. It's very much an independent business.
> and
> My own personal feeling is that the student has got to be independent enough to make their own decisions.

When a project does not work, the supervisor: role is to *advise*, not change the project.

She spent a couple of years doing fieldwork, and eventually sent back one fieldwork report on the geology of the place... She kept writing to say she was floundering and I kept writing to her to suggest angles of approach and she didn't seem to take them on.

Here supervisors explicitly place ownership of the research on the student, and see their role as essentially advisory, not managerial or, indeed, supervising. They are behaving like the members of a personal family: where achieved statuses are paramount, and social control is implicit and negotiated. The PhD student 'owns' his or her project, as an individual. Not only are any publications the student's own responsibility and property: the thesis may be the 'lifework'. In anthropology this is very common: Cowan (1990) is an expert on Sohos, Kenna (2000) on Nisos, Herzfeld (1985) on Glendi for life. However it is also the case in other disciplines, so that the doctoral thesis on transport in Balham gives a basis for reputation and expertise a decade later. Failing students in social science were those who did not thrive in the 'personal' research style. Our most disillusioned respondent recognized that:

> I realized just how much submerged knowledge there is.... And nobody would tell me because, I got the impression, they all presumed I must know. If I'd come this far I must know...I really couldn't get any response from anyone, even direct questions were met with a load of theoretical waffle...A lot of mistakes I've made are the result of me not asking questions and people not putting me right. They presume I must know...Nobody bothered to tell me and nobody *has* told me.

This candidate was an extreme case, in that he was *articulate* about the clash between the regime he expected and the reality he found.

For the successful social scientists, the pride in the ownership of their own research and the sense of professional adulthood when they finished their theses and passed, were evident. Doing Travers, of Southersham, was finished when interviewed:

Before you go away you are just one of the kids and are treated as such, but when you come back you can be talked to like an adult. You have passed your initiation.

Similarly Nancy Enright, who did her PhD at Kingford and then got a lectureship at another fieldsite, waxed lyrical about the discipline despite an unpleasant viva. Becoming a human geographer or an anthropologist may involve loneliness on the way through, but, for the successful, inculcates a joy in the eventual disciplinary membership.

The contrast between life in a positional culture (the science research group) and a personal one (the social science *non*-group) is starkly revealed in the ways writing up the thesis is discussed (or not discussed) by supervisors and students. For the scientists, as long as there are results to describe there is 'nothing to it' except following rules and getting it done. *And* because of the research group there has been more sharing of writing all along: colloquia debate texts, group members share 'writing up' and publishing. The style and format of writing, whether for a conference poster, an article or a thesis, are also much more clearly defined and more public. For the social scientist, writing is more personal, and more negotiable. Because 'the best work, the best texts, come out of very solid fieldwork' (Dr Fustian); the students have to be 'prepared to live with' the data they have collected when they write them up. Both the data collection and the writing up are 'tests' of the individual student's personal qualities. Being 'able to write' is an achieved status that the social scientist must work towards to gain the status of the full grown scholar.

Bernstein argued that personal and positional families were found in different sectors of society, drawing on different experiences of the labour market and serving to reproduce different sectors of it. Thus the old middle class reproduces itself through positional families, while the new middle class reproduces itself through the personal family. So too the various academic tribes reproduce themselves through positional and personal management systems for PhD students.

A Research Agenda

It is over ten years since the ESRC funded the programme of research on 'The Social Science PhD' (Burgess, 1994) and the Spencer Foundation funded its five nations study (Clark, 1993). In Britain the policy context has changed considerably, especially since the Harris Report (1996). There is a need for new research on a range of higher degree issues.

Humanities/Arts Disciplines

Although there is the survey done by Sandra Harris for UKCGE (2000), there is no social science research on MPhil/PhD research students and their supervisors in those disciplines. History was included in the five nation Spencer funded study (Clark, 1993; Becher, Henkel & Kogan, 1994), but there is no research on English, Ancient or Modern languages, or other arts and humanities disciplines. The establishment of the AHRB may or may not have changed the everyday lives of students and supervisors in these disciplines. As I write the BA and the AHRB are conducting enquiries into the area of graduate education: the lack of research base must be hampering both enquiries.

'Vocational' Disciplines

There are few studies of the place of doctoral studies in disciplines such as social work, nursing, librarianship, agriculture, forestry, dentistry, medicine, architecture...Why do people in such fields *do* graduate work? We do not know.

Professional Doctorates

There is now a range of 'professional' doctorates including the DClinPsych and the EdD. We have not yet done the research on these degrees that they deserve.

The Examination Process

Tinkler and Jackson (2000) are convinced that the examination process needs thorough investigation. There are severe ethical problems around studying real examination processes, but Tinkler and Jackson are correct to raise the need for investigations here.

Ethnographic Research

I argued at HECUI that while the UK had led the world in the number and quality of its ethnographies of schools and schooling (Delamont & Atkinson, 1995), there was a dearth of ethnographies of higher education settings. The few that exist are not well known. The UK needs studies such as Moffat (1990) and Holland and Eisenhart (1990).

References

Atkinson, P.A., Davies, B. and Delamont, S. (eds), (1995), *Discourse and Reproduction: Essays in Honour of Basil Bernstein*, Creskill, NJ: Hampton.

Becher, T., Henkel, M. and Kogan, M. (1994), *Graduate Education in Britain*, Jessica Kingsley: London.

Bernstein, B. (1977), *Class, Codes and Control vol. 3.*, Routledge and Kegan Paul: London.

Bourdieu, P. (1988), *Homo Academicus*, Polity: Cambridge.

Bourdieu, P. (1996), *The State Nobility*, Polity: Cambridge.

Burgess, R.G. (ed.), (1994), *Postgraduate Education and Training in the Social Sciences*, Jessica Kingsley: London.

Charlesworth, M., Farrall, L., Stokes, T., and Turnbull, D. (1989), *Life Among the Scientists*, Oxford University Press: Melbourne.

Clarke, B.R. (ed.) (1993), *The Research Foundations of Graduate Education*, California University Press: Berkeley, CA.

Cowan, Jane (1990), *Dance and the Body Politic in Northern Greece*, Princeton University Press: Princeton.

Deem, R. and Brehony, K. (2000), 'Doctoral students' access to research cultures'. *Studies in Higher Education*, vol. 25(2), pp. 149-168.

Delamont, S. (1987), 'Three Blind Spots?' *Social Studies of Science*, vol. 17(1), pp. 161-170.

Delamont, S. (1989), *Knowledgeable Women*, London: Routledge.

Delamont, S. (2000), 'The Anomalous Beasts', *Sociology*, vol. 34(1).

Delamont, S. and Atkinson, P.A. (1995), *Fighting Familiarity*, Hampton Press: Cresskill, NJ.

Delamont, S. and Atkinson, P.A. (2001), 'Doctoring uncertainty', *Social Studies of Science*, vol. 31(1), pp. 87-107.

Delamont, S., Atkinson, P.A., and Parry, O. (1997a), 'Critical mass and pedagogic continuity', *British Journal of Sociology of Education*, vol. 18(4), pp. 533-550.

Delamont, S., Atkinson, P.A., and Parry, O. (1997b), 'Critical mass and doctoral research', *Studies in Higher Education*, vol. 22(3), pp. 319-332.

Delamont, S., Atkinson, P.A., and Parry, O. (1997c), *Supervising the PhD*, Open University Press: Buckingham.

Delamont, S., Atkinson, P.A., and Parry, O. (2000), *The Doctoral Experience*, Falmer: London.

Douglas, Mary (1975), *Natural Symbols*, Barrie and Rockcliffe: London.

Downey, G.L. and Lucerna, J.C. (1997), 'Engineering selves' in G.L. Downey and J. Dumit (eds), *Cyborgs and Citadels*, School of American Research Press: Santa Fe.

Hacking, I. (1992), 'The self-vindication of the laboratory sciences' in A. Pickering (ed.), *Science as Practice and Culture*, Chicago University Press: Chicago.

Harris, M. (1996), *Review of Postgraduate Education*, Bristol: Higher Education Funding Council for England.

Herzfeld, Michael (1985), *The Poetics of Manhood*, Cambridge: Cambridge University Press.

Holland, D.C., and Eisenhart, M.A. (1990), *Educated in Romance*, Chicago: The University of Chicago Press.

Kenna, Margaret (2000), *Fieldwork on Anafi*, Harwood: London.

Kevles, D.J. (1998), *The Baltimore Case*, New York: W.W. Norton.

Moffat, N. (1990), *Coming of Age in New Jersey*, Rutgers University Press: New Brunswick, NJ.

Sadovnik, A. (ed.), (1995), *Basil Bernstein*, Norwood, NJ: Ablex.

Seymour, E. and Howith, N.M. (1997), *Thinking about Leaving: Why Undergraduates leave the Sciences*, Boulder, Co., Westview.

Tinkler, P., and Jackson, C. (2000), 'Examining the doctorate', *Studies in Higher Education*, vol. 25(2), pp. 167-180.

Tobias, S. (1990), *They're not Dumb, they're Different*, Research Corporation: Tucson, Az.

Traweek, S. (1993), *Beamtimes and Lifetimes*, Harvard University Press: Cambridge, MA.

Winfield, G. (1987), *The Social Science PhD*, (2 vols) ESRC: London.

Chapter 7

Policy Driven Curriculum Restructuring: Academic Identities in Transition?

Rob Moore

Reflections on Method: Analysis of Interviews

My research involved exploring how two universities were responding to recent curriculum policy, with a particular interest in the responses of academics to the pressures placed on them to collaborate across disciplinary boundaries to produce multi- or interdisciplinary programmes that were responsive to South Africa's economic and social development needs, and that conformed to outcomes-based approaches to curriculum design.

The issue that I came across again and again was the distinction between public discourse (the 'best face forward' accounts) and the more private disclosures which offer clearer insight into the actual responses of academics and the processes that were followed in attempting to fulfill the policy. This is, I'm sure, a fairly perennial challenge facing qualitative researchers. I think some conditions may have sharpened the problem in my case. Probably most important was the fact that the changes were policy-driven, with the promise that eventually state subsidies would be tied to enrolments in 'programmes' approved by the state, rather than simply on enrolments generally, as in the past. Thus external perceptions of the 'strength' of particular programmes could be important in determining the credibility (and thus fundability) of particular programmes.

Thus there was an understandable impulse on the part of many respondents (especially more senior ones) to offer 'public discourse', rather than the more nuanced accounts needed for qualitative enquiry. But as the process proceeded, I became conscious of particular strategies I was adopting to counter this, and of the sometimes changing responses from my informants as their perceptions of me shifted during the course of an interview. I became aware that the identity I presented during interviews may have conditioned the openness (or otherwise) of respondents, and I realized that the way I framed the purpose of interviews for respondents at the outset changed somewhat as the data-gathering proceeded. I also became aware of my own comportment during interviews, especially ways in which I endeavoured to put informants at ease, and encouraged particular kinds of response.

Interestingly my awareness of these issues grew at about the same time as I became interested in the issue of identity (not originally a theme foregrounded in my planning for the project, but subsequently central to my analysis), and the ways in which the policy was asking academics to adopt changing identities, to comport themselves differently in their relationships with each other and the outside world, and to prioritize changing values. As my awareness of this theme deepened, I began to see the interview as a dance of identities, with each of the two players projecting particular personas. In some cases the responses of the colleagues remained fairly consistent throughout (sometimes strongly assertive, sometimes persistently evasive), but in other cases, a respondent would begin with a 'public' account, but would relax during the course of an interview and feel confident enough to offer insight into the messier, more complex realities behind the public face. These would often be some of the more rewarding interviews because they reflected much of the broader pattern of the policy responses generally: apparent compliance at the level of public rhetoric, working to camouflage widespread business-as-usual on the ground, or in very rare instances, highly conflictual and traumatic attempts to bring about significant change.

Introduction

Recent debates over curriculum have increasingly raised the issue of the implications of curriculum reform for the forms of social organization and identity associated with changing forms of knowledge. For example, Rob Moore (of Homerton College, Cambridge) and Michael Young (2001) note how contending pressures for change are exerting pressure on both modes of knowledge production and forms of curriculum organization, usually towards increasing integration. This pressure for integration includes increasing connectivity between disciplines, between knowledge and its application, and between the academy and the outside world. Moore and Young remind us that knowledge is essentially social in character, and derives from particular sets of codes and values pursued systematically within specialist communities and networks. These codes and practices historically found organizational form in university subject departments and specialist professional and academic organizations concerned with knowledge production. Moore and Young argue that claims for shifting forms of knowledge in the curriculum should not be considered apart from 'the role of specialist communities, networks and codes of practice' that are needed to sustain these (2001: p. 16). In other words, attempts to change curriculum towards more integrated forms of knowledge has implications for the forms of social organization that underpin curriculum delivery. This has potentially far-reaching implications for the higher education sector, where the organizational base for curriculum is often related to that for knowledge production.

In her study of how academic identities are responding to policy shifts in higher education in the UK, Mary Henkel (2000) argues that the primary resources for academic identities are the discipline and the institution. Following Bourdieu, Mary Henkel notes that the processes of identity formation in the field of science are essentially competitive: 'Competitors have both to distinguish themselves from their predecessors and their rivals and to integrate the work of these groups into a construction that transcends it. The achievement of identity is therefore instrumental to the way in which science works' (Henkel 2000, p.18). Bourdieu argues further that the various scientific fields have strongly differentiated power and status, stand in competition with one another, and are 'the locus of competitive struggle' for individual scientists located within the fields: 'What is at stake is the power to impose the definition of science ... best suited to [the individual scientist's] specific interests' (Bourdieu 1975, p. 23, cited in Henkel 2000, p. 17). Henkel then draws on the work of Burton Clark (1983) to argue that academics stand in a matrix 'formed by the cross-cutting imperatives of discipline and enterprise (the university or college)', and that the institutional form of this intersection is the academic department. Academics thus experience 'the complexities and tensions inherent in two major sources of identity, one local, visible and tangible, the other cosmopolitan, largely invisible and disembedded' (Henkel 2000, p. 19). The forms of social organization in which academics are located thus perform the dual function of ensuring the epistemological integrity of knowledge production and transmission, and of constructing and sustaining the professional identities of academics.

In a paper which outlines what he calls the 'slide' toward 'performativity', Ronald Barnett (2000) notes the multiple forces competing for influence on contemporary curriculum – coming from, amongst others, the state, the labour market, knowledge fields and institutions. He develops a set of hypotheses that aims to predict the broad trajectory of curriculum change in higher education. Drawing on the work of Basil Bernstein, he distinguishes between curricula that are 'inward-looking, reflecting a project of introjection where they are largely the outcome of academic influence' and curricula that are 'outward looking, reflecting a project of projection, where they are subject to external influences' (Barnett 2000, p. 263). Barnett predicts that at the macro level (state and institutional policies), change will be in the direction of projection (clearly the case in the South African context, as we shall see below) and (again drawing on Bernstein) from insulated singulars towards increasingly multi-or inter-disciplinary regions. However he notes that despite the multiple claims from outside the academy, 'the discipline (or knowledge field) constitutes the largest claim on the identity of academics' (p. 264) and consequently the micro level of actual curricular changes will reflect both the extent to which disciplines within institutions are yielding their insularity, and changes within disciplinary fields of inquiry (p. 264). He further predicts that changes will depend on the relative strength of institutions against that of their constituent disciplines, and the positioning of individual institutions within the higher education system. Barnett thus generates a complex picture of how curricular change will come about, predicting – in spite of the drift to projection and performativity – the salience of strongly-established disciplinary identities, particularly in situations where institutions are powerfully-positioned in the national hierarchy of universities.

This chapter explores one context of curriculum restructuring in higher education, and reports on a study which looks at how academics in two South African universities have responded to national curriculum policy, both in terms of the extent of curriculum changes, and in terms of the implications for academic identities and forms of academic organization. The chapter will firstly outline the South African higher education curriculum policy context. I will then draw on the work of educational sociologist Basil Bernstein to propose an interpretive frame for the study, illustrating this with some examples. Finally I will present a case study of attempts to change curriculum in response to the policy which illustrates issues of identity and social organization, and which – in conclusion – proposes conditions under which significant curriculum change can be achieved.

Policy Context

Since the transition to democracy in 1994, higher education in South Africa – like other sectors – has been subject to a series of policy papers and bills which seek to reconstruct the field in various ways. These policy moves reflect two broad imperatives: a response to global developments and the changing role of higher education internationally, and a local concern for economic development, social reconstruction and equity. Higher education is seen as a means of helping to integrate South Africa into the global economy on the one hand, and as a vehicle for correcting the social and economic imbalances inherited from apartheid on the other. A central ambition of the policies has thus been to enhance levels of state control over the higher education system so as to steer the system more effectively towards these goals. The key means by which the state plans to exert this enhanced control is the academic 'programme'. The Draft White Paper on Higher Education notes that 'the most significant conceptual change is that the single co-ordinated system will be premised on a programme-based definition of higher education' (Department of Education [DoE] 1997: paragraph 2.4). Programmes would thus become the unit by which the system would be planned, governed and funded, enabling a greater responsiveness of the system 'to present and future social and economic needs, including labour market trends and opportunities, the new relations between education and work, and in particular, the curricular and methodological changes that flow from the information revolution' (DoE 1997: paragraph 2.6). Programmes are thus not only a structural device to enable better steerage of the system; they are intended to be a vehicle for a qualitatively different form of curriculum.

   One of the arguments advanced for curriculum reform are claims about the changing nature of knowledge, and where and how it is produced. For example, Cloete and Bunting (2000) argue that science has come to depend more on applied knowledge and less on dramatically novel knowledge, typically produced 'by trans -disciplinary groups, or teams who are from within and outside of higher education, where the organizational structures and teams are less hierarchical. ... This new social organization of knowledge requires a differently equipped cadre of knowledge workers than those who are currently based in universities. The new cadre must consist of problem-identifiers, problem-solvers and problem-brokers' (Cloete & Bunting 2000: 39). In this way arguments are made not only for changing knowledge forms, but also for changing organizational forms and academic identities.

The counterpart in curriculum policy to this discursive trend is thus a shift away from discipline-based degrees towards more vocationally purposive 'programmes' – 'It would also break the grip of the traditional pattern of qualification based on sequential, year-long courses in single disciplines'. (DoE 1997: para 2.6) – a shift of particular significance for the natural sciences and humanities, and a trend roundly critiqued in, for example, Muller (2000). A further justification for the shift towards programmes is the argument that curricula need to be *responsive* to the needs of society. For example, the report of the National Commission on Higher Education (NCHE) which preceded (and informed) the regulations subsequently issued by the South African Qualifications Authority (SAQA) makes a connection between a particular notion of educational design and the goal of greater responsiveness to economic and social needs. Programmes, we are told:

> are almost always invariably trans-, inter- or multidisciplinary.... The demands of the future of South Africa as a developing country require that programmes, while necessarily diverse, should be educationally transformative. Thus they should be planned, coherent and integrated; ... they should be learner-centred, experiential and outcomes-oriented; they should develop attitudes of critical enquiry and powers of analysis; and they should prepare students for continued learning in a world of technological and cultural change. (NCHE in SAUVCA 1999: p. 7)

A third justification for the emphasis on programmes draws on the discourse of accountability. The NCHE report expresses this theme in terms of 'responsiveness', again asserting a need for changes in organization and practices:

> In essence, increased responsiveness and accountability express the greater impact of the market and civil society on higher education and the consequent need for appropriate forms of regulation. ... Overall, greater responsiveness will require new forms of management and assessment of knowledge production and dissemination. It has implications for the content, form and delivery of the curriculum. (NCHE 1996: pp. 6 – 7)

The NCHE report is explicit that the consequences of 'responsiveness' for academic disciplines is a weakening of the autonomy of disciplines and institutions, and a shift of regulative authority toward more negotiated forms:

> At an epistemological level, increased responsiveness entails a shift from closed knowledge systems (controlled and driven by canonical norms of traditional disciplines and by collegially recognized authority) to more open knowledge systems (in dynamic interaction with external social interests, consumer or client demand, and other processes of knowledge generation). (NCHE 1996: p. 6)

The subsequent regulations governing academic programmes issued by SAQA blend the discourses of outcomes-based approaches and accountability. The regulations require a qualification to (amongst other things) have a 'defined purpose', consist of 'planned combinations', produce in learners an 'applied competence' which is made visible in 'integrated assessment ... to ensure that the purpose of the qualification is achieved'. The body representing university top executives (the South African Universities' Vice Chancellors' Association – SAUVCA) notes that these developments would make it 'feasible for massive improvements in quality to be achieved' through 'putting into place the most important requirement of any quality assurance system: clearly defined outcomes against which the quality of student performance and institutional provision can be assessed' (SAUVCA 1999: p. 26). Thus while reserving judgement on the feasibility of the inclusion of university qualifications on a tightly formatted qualifications framework, SAUVCA sees advantages of programmatization lying in its potential for increasing levels of accountability and (by implication) centralization of control.

SAUVCA has published a Facilitatory Handbook (SAUVCA 1999) intended to guide the implementation of the policy in South Africa's universities. The handbook is explicit about the implications of the policy: what is required is nothing less than

> a new model of Higher Education practice. For example, academics will now have to make explicit their learning outcomes and assessment criteria and offer these for public scrutiny. When designing curricula, they will be required to work in programme teams rather than as single individuals.... The demand for summative integrated assessment, across specific course outcomes and across modules within a programme will be particularly demanding in relation to design and implementation, given traditional territorial and individualistic approaches to teaching.... (SAUVCA 1999: pp. 27-8)

The policy of programmatization[12] was thus anticipating significant shifts in the nature of academic practices, in the professional identities of academics, and in the forms of authority that are invoked to regulate curriculum decisions. In particular, it anticipates a weakening of the insulations between disciplines, and that academics will participate in collectives which cross disciplinary boundaries, and which are predicated on serving external accountabilities. This accountability has at least two dimensions: firstly a responsiveness to broader social and economic goals, and secondly an accountability for achieving the cross-cutting learning goals stipulated for academic programmes as a whole (rather than simply discipline-specific ones). Both of these dimensions ask for a weakening of prior

---

[12] Whilst the account I have given here of the policy draws from national level policy discourses, and while the study referred to in this chapter looks at how institutions have responded to the policy environment, it is clear that there is no one-way linear pattern of 'policy -> response' at work here (Muller 2001). South Africa's policies are themselves responses to wider global discourses, and (as I have shown in a prior paper) at least one of the institutions under study had embarked on a process of programmatization *before* the national policy was published (Moore 2002).

insulations between departments or disciplines as academics meet to agree on graduate identities deemed suitable for the contemporary workplace, translate these into overarching outcomes that curricula should achieve, and then (at least) modify disciplinary curricula or (preferably) collaborate in interdisciplinary or multi-disciplinary curricula to achieve these outcomes.

We have come to learn, however, that the good intentions of policy are seldom if ever translated straightforwardly into practice (Ball, 1993). Muller (2001) suggests that the exogenous pressures of policy or the market are limited in their conditioning effect on higher education institutions by the state of play of two endogenous factors. These are, firstly, the changing dynamics and relative strengths of disciplines (intellectual capital) and, secondly, the systemic capacity for change (managerial capital). The differing dispositions of these two forms of capital translate intended policy into enacted policy. Muller concludes by noting that institutions may be varyingly responsive, or unresponsive, to policy as a result of either weakness or strength in these areas, and that these institutional dispositions are 'inscribed in people and practices' (Muller, 2001: p.12).

Confirming the lack of linearity in policy processes, Ensor's study of curriculum restructuring across South Africa's universities shows that despite the policy pressure towards interdisciplinary curricula, there is little evidence of interdisciplinarity:

> The credit exchange discourse has pressured faculties of science and humanities to provide a professional or vocational face to their academic provision. ... Overall, though, it would seem that curricula have been re-packaged and redesigned ... but remain recognizable in terms of their disciplinary origins. (Ensor, 2002: p. 290)

And confirming the centrality of 'people and practices', Ensor's (1998) study of an attempt at interdisciplinarity suggested that the high levels of conflict noted in her study were the consequence of the difficulty of reconciling opposing principles for the construction of curriculum, and that these were 'interwoven with equally potent issues of disciplinarity and identity' (Ensor, 1998: p.103). The opposing principles of curriculum construction are closely bound up with differing identity positions, and the vindication of one principle above another has consequences for the respective identities. Although new forms of curriculum were being demanded, no new mechanisms were in place to manage the competing claims, with the consequence that 'the debate polarized very rapidly and resolution became impossible' (Ensor, 1998: p.103). The study reported below is thus an effort to explore in closer detail how 'people and practices', and particularly how academic identities, work to condition policy responses. For this purpose I need to turn briefly to a discussion of identity.

An Interpretive Frame

I now turn to the work of educational sociologist Basil Bernstein to develop an interpretive frame through which to give an account of the data emerging from the study. Bernstein argues that initiatives of curriculum reform are concerned to change the 'bias and focus of official knowledge', and that these competing initiatives attempt to construct different pedagogic identities: 'thus the bias and focus of this official discourse is expected to construct in teachers and students a particular moral disposition, motivation and aspiration, embedded in particular performances and practices' (Bernstein 1999, p. 246). Bernstein emphasizes that the construction of identity is not a purely solitary and inward psychological construction, but that it is formed through social processes. Identity, he says, 'is the dynamic interface between individual careers and the social or collective base.... [I]dentity arises out of a particular social order, through relations which the identity enters into with other identities of reciprocal recognition, support, mutual legitimization and finally through a negotiated collective purpose' (1996: p. 73). This is consistent with Henkel's (2000) 'communitarian' view which sees identity as shaped by the communities it is embedded within, and which provide the normative space for individual choices. From this view, the various institutional communities (and their values and practices) that academics locate themselves in thus play a major role in shaping their professional identities. How these communities are realized at local levels, and attempts to change these social forms as suggested in the policy discourses outlined above, can thus have significant influence on identity formation.

Bernstein distinguishes between two 'official' identities projected by the discourse of the state, and two 'local' identities generated within institutions, particularly where these institutions (like the two universities in this study) have a degree of autonomy. The two official pedagogic identities are the retrospective, and the prospective. *Retrospective* identities are 'shaped by national religious, cultural grand narratives of the past ... appropriately recontextualized to stabilize that past in the future'. Importantly, notes Bernstein, the discourse of this identity 'does not enter into an exchange relation with the economy. The bias, focus and management here leads to a tight control over the *inputs* of education, that is its contents, *not* over its *outputs*' (1999: p. 248). By contrast, the *prospective* identity is essentially forward-looking, and is oriented to deal with cultural, economic and technological change, and is usually motivated by the need to maintain or improve economic performance. Because of this emphasis on economic performance, the promotion of these identities 'requires the state to control both *inputs* for education and *outputs*' (1999: pp. 248-249). From this view, the South African policy discourses noted above thus articulate a broadly prospective position, in comparison to the retrospective position of, say, the era of grand apartheid.

Bernstein calls the two local identities, which can be generated within reasonably autonomous institutions, the therapeutic and market positions. Whereas the two official identities distinguished above recontextualize various resources from the past, these two local identities are concerned with the present, although different versions of the present. With the *market* identity, the institution shapes its pedagogy and management to produce products which have an exchange value in a market. Management tends to be explicitly hierarchical, and acts to monitor the effectiveness of the components of the institution in satisfying and creating local markets, and to reward and punish accordingly.

We have here a culture and context to facilitate the survival of the fittest as judged by market demands. The focus is on the short term rather than the long term, on the extrinsic rather than the intrinsic, upon the exploration of vocational applications rather than upon exploration of knowledge. The transmission here views knowledge as money. And like money it should flow easily to where demand calls.... [This] position constructs an outwardly responsive identity rather than one driven by inner dedication. Contract replaces covenant.... The [market] position projects contingent, differentiated competitive identities. (Bernstein, 1999: pp. 250-251)

By contrast, the *therapeutic* position emphasizes 'an integrated modality of knowing and a participating co-operative modality of social relation'. Compared to the competitive identities of the market position, this position projects (ideally) stable, integrated identities with adaptable, co-operative practices: 'the management style is soft, hierarchies are veiled, power is disguised by communication networks and interpersonal relations' (1999: p. 251). Bernstein notes that the pedagogy of this position (because of its collaborative and student-centred approaches) is relatively costly, and that this identity position is sponsored by a social group with relatively little power.

I want to suggest that the official policy discourses discussed earlier, whilst of a generally prospective orientation, contain within them signals which could be drawn on to make the case for *both* of these local identity positions, although more strongly for the market than the therapeutic position. As the case study presented below will suggest, the discourse of some individual academics in the two institutions under study can be shown to reflect one or another of these orientations. However, it is also necessary to consider other, *still-current* identity positions, in particular the traditional position of academics in a dispensation of minimal state or other outside intervention in higher education, or what I'll call the 'old collegium'. This is a position of high levels of individual autonomy within institutions, with clearly-defined disciplinary bases as the chief locus of social integration, and with relatively strong insulations between disciplines, and between the academy and the outside. This is the position that the policy discourses invite academics and institutions to move *from*, towards the new prospective position that the policy advocates. I also want to distinguish between those positions in the old collegium that are relatively introjected or inward looking (the *disciplinary* position), and those that are more projected or outward looking (typically the *professional* disciplines).

To illustrate this, I'll provisionally represent these four theoretically-derived positions diagrammatically (adapting Ensor's 2002 diagram). For the axes of Figure 7.1 below, I use the two key pressures for change embedded in the policy: the shift from an insular *introjected* orientation towards a more outwardly integrated and responsive *projected* orientation, and the shift from high levels of personal autonomy within disciplinary groupings to patterns of teamwork across disciplinary boundaries. For this latter distinction, I'll use Durkheim's notion of *mechanical* and *organic* solidarities, rather as Bernstein (1975a) discussed them.

Figure 7.1 Contemporary identity positions in the academic field

	Introjected	Projected
Mechanical	Disciplinary (old collegium)	Professional
Organic	Therapeutic (new collegialism)	Market (entrepreneurial)

The policy thus attempts to exert pressure for (especially) academics in the formative disciplines (the 'disciplinary/old collegium' section) to move towards the bottom two quadrants. Although Bernstein argues that the therapeutic position is a relatively weak one, it is one that is nevertheless articulated in the advocacy literature on higher education (see for example Harvey and Knight's 1996 account of 'new collegialism' as the social form to replace what they call the 'cloisterism' of the past).

While this diagram helps to distinguish these respective ideal-typical discursive positions, this representation doesn't reflect various nuances that will be illustrated in the data below. In particular, I want to make two points at this stage. Firstly, these positions are *in practice* very differently realized, with the disciplinary and professional positions being very strongly institutionalized, whilst the market and therapeutic positions are very weakly represented in the two institutions under study. Secondly, I will argue below that the market and therapeutic positions are necessary but transitional positions in the movement of some introjected disciplinary singulars towards projected professional or vocational regions (see Figure 7.2 below). In order for singulars to collaborate across disciplinary boundaries in an interdisciplinary project, which eventually becomes codified and institutionalized as a newly-emerging region, it is necessary for discipline-based academics to abandon insularity in pursuit of the 'vocational applications' of the market position, and the 'integrated modality of knowing and a participating co-operative modality of social relation' of the therapeutic position. Once the new region has coalesced and found stable organizational forms, then the social relations of academics within that form begin to take on the features of the professional position, with increasing forms of specialization within an established field with an identity in its own right. But such a transition has as its primary engine the processes of knowledge production, rather than transmission. Interdisciplinary curriculum which does not ride on the coat-tails of a regionalising field of knowledge production and/or a field of practice would seem to have a flimsy base for the achievement of cross-border consensus, and may be consequently quite unstable in the absence of authoritative criteria for recontextualisation (Muller 2001).

Figure 7.2 Potential transitions of identity

```
                        Therapeutic
Disciplinary (singulars)  →                    →Professional (regions)
                          Market
                    (transitional positions)
```

In the case study below, I will use this interpretive frame of varying identity positions to interpret the identity aspirations articulated in the discourse of academics who are responding to the policy-driven pressures. In the account, it will become clear that while some academics have a view of the new identity positions and the practices they imply, few are willing to make the transition, and those who do aspire to shift to these positions find considerable obstacles in their way. The case study will conclude with some suggestions for the conditions under which substantive shifts in academic identities and practices might be achieved, conditions which are likely to find realization only rarely.

The Case Study

This chapter reports on a comparative study of the implementation of this curriculum restructuring policy in the science and humanities faculties of two South African universities with a particular interest in the responses of academic staff. This study aims to explore the programmes implementation process, seeking to understand some of the motivations and conditions that have driven the responses to the policy. Compared to the other universities in the country, the two chosen for this study are relatively well-established institutions with strongly entrenched traditions of discipline-based departments, and with good research track-records. These institutions were chosen for the study in the knowledge that the assumptions of the policy about weakening of disciplinary identities would be particularly challenging for universities with strong departmental cultures. In 2000, the year of principal data gathering, the two institutions (UniA and UniB) were respectively in their first year and second year of programme implementation, although effectively both were implementing the changes at second-year undergraduate level. Data for the broader study included in-depth interviews with academic staff at all levels associated with the programmatization process, as well as institutional documentation of various kinds, where this was available.

This chapter reports on a component of the broader study, drawing on interviews with humanities-based academics in each institution associated with newly-produced programmes in development studies. Prior to the programmatization process, development studies as a focus of interest had been pursued only by individuals within departments, usually without reference across departmental boundaries. Although this period (the 2000 academic year) marked the first time that such programmes were listed in the respective handbooks of the two institutions, it is not the first time that attempts had been made to forge similar multi- or interdisciplinary curricula in this broad area.

Questions motivating the study thus include: Are insulations between departments and disciplines weakening, and are academics meeting across disciplinary boundaries to achieve consensus, and to monitor and adjust their curricula? If so, is there evidence that new communities of practice are forming which may be signalling the emergence of new academic identities?

The Case of UniA

At UniA, for example, efforts four years previously to form development studies had been 'scuttled ... because of turf battles'. The field was seen by one department as 'their disciplinary domain, and they didn't really want to open up their field of academic activities to other departments' (AH11: p. 1). A further constraint seems to have been the system where student enrolments are used to calculate staffing levels in departments, prompting a reluctance from academics to 'share' students across departments. The context of programme implementation at UniA in 1999 and 2000, however, placed a greater pressure on academics to respond to the policy. Although South African higher education generally was experiencing declining enrolments, UniA's student numbers had dropped further than those of comparable institutions, and the programmatization exercise was presented as an opportunity to attract more students. In particular, the Arts Faculty in this institution felt under pressure as a consequence of a restructuring exercise that had closed or merged some departments, retrenched a number academics, and introduced a staffing formula which suggested that the faculty was still 'overstaffed'. This faculty responded to the policy much more promptly than others, and faculty leadership played a strong role in galvanizing compliance and establishing procedures which, in retrospect, most informants agree were transparent and fair.

By the beginning of 2000, the range of offerings in the faculty handbook had, on the face of it, been transformed into multidisciplinary programmes of various kinds. These programmes could be divided broadly into two groups: loosely-structured programmes that allowed students some limited choice in their combination of majors and electives, and tightly-structured programmes with few or no such options available. The *Development and Environment* programme is of the latter type, and consists of three compulsory majors in Geography and Environmental Studies, Sociology, and Public and Development Management. Students are also required to do a year of Economics, either the mainstream version or a less numerate version designed for humanities students. Apart from this, students only have space to choose one additional one-year subject from a very limited list of electives.

The process of developing this programme drew academics into the cross-border negotiations envisaged by the policy, and thus into the new academic relationships and practices, potentially characteristic of a new identity. Staff most closely involved in the initiatives understood in theory what the new role required of them:

[It required] actually getting consensus on what a programme entailed. I think the central theme, really, was the outcome. There's a little person that you have to produce at the end of the day ... to produce someone who would be able to go out there and do a specific job. We looked for a niche out there where we think we would be able to place people,... and then you said, okay, if this is the field in which there is an opening, then what do you require to be able to be trained for that purpose? (AH1: p. 2)

In addition to the discourse of an outcomes-based approach to education, academics also suggest that the new role involves a shift towards what Bernstein calls 'invisible pedagogies': student-centred, small-group learning where the academic is decentred into the role of facilitator: 'From the sage on the stage, to the guide on the side', as some respondents put it. Further, courses in some departments have moved from a discipline-based structure to a problem-based structure. But my informants note considerable problems with their attempts to assume this new role.

While some academics are able to articulate an 'outcomes' discourse, they also acknowledge that they quickly came up against conditions which limited opportunities for entirely custom-designed curricula. Apart from some cases where new modules were designed from scratch, academic staff drew on existing courses as the basis for their participation in a number of programmes. The key issue of limited resourcing, and the need for disciplinary courses to serve *several* programmes at once so as to maintain optimal enrolment levels, set limits on the customization of curricula:

People might say, okay we should do this or that in terms of a specific module, and we would say, well, you can't really do that because you already are in programme elsewhere, for which your particular module was found to be coherent with the outcome of *that* programme. You can't just unilaterally change that now, because then you are disrupting the fabric of that programme. ... I think the moment you narrow the focus down to specifics, then you get a problem with coherence in specific programme packages. It is a lot easier to keep things rather broad, rather vague, and then it seems coherent. (AH1: pp. 2, 9)

It is also clear that in the context of this undergraduate programme disciplinary insulations have remained strong, and that no interdisciplinary integration is attempted at any point. Indeed they even note how the shift towards problem-based curricula in one department limited that department's capacity to offer modules across faculty boundaries, where such pedagogic shifts have not been made:

We are working with a problem-driven approach ... we have a third-year module on water in the environment. The guys [in the Science Faculty] would say 'we want you to produce us a module in Bio-Geography'. Bio-Geography is a sub-discipline that is not problem-driven, it is discipline-specific. It deals with a specific disciplinary field, but it is not a specific problem. We have basically made this disciplinary adjustment, and that works in this [Arts] Faculty, but we can't take that same thing and just package it across the border. They want something else from us, and we have either got to produce that specific module separately – and that runs contrary to the White Paper-driven principles, where we were told we have got to decide what it is that you are, you have got to decide your specialization, stuff like that. So we really can't serve two masters at this stage. (AH1: p. 8)

Significantly, informants note that while disciplinary insulations have remained strong in the development of this vocationally oriented undergraduate programme, they indicate by contrast an instance where an interdisciplinary programme in Ecology at postgraduate level has grown out of an intellectual convergence involving some of the same departments. In this case, the intellectual logic of the project provided a credible, authoritative basis for cross-border collaboration. This fact, that some disciplinary integration is achieved when driven by internal intellectual criteria, but not when driven by external market-driven vocational criteria, suggests the relative strength of these two forms of authority in commanding the allegiance of academics. But it also reflects the desire of academics to preserve the undergraduate taproot of discipline-based training which provides a pool of potential postgraduates (and thus serves the reproduction of the discipline), and which forms the necessary disciplinary basis for postgraduate approaches to interdisciplinarity.

This issue of authority, and the organizational base for decision-making, is identified by many respondents as a fraught issue. Given that multi-disciplinary 'programmes' are the new organizational base for curriculum delivery, what should be the relationship between the old (but still existent) organizational base and the new? In the excerpt below, an academic wrestles (unsuccessfully) with the problem:

I don't think the departments can really proceed effectively in the new system as they are at the moment. I think you have just to get rid of the idea of a department. From a managerial perspective, which is the business we are in, you can do it either way. You can retain the department as a unit of organization, or you can just rub them out and replace them with ... programmes. The point is that somewhere, somehow, you have to recognize disciplinary boundaries still. These programmes, as I interpret them, are not designed to really replace separate disciplines. It is a question of integrating them at a certain level, and below that level you will continue to have these disciplinary groups. ... That's a tension that exists, and I know it is a difficult one to deal with. As long as the department is still seen as a structure with hard boundaries, it is bound to create turf battles, especially with programme convenors who see opportunities ... that may threaten the autonomy of the departments. I personally am not in favour of retaining the structure of the department or the head of a department as it is now, in such a new system, because I think it just creates more problems than it will solve. But it is a difficult one with an inherent tension in it. I don't think there's an easy way to resolve that. (AH11: p. 8)

This tension between these two organizational forms, and their potentially conflicting interests and forms of authority, remains unresolved for multi-disciplinary programmes. It seems that the integrated practices of the 'therapeutic' position have found effect in only limited ways, usually in terms of the negotiation of space in new programme structures. There is little evidence of a continuity of integrated practices in intellectual or pedagogic collaboration, or in sustained organizational forms. Once structural inclusion has been effected, the disciplinary identities and practices are again the dominant ones. Whilst some academics are able to identify the characteristics of a new 'therapeutic' form of academic identity, it seems clear that this is not a widely-developed position, and many structural constraints (particularly resourcing, and the strong 'gravity' of existing discipline-based structures) inhibit opportunities for this identity to grow over time. The logic of disciplinary forms of organization thus remain as the most established and compelling social bases for identity, practice and solidarity.

The Case of UniB

In the account of the development of this programme at UniA we glimpse the key themes of this chapter, but these themes are developed in more nuanced detail in the data arising from the counterpart programme at UniB. This may be because the process of programmatization at UniB seems to have been much more contested and problematic. While in both contexts we have seen academics respond negatively to the policy, resentful at their loss of autonomy, at the challenge to well-established roles and identities, and at the escalation of their administrative loads, these were features of the UniA context mostly at the start of the programmatization process, and by early 2000, these resentments seem to have been replaced by a general acceptance, even enthusiasm in some quarters, for the new arrangements. At UniB, by contrast, protests, challenges and conflict have been much more persistent, and some of the programme constructs have been much more unstable as a consequence. In several instances, when I interviewed informants, the programme structures under discussion no longer followed that laid down in the Faculty Handbook for that year. Indeed, soon after my main round of data-gathering, a major review of programmes in this Faculty proposed significant changes to curriculum structures, reversing much of the programmatization process.

At the time of data-gathering, the programme in *Development Studies and Social Transformation* (DSST) was a multi-disciplinary structure, composed mainly of contributions from the four departments of Sociology, Social Anthropology, Environmental and Geographical Studies (EGS), and Political Studies. The structure of the programme is complex (reflecting the many compromises embedded within it): students are required to complete four compulsory DSST 'core' courses, and these can then be combined with studies in any one of the four participating disciplines. On the face of it, it would seem that a programme in development studies in this context would provide an ideal basis for interdisciplinary collaboration, and thus for therapeutic identities to emerge. Individual academics in all four departments have a history of interest in development, and the field of development studies, although broad, should be a compelling one in South Africa's post-apartheid context.

But the history of the four 'core' courses reveals the difficulties inherent in weakening disciplinary insulations. The original proposals for this programme envisioned that the core would be truly *inter*disciplinary, involving collaborative input from all participating disciplines. However this ambition foundered on the twin rocks of a shortage of resources and epistemological differences. The resource problem came from the fact that few of the participating academic staff had the time to involve themselves personally in the development of the core; they were simply too stretched trying to maintain existing commitments. The epistemological problem was reflected when none of these would permit academics from the one department (Sociology) – who did seem to have the staffing capacity – to represent the intellectual field of development studies, concerned that other disciplinary claims to the field may be compromised or occluded. The accounts from various respondents suggest that the social dynamic characterizing the negotiations between these participants focused not on how the different disciplinary positions would *contribute* to an integrated approach (what Bernstein calls 'similar-to relations', or the basis for uniting difference in an organic solidarity), but instead focused on the epistemological *differences* in the respective approaches to development (an emphasis on 'different-from relations' which anchors individuals in the mechanical solidarities of their home base). One account of the contest is as follows:

> Okay, so instead of having a [single] carefully constructed notion of Development Theory, there was a very different notion of a discipline, which says instead – EGS has got a course called Cities of the South but embedded in it, it has a whole lot of Human Geography theory about where cities come from and so on. [Politics] has got a course in Development Management which has its own set of theories. Anthropology has got another one. Sociology has got something called Introduction to Development Theory. And they all said 'These things all enjoy equal status' and then there was a very interesting argument about a discipline which said 'In other disciplines we don't treat theory in the same kind of way as you do'. Okay? ... We have to accept the notion that we treat theory in different kinds of ways – I mean there are some ways – what's distinctive about Anthropology you know, is the methodological approach. So you know, meeting the other disciplines threw up all sorts of hellava interesting meta-theoretical things, and [one colleague] came through and said 'There's no reason why theory is necessarily the core'. Right, so all of a sudden we had a multi-disciplinary core. (BH15a: pp. 8-9)

The compromise was to include an existing course from each of the four participating disciplines, to make up the 'core', but as in the UniA case, these courses would be serving several programmes simultaneously:

> We had a situation where people were saying we are not going to offer anything new, we are just going to take our existing courses and shove them in ... and we'll pretend that they fit together, but they didn't. There was no way that they were designed together. In fact, we had quite a strong argument from people here who were saying we don't have time to make them fit together. We refuse to have meetings, or even to circulate our course outlines to each other to see what each of us is doing. There was that level of recalcitrance and disillusionment, and I think with the whole process of the programmes anyway. (BH15b: p. 5)

A further structural factor which helped to emphasize disciplinary identities rather than integrated positions was the university requirement that all course codes should be departmental ones, with the result that student enrolments in those courses would be credited to a single department, rather than shared across contributing departments. In a context where programmatization was widely suspected to be a stalking horse for retrenchments, academics were concerned to maintain or strengthen student numbers in their courses. One respondent from a small department compares his involvement in another programme where the grouping of contributing disciplines is based on neither an intellectual convergence nor a projected field of practice; instead:

> It is an arrangement of convenience to make sure that majors survive. It was a means of having a relationship with two other disciplines which were going to attract [large student numbers]. ... We know if we put ourselves alongside both of those two, they won't be threatened. They don't care if they lose a few students to us [when they choose their majors]. (BH11: pp. 9, 16)

This respondent notes that this latter 'marriage of convenience', characterized by no coherence or co-ordination across disciplines in any form, is an entirely amicable arrangement. By contrast, the DSST programme, which is referenced to an existing field of practice, and which has potential intellectual commonalities across disciplines, is fraught with tension and mistrust. It seems that the reason that the explicit 'marriage of convenience' model works is that neither resources nor trust need be an issue: all participants continue as before, within their established disciplinary positions. The reason DSST has difficulties is that the high cost of forging integration immediately thrusts issues of resourcing, trust and identity to the fore, in a context where such transitions have not been provided for.

A key factor supporting (or frustrating) attempts at such transitions is that of authority, which in this context takes at least two related forms: discursive and organizational. At the level of discourse, I've noted above how academics in disciplinary and (I would argue) therapeutic positions are more inclined to respond to intellectual projects than those driven by the market. However, a major feature distinguishing a disciplinary position from a therapeutic one is the degree of credibility commanded by pedagogic discourses. While a disciplinary position requires that the structure of a curriculum be determined by the discursive structures of the discipline itself, the therapeutic position would argue that the recontextualization of disciplinary knowledge into a curriculum should be guided also by pedagogic considerations. One respondent, arguing (in a context where only mainstream Economics is on offer, with high entry requirements and high failure rates) that Economics can be made accessible to any motivated university student, expresses her faith in pedagogic method as follows:

> I think what appalled me was the inability of someone in this university to say that we can make people who are not numerate, numerate and this is how we can do it. If you want that to happen in your programme, this is the time you have to give to it, this is the staff you will need. ... If you say that they must be able to read graphs and they

must be able to do ratios and stuff like this, this is what needs to be in place. (BH18: p.11)

This argument rests on the assumption (identified by Bernstein as the 'competence' model) that all learners have an equal capacity for acquisition, and that pedagogy can compensate for difference and disadvantage. The contrasting assumption of the disciplinary position (the 'performance' model in Bernstein's terms) inclines to the elitist 'sink-or-swim' orientation, and thus discounts pedagogic arguments. The implications of the therapeutic position on pedagogy is the 'new collegial' team structure of relationships, where disciplinary knowledge and pedagogy come together in a form of collegial peer review. In the extract below, a respondent describes the process as she has experienced it elsewhere, and regrets its absence in the DSST context:

> Sitting down and saying we are teaching things together. This is a programme we are teaching – can we go on a bosberaad [retreat] and sit down and say: What it is we are doing? Textbooks, integration, what are the issues and how are they being looked at? It has to happen every year actually. It is consensus, in a sense. We used to sit down every year and say – this is what we are doing in the first year, second year and third year and postgraduate. The questions that arose – where are these questions picked up again and where are they amplified? What gets dropped? ... To say this is what we are reading, these are the new books. And we would spend two to three days doing it. And we would then require after that, that people bring the essay questions for their courses, their topics and those would then be thrashed through. ... The interesting thing is that I don't have this here because I do it all by myself now – I don't have anybody to share this with. So, in that sense, I am not kept on my toes – I am only as good as my best students are. ... I dread to know when I am going to get the first DSST people – I may get them in the next semester – and I won't know what they have learned. (BH 18: pp. 19-20)

It seems the DSST programme development process started out in collegial form, and was driven by a triumvirate of colleagues from three different disciplines. But when a ruling came from the university administration that a single programme convenor be identified, it fell to one of the three, at that time also the head of a department, to lead the programme. Here the tension (noted in the UniA case above) between the roles and interests of programme convenor and department head became evident: 'He couldn't change hats fast enough' (BH11). Various accounts suggest that the individual came under fire from his colleagues in the programme, as well as his colleagues in his department, as he sought to cater to these conflicting interests, and to give expression to his own personal intellectual bent. As he attempted to travel from a disciplinary position to a therapeutic one, he became caught in an organizational 'no-man's' land. On the one hand he was accused of betraying the interests of the discipline – he was committing 'academic exterminism' (BH19), or he was colluding in the production of 'Kentucky Fried Knowledge, standardized, nugget-sized pieces expertly designed to meet the demands of the market' (BH20). On the other hand found no 'new collegial' community as a stable collective social base on which to forge a programme-based alternative. My reading of the situation is that this individual was personally prompted towards a therapeutic position, but was hung by his colleagues for being a marketeer. This experience carried a high personal cost for the individual concerned, and he has since withdrawn from his leadership positions and is considering leaving academia.

Further exploration of the data suggests that those academics (like BH4 and BH18 above) who have claimed successful therapeutic-style collaboration with colleagues have experienced this initially in disciplinary departmental contexts, where epistemological common ground is more readily established. More difficult has been efforts by these individuals to pursue therapeutic-style negotiations across disciplinary contexts where epistemologies are less easily reconciled. It is in this regard that we recall Moore and Young's warning (outlined at the start of this chapter) that policy arguments for changing forms of knowledge in the curriculum should not be considered apart from 'the role of specialist communities, networks and codes of practice' that are needed to sustain these (2001: p. 16). This is at the heart of the issue of authority, or the base from which competing epistemological claims may be adjudicated. Collaborative practices within disciplines may call on a set of specialized codes and practices to validate new curricula, but to achieve this across disciplinary boundaries requires the painstaking establishment of a new authoritative social and normative base.

Conclusion

What might be the conditions for a sustained transition to a new identity position? It is worth turning to Durkheim and reviewing some of his comments about the transitions from mechanical to organic forms of solidarity to enable more complex divisions of labour. He argues that although organic forms of organization arise from prior mechanical forms, and that attempts might be made to reconcile the two forms of organization,

> there is an antagonism which necessarily ends in a break. ... [The division of labour] can only grow by freeing itself from the framework that encloses it. ... The substance of social life must enter into entirely new combinations in order to organize itself upon completely different foundations. (cited in Giddens, 1972: p.144)

This suggests that the basis of solidarity in the two organizational forms of the disciplinary department and the programme need to be understood as quite distinct, and requiring substantially different assumptions and relationships to maintain the cohesion in each case. To travel from the one context to the next would require of an individual to either 1) permanently relinquish one frame of reference for another, or 2) to be content to hold two contrary frames of reference simultaneously, and to invoke these separately as the context requires. Durkheim further outlines the conditions under which a new organic frame of reference is established. Time and space is required for the development between individuals of a common understanding and purpose, what he calls 'moral density':

But this moral relationship can only produce its effect if the real distance between individuals has itself diminished in some way. Moral density cannot grow unless material density grows at the same time, and the latter can be used to measure the former. (1972: p.151)

In other words, developing what Bernstein calls 'ideological consensus' amongst a group depends on the communicative opportunities available for this purpose, and these need to be dense enough to constitute a community of practice. Crucially, consensus is unlikely to be achieved in a context of competition for resources. As resources shrink, so conflict between individuals becomes more intense. 'Similar occupations are as competitive as they are alike' (Durkheim, cited in Giddens, 1972: p.154).

Bernstein similarly suggests conditions for the successful establishment of an integrated-type curriculum: staff participating in such an arrangement 'are part of a strong social network (or it *must* be strong if the transmission is to work) which should be concerned with the integration of difference. And this is no easy activity' (Bernstein 1996: 25, emphasis in original). He stipulates four conditions of social organization necessary for an integrated-type model to succeed, and it is worth quoting these in some detail.

1. There must be consensus about the integrating idea and it must be very explicit.... It may be that integrated codes will only work when there is a *high* level of ideological consensus among the staff. We have already seen that, in comparison with collection, integrated codes call for greater homogeneity in pedagogy and evaluation, and therefore reduce differences between teachers in the form of transmission and assessment of knowledge... Where such ideologies are not shared, the consequences will become visible and threaten the whole at every point.

2. The nature of the linkage between the integrating idea and the knowledge to be co-ordinated must be coherently spelled out... *The development of such a co-ordinating framework will be the process of Socialization of the teachers into the code.*

3. A committee system of staff may have to be set up to create a sensitive feed-back system and which will provide a further agency of Socialization of the code.

4. One of the major difficulties that inhere in an integrated code arises over what is to be assessed and the form of the assessment... Of greatest importance, very clear criteria of evaluation must be worked out. (Bernstein 1975b: pp. 84 and 107-108; emphases in the original)

In short, for an integrated-type model to establish itself, the conditions have to be created in which a community of academics united in a common project can come to agreement on what is to count as valid knowledge, why, and how it is to be recognized in the context of that programme: in other words, to arrive at a social epistemology of curriculum which provides the basis for continuing collective practice over time, and for a stable and sustainable academic identity.

We have here two examples of policy-driven attempts to create more-or-less integrated models of curriculum, which index the distinct, if diverse, field of development studies. In neither case does an *inter*disciplinary model ensue; instead strongly insulated *multi*-disciplinary models are the result. Seen through an identity-based frame of reference, it is clear that, despite the policy injunctions, disciplinary identities remain resilient social and normative positions for practice and solidarity. Although therapeutic positions are articulated by several respondents, these are not realized in any sustained way in these cases. There is little or no evidence here of market positions in the discourse of these academics, although this is a feature of the increasingly managerialist practices of the institutional administrations. The authors and implementers of curriculum policy thus need to consider more carefully the collective social and normative bases (and their costs) that are required to sustain the delivery of particular curriculum models.

References

Ball, S. (1993), 'What is policy? Texts trajectories and toolboxes', *Discourse,* vol. 13(2), pp. 10-17.

Barnett, R. (2000), 'Supercomplexity and the curriculum', *Studies in Higher Education,* vol. 25(3), pp. 255-265.

Bernstein, B. (1975a), 'Open schools – open society?' *Class, Codes and Control,* vol. 3. *Towards a Theory of Educational Transmissions,* Routledge and Kegan Paul, London.

Bernstein, B. (1975b), 'On the classification and framing of educational knowledge', *Class, Codes and Control.* vol. 3. *Towards a Theory of Educational Transmissions,* Routledge and Kegan Paul, London.

Bernstein, B. (1996), *Pedagogy, Symbolic Control and Identity: Theory, Research, Critique,* Taylor and Francis, London.

Bernstein, B. (1999), 'Official knowledge and pedagogic identities', In F. Christie (ed.), *Pedagogy and the Shaping of Consciousness: Linguistic and Social Processes,* Continuum, London.

Bourdieu, P. (1975), 'The specificity of the scientific field and the social conditions of progress of reason', *Social Science Information.* vol. 14(6), pp. 299-316.

Clark, B. R. (1983), *The Higher Education System: Academic Organization in Cross National Perspective,* University of California Press, Berkeley, CA.

Cloete, N. and Bunting, I. (2000), *Higher Education Transformation: Assessing Performance in South Africa,* Centre for Higher Education Transformation, Pretoria.

Ensor, P. (1998), Access, coherence and relevance: Debating curriculum in higher education, *Social Dynamics,* vol. 24(2), pp. 93-105.

Ensor, P. (2002), Curriculum restructuring in higher education in South Africa in the 1990s, in N. Cloete, D. Fehnel, P. Gibbons, P. Maassen, T. Moja, and H. Perold (eds), *Higher Education Policy, Institutions and Globalization: New Dynamics in South Africa after 1994,* Cape Town, Juta. pp. 33-57.

Giddens, A. (1972), *Emile Durkheim: Selected Writings,* Cambridge University Press, London.

Henkel, M. (2000), *Academic Identities and Policy Change in Higher Education,* Jessica Kingsley Publishers, London.

Moore, R. (2002), 'The (re)organization of higher education curricula: contrasting models of implementation', *Journal of Education*, vol. 28, pp. 33-57.

Moore, R. and M. Young. (2001), 'Knowledge and the curriculum in the sociology of education: towards a reconceptualisation', *British Journal of Sociology of Education*, vol. 22(4), pp. 445-461.

Muller, J. (2000), *Reclaiming Knowledge: Social Theory, Curriculum and Education Policy*, Routledge and Falmer, London.

Muller, J. (2001), 'Responsivity and innovation in higher education', a paper prepared for the Centre for Higher Education Transformation (CHET), Pretoria. Mimeo.

National Commission on Higher Education. (1996), *An overview of a new policy framework for higher education transformation*, Human Sciences Research Council, Pretoria.

South African University Vice Chancellors' Association. (1999), *Facilitatory Handbook on the Interim Registration of Whole University Qualifications by June 2000*, SAUVCA, Pretoria.

Trowler, P. (1998), *Academics Responding to Change: New Higher Education Frameworks and Academic Cultures*, Society for Research into Higher Education and Oxford University Press, Buckingham.

PART III
ORGANIZING AND MANAGING
HIGHER EDUCATION

Chapter 8

Improving the Quality of Education: What Makes it Actually Work? A Case Study

Veerle Hulpiau
Kim Waeytens

Reflection on Method: Documentary Analysis

The research questions addressed in this chapter concern the type of problems that appear during evaluations of educational activities, and about the relationship between these problem-types and the subsequent actions to rectify them. These data consisted of internal and external evaluations of university educational programmes. There were successive evaluation and follow-up reports, five reports for each of the six cases under scrutiny. In total this involved about eight hundred full text pages. We used qualitative documentary analyses techniques to help us answer the questions we had. However this presented us with several challenges.

The reduction and representation of the data generated a first challenge. The relevant problem-types and follow-up activities were coded independently by two researchers, generating considerable work. But in addition the linkage of these across the successive reports, and their representation in a surveyable way, presented a particular challenge. At first sight the linkages between these data were not obvious due to the specific context and target group of each report. Generic categories had to be developed to link the data across the reports. As far as the representation of the data was concerned, we were permanently confronted with the tension between the surveyable representation of the data on the one hand and the preservation of sufficient information needed to contextualize the data accurately on the other.

The key question about problem-types and subsequent actions to resolve them was whether problems that are detected in the course of the evaluation process are finally followed-up. In spite of the fact that the reports logically succeeded each other in time and build upon one another, some problems seemed to disappear and were never followed up. However we found that in reality there had in fact been undocumented follow-up in some cases. Problems that came about at the start of the evaluation process were judged of such an importance by the authors that these problems weren't mentioned in the subsequent report for the external visiting committee, for example. Hence they were made to 'disappear' from the documentation. However this does not necessarily mean that there was not action taken to resolve the issues by those responsible for the programme. These kinds of gaps in the documentary data, and the reasons for them, may be identified through interviews with privileged witnesses.

However, these interviews raise further problems. There is a gap of variable length between the termination of the evaluation process and the point at which these interviews will be conducted. Respondents' recall of the events can become limited, and somewhat selective, as a result of this time gap. This problem is compounded by the fact that the evaluation process itself can take as long as two and a half years.

As well as the very specific and limited nature of the goals of each type of report, evaluating specific programmes and making recommendations for action, the reports involved a further limitation which presented problems for our analysis – the discourse in which they were framed. This only became apparent to us as we became immersed in the data: gradually we gained a feel for the way in which a veiled and sometimes specific language is used in the reports ('...seems to be an element that is open to improvement', 'There are reasons for some concern about...', 'The fostering of self-activity of the students remains a challenge').

To conclude: our experience showed that documentary analysis is a labour-intensive and time-consuming task. Despite this we found, ultimately, that using the approach enabled us to achieve our goals. The experience of using this approach was in itself educative and when conducting analogous research, in the future our application of documentary analysis will be more efficient as we will not need to go through the learning process that occurred during the research reported in this chapter.

Introduction

Quality assessment systems in higher education usually serve two major purposes. On the one hand they aim at improving the quality of teaching and learning. On the other hand they provide accountability to the outside world regarding the quality of the teaching activities and the use of the resources provided to this end. Quality improvement and accountability are, in Flanders as elsewhere, the underlying principles of the quality assurance systems in Higher Education. Although initiatives in the field of quality assessment date from the eighties, a systematic and overall approach at the Flemish universities was introduced by a decree only in 1991. Flemish universities obtained more autonomy in exchange for adopting a more systematic approach to quality assurance and enhancement. Universities were made explicitly responsible for the regular internal and external quality assurance of the teaching activities and for the follow-up of these activities. The government may organize meta-evaluations in order to judge the quality assessment initiatives of the universities and may undertake comparative studies on the quality of education through a committee of independent experts.

The first objective of the quality assurance movement, i.e. quality improvement, is the primary goal for the institutes themselves. They invest a lot in systems to assess and improve the quality of their activities, i.e. teaching (Boyle & Bowden, 1997). In this context, it is somewhat surprising that only limited research has been carried out on the extent to which results of both internal and external evaluations are actually used. The impact of quality assessment on actual educational processes has not sufficiently been investigated (Frederiks, Westerheijden & Weusthof, 1994; Westerheijden, 1999). Hence our research that pertains to the use of these results has an explorative character.

There is a need for better insight into the extent to which the results of evaluations are actually used to improve teaching. In 1998 an external audit committee was commissioned to investigate whether the Flemish universities are fulfilling their obligations regarding quality assurance. It came to the conclusion that a defensive attitude towards (some of the) findings of the visiting committees is still tempting for universities and that the adoption of a more proactive attitude would be desirable (Audit Commission, 1998). The academic authorities of the University of Leuven concluded on the other hand that the ways in which the follow-up of educational evaluations could be strengthened needed to be investigated in order to develop a more efficient policy towards educational improvement.

The material for such an investigation was available. In 1993-1994 a system of periodic internal evaluations of the educational activities was introduced at the University of Leuven. Once every four years the educational programmes are evaluated internally. In view of enhancing the feelings of ownership, faculties have been made responsible for the quality of their education in general and for the internal evaluation in particular. Several elements illustrate this. First, the internal evaluation is coordinated by an evaluation committee at the level of the programme under scrutiny and consists of a delegation of tenured and untenured faculty members and of students. The evaluation committee is coached by a member of the educational support office. Second, the internal evaluation follows some university-wide guidelines. But these guidelines leave ample scope for the evaluation committee to determine what exactly will be evaluated and how the evaluation will be performed.

The evaluation is based on the educational goals and quality criteria specified by the curriculum committee that is permanently responsible for educational quality. The internal evaluation system takes the study programmes as basic evaluation units. The evaluation pertains to the study programme as a whole as well as to the specific courses.

One of the major underlying principles of the system is its focus on quality improvement rather than on sanctioning. In this respect specific attention is paid to the conception of follow-up plans at the level of the individual courses and at the level of the whole programme.

The whole evaluation process takes two years. In the first year the evaluation committee decides upon the content of the evaluation and on the instruments that will be used. The evaluation data are gathered, interpreted and the results are reported in a global report as far as the evaluation of the curriculum is concerned, and in individual reports as to the evaluation of the individual courses. The second year is almost entirely devoted to the follow-up of the evaluation results.

Once every eight years such an internal evaluation is followed by an external one performed by a visiting committee. In this case the editing of the global report will be followed by writing a self-study in accordance with the guidelines of the Flemish Interuniversity Council. The latter acts as the coordinating agency for the external evaluations, which are organized at interuniversity-level and are carried out by visiting committees. An external committee visits each university that provides the programme(s) under evaluation. A visiting committee consists of five independent members. During its two day visit this committee talks to the representatives of all actors involved in the educational process and visits the educational infrastructure. At the end of the visit the external committee orally reports on the results of its visit. When all universities concerned have been paid a visit, the committee publishes its final report.

If an internal evaluation at the University of Leuven is followed by an external one, those responsible for the study programme have to report after a one-year period to the academic authorities on the follow-up given to the evaluation.

Follow-up is a central issue within the evaluation procedure, in the context of the internal evaluation just as in the external one. However, one should know that although a follow-up procedure has been set up, means to 'force' curriculum committees or individual faculty members to make use of the evaluation results are almost nonexistent and follow-up is not to be expected to occur automatically.

Research questions

Strengthening the follow-up of educational evaluations assumes that one knows the strengths and weaknesses of the actual approach. This was not the case. Since the introduction of systematic internal evaluations in 1993-1994 numerous data were gathered containing information on several aspects of the educational quality, i.e. the problems that are detected during the evaluations, the way those responsible for the programmes and the individual faculty react to these problems. However these data had never been analyzed before from a perspective beyond the particular programmes.

Knowledge of the problems education is often confronted with, or the difficulties encountered by those responsible for the programmes while trying to solve these problems, facilitates policy-action directly oriented to these aspects. Furthermore, as far as the major goal of the evaluation system, quality improvement, is concerned, it is important to know whether the investment of considerable resources in the system is worthwhile.

Thus, our research relates to the outcomes and impact of evaluations of educational activities. The following research questions were selected: What types of problems regarding teaching and learning systematically come up in the course of educational evaluations? Is there a relation between the nature of the problem-types and the one who detects these problem-types or in other words the location of the problem detection? What types of problems are dealt with and what types of problems remain unaffected?

The notion of impact, however, is not one without pitfalls. Brennan and Shah argue that a distinction is to be made between intention and outcome, between organizational action and educational consequence. Moreover statements on improvement need to be made against the background of quality criteria and values (Brennan & Shah, 2000). Whether intentions and initiatives result in the improvement of the educational quality was not the focus of our study. The notion 'follow-up' refers to explicit intentions and actual initiatives, or their absence, in order to improve the quality of education, independent of the question whether the improvement actually occurred or not. Focusing upon the follow-up process, instead of quality improvement, is contextually legitimate with respect to the explicit attention paid, within the evaluation process, to the follow-up activities in response to an internal or external evaluation.

Methodology

In order to obtain a better insight in the follow-up process use was made of existing material with respect to internal and external evaluations of educational programmes that were organized at the University of Leuven. The research material already available consists of the successive evaluation and follow-up reports that are drawn up during the evaluation process of several programmes (Figure 8.1). The nature of these data lends itself to a qualitative approach by means of document analyses.

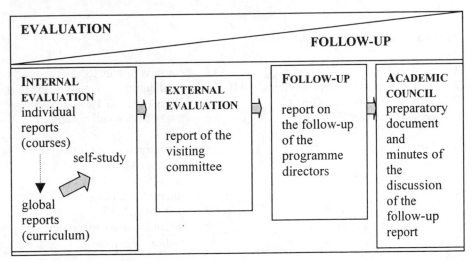

Figure 8.1 Successive reports in an evaluation-process

Only the programmes that went through the whole evaluation process, which takes approximately three years from the very start to the end, were eligible for our study. Out of 18 possible programme evaluations, six were chosen taking into account that each disciplinary group (human, exact and bio-medical sciences) should be represented within the study.

A qualitative content analysis of the relevant documents, 36 documents/reports in total, was carried out (Krippendorff, 1980). The successive evaluation and follow-up reports were analyzed by producing within-case matrix displays (Miles & Huberman, 1994) with the problems described in the different documents on the one hand and with the recommendations, intentions or measures towards improvement or reactions on the other hand as units of information. A problem is defined as a condition that does not meet predefined expectations, standards and has to be improved. As to the use of the evaluation results, four possible ways to react to problems are specified: intention, measure, reaction or nothing at all. Thus for each problem it is indicated whether those who are responsible intended to take action (intention), whether they formally decided to take action or already had taken action (measure), whether they only made some comment on the given problem (reaction) or whether there was no (re)action at all. The notion of recommendation has only been used in the case of the report of the visiting committee. This notion refers to possible measures that the visiting committee puts forward in order to solve a specific problem. All problems and intentions, measures or recommendations were coded. The basis for the coding was the checklist of the Flemish Interuniversity Council that is used by visiting committees when evaluating the programmes at the end of a site-visit. This checklist distinguishes 87 possible types of problems which are grouped into 20 broader categories (Table 8.1).

Table 8.1 Categories of problems

1.	goals (GO)	11.	Success ratings (SR)
2.	characteristics of the programme (CH)	12.	total duration of study (TDS)
3.	programme-structure (PS)	13.	study time (STT)
4.	programme-content (PC)	14.	study advice and coaching (SA)
5.	instructional methods (IM)	15.	infrastructural facilities (IF)
6.	assessment (AS)	16.	alumni (AL)
7.	skills (SK)	17.	staff (ST)
8.	thesis (TH)	18.	internationalization (INT)
9.	practical training (PT)	19.	self-study (SST)
10.	number of students (NS)	20.	internal quality assurance (IQA)

Cross-case analyses of the above mentioned within-case matrices were directed towards detecting specific patterns: which problems appeared at which stage in the evaluation process; whether and in what stage reaction upon these problems occurred. As a result of this approach each problem was observed through the evaluation procedure, from the beginning of the process with the internal evaluation to the end with the discussion of the follow-up report in the Academic Council.

In view of the data reduction the occurrence of problems, recommendations, measures, intentions, reactions or absence of any follow-up were represented schematically per programme. These schemes make it possible to detect what types of problems systematically come up in educational evaluations, whether the internal evaluation committee, the external committee or both detected the problems and what use was made of the evaluation results.

Results

Problems

Frequent problems Our first research question regards the types of problems that are detected systematically in the course of educational evaluations. In order to learn what problem-types those responsible for the programme are often confronted with, the number of programmes in which a problem-type appeared as well as the number of problems per problem-type and per evaluation were counted. The use of the above mentioned classification-framework was necessary in order to determine possible problem-types and to know the maximum of possible problem-types. In fact the chosen framework appeared to be appropriate for the classification of the research data although during the codification process a small number of problems occurred with the framework. There was no problem-type in which problems concerning study materials and pedagogical materials could be properly classified. Similarly problems related to student characteristics (prior knowledge) could not be attributed to one of the predefined problem-types. None of these appeared frequently within the evaluations.

Another problem with respect to the checklist bears upon the scope of the different problem-types. A problem-type, e.g. the number of students, is quite narrow whereas the coaching of thesis students could refer to a variety of aspects such as quality, frequency and initiative.

A problem-type is considered as frequently occurring when it appears in four or more programmes (on a total of six examined programmes). This choice is an arbitrary one. Therefore separate information will be provided with five and six programmes as an alternative standard.

Table 8.2 contains the frequently appearing problems (FAPs). The first column refers to the broader problem-category (see also Table 8.1). The columnheads in the second column describe the problem. The third column mentions the number of programmes in which the problem-type appeared. The fourth indicates the total number of problems that were mentioned within these programmes and belong to the problem-type concerned. Indeed, within one problem-type several problems may occur. One and the same problem-type may show several problems as in the case of the curriculum committee: the frequency of the meetings may be problematic and at the same time its determination to act. The analyses reveal that the FAPs are of a pedagogical type or relate to educational and organizational conditions.

Table 8.2 Frequently appearing problems

Problem-category Problem-type		Nr. progr.	Nr. probl.
PEDAGOGICAL PROBLEMS			
Characteristics of the programme	problem solving	4	4
	independent and critical attitude	4	4
	self-activation	6	6
	future professional field	6	9
Programme structure	sequential structure	6	11
	coherence	5	10
Programme content	up-to-date	5	19
Instructional methods	adequacy	4	5
	use	5	19
Assessment	accordance (with educational goals)	4	6
	comprehension	6	6
	organization	4	6
	criteria	4	9
CONDITIONS			
Educational conditions			
Number of students	number freshmen	5	6
Study time	conformity	6	18
Study advice and coaching	study-advice	6	7
Alumni	contacts alumni	4	7
Organizational conditions			
Infrastructural facilities	classrooms	5	9
	computer	4	4
Staff	educational professionalization	5	6
Internationalization	organization	4	6
Internal quality assurance	curriculum committee	5	6
	student involvement	5	6
	evaluation-procedure	5	9

Pedagogical problems   Frequently occurring pedagogical problems (FAPs) relate to the characteristics, the structure and content of the programme, the instructional methods, and the assessment of the students.

FAPs in the field of programme-characteristics concern the extent to which the programme supports the development of academic skills such as problem solving, an independent, critical attitude and self-study. Also the degree in which the programme contains links with the future professional field of its students systematically appears as a problem or needs to be improved. Lifelong learning alone did not appear as a FAP in this problem category.

Typical problems with the curriculum structure concern its sequential nature, i.e. the extent to which courses and study-years build on the previous-ones, and the coherence or horizontal consistency within the programme. Overlap between courses within a study-year is an example of lack of horizontal consistency.

During evaluations the internal committees as well as the visiting committees often report the existence of gaps within courses or within the programme as a whole, which negatively impacts the up-to-dateness of the programme. This was the only FAP out of five in the programme-content category. The other four problem-types in this category relate to the quality level of the programme and did not appear as FAPs.

With respect to the category of instructional methods the frequently appearing problems relate to the adequacy of these methods and to the use that is made of these methods. The adequacy of the instructional methods pertains to the relationship between the methods and the educational goals. Problems regarding the use of these methods refer to the actual application of the chosen methods. There might be, as an example of the latter, a lack of feedback on written reports delivered by students.

Four out of five problem-types with respect to assessment are problematic. These deficiencies relate to the accordance between examination methods and goals of the programmes, the organization of exams and (mainly lack of clarity on) the criteria. The extent to which the exams assess students' comprehension of the subject matter rather than factual knowledge, is mentioned for all programmes.

Out of 42 possible pedagogical problem-types, 13 (31 per cent) problem-types frequently appeared within the programmes. Out of 13 pedagogical FAPs four systematically occur in all programmes, seven in five or more programmes.

Many problem-types only occur now and then or do not occur at all. Some (broader) problem categories do not contain FAPs. This is the case for the categories: 'goals' (formulation, realizability, academic level, minimal standards, acquaintance of students, implementation within the programme), 'skills' (in writing, speaking, computer, social skills, foreign languages), 'thesis' (level, weight, coaching, assessment) and 'practical training' (level, weight, coaching, assessment). The fact that some study programmes do not require a thesis or practical training may explain why these problem categories do not contain problem-types that appear in four, five or six programmes, which is not the case for the other problem categories.

Educational conditions Frequently appearing problems regarding the educational conditions involve the problem-types: number of students, the study time, study-advice and -counselling, and the alumni.

The number of freshmen can be problematic because it is either too low or too high. In some cases the small number of students questions the viability of the programme. In other cases similar questions arise in relation to the expected inability to meet future societal demands of graduates. In one case the number of freshmen was found to be high in relation to the job opportunities of the graduates. The other problem-types within the problem-category 'number of students', namely evolution of student numbers, the total number of students and the ratio of male-female-students, stayed blank.

Universities have to define in advance how much time the average student will need to spend on the programme as a whole and on each course in particular in order to be successful. This study time is translated into study points. By decree universities are obliged to assess regularly the correspondence between estimated and actual study time. The document analyses reveal that this problem-type systematically appears in all evaluations. However, the distribution of study time within and over study year(s) poses no problems. Neither is the ratio of time devoted to self-study on the one hand and to class activities on the other, an FAP.

Students need better study-advice during their studies. In several cases this comment pertains to advice on specific choices students need to make during their studies. Problems regarding study-advice to school leavers, the quality of the study guides, coaching of students in their first year or later do occur but not frequently.

Finally the lack or insufficiently developed contacts with alumni in order to improve the quality of the programmes appears as a FAP.

On a total of 19 problem-types regarding the educational conditions, four (21 per cent) problem-types frequently appeared within the programmes. Of these four FAPs two systematically occur in all programmes, four in five or more evaluations.

Again, many problem-types only occur now and then or never occurred. There are no broader problem categories that stayed blank.

Organizational conditions   Finally the analysis frequently identifies problem-types with respect to organizational conditions such as infrastructural facilities, staff, internationalization and integral quality assurance.

The broader category of infrastructural deficiencies contains classroom facilities, labs, libraries and computer facilities as problem-types. Problems with classroom and computer facilities frequently occur. Deficiencies concerning classrooms are diversified: into lack of space, old rooms, geographical spread and deficient accessibility for handicapped persons. Computer facilities generally concern the number of computers available for students in classrooms. Outdated infrastructure was mentioned only once as a problem.

Out of 11 problem-types in the staff-problem category only one, namely professionalization of the staff is to be considered as a FAP. The extent to which staff members attend faculty training programmes is almost systematically found to be problematic, sometimes in relation to deficiencies of teaching abilities of staff members. The lack of awareness of the importance of participation and the lack of commitment to these activities are considered as possible explanations by visiting committees.

Organizational problems regarding internationalization are of a very diverse character (the amount of administrative work, exchange of information between partners, and so on). When it comes to integral quality assurance three problem-types are frequently detected: the permanent curriculum commissions, the involvement of students within these committees and the procedure of internal evaluations.

Permanent curriculum commissions are responsible at the programme level for the continuous monitoring of the educational quality. These commissions are composed of tenured faculty, untenured faculty and a student delegation. Problems mentioned are once more of a quite diverse nature: the frequency of meetings, the consensus-oriented style of decision making, the number of members, lack of involvement of tenured faculty, etc. The involvement of students within these permanent curriculum commissions is often assessed as problematic or to be improved.

Finally the procedure of the internal evaluations reveals a diverse set of problems: involvement of students in the follow-up of evaluations, the transparency of evaluation results and follow-up initiatives, and the frequency of the evaluations.

Out of 26 organizational conditions, seven (27 per cent) problem-types often appear. Five of these came up in five evaluations. Only one small problem category, namely self-study, which regards the quality of the self-study viewed by the visiting committee, stayed out of our scope of FAPs.

Conclusion Out of 87 problem-types, 24 or 28 per cent frequently appeared to be problematic or required improvement. The highest percentage of these FAPs (15 per cent) is located within the category of pedagogical problems. Eight per cent of the FAPs regards organizational conditions and five per cent educational conditions.

Table 8.3 FAPs per problem category and in total

	nr PT	Criterium = min. 4		Criterium = min. 5		Criterium = min. 6	
		FAPs nr.	% on total of 87 FAPs	FAPs nr.	% on total of 87 FAPs	FAPs nr.	% on total of 87 FAPs
Pedagogical problems	42	13	15%	7	8%	4	5%
Educational conditions	19	4	5%	3	3%	2	2%
Organiz. conditions	26	7	8%	5	6%	-	-
Total	87	24	28%	15	17%	6	7%

PT= problem type
FAP= frequently appearing problem type

These figures show that most problem-types (63) only occur now and then or even never occur. There are even a few problem categories for which no problems were detected.

Problem detection   The second research question regards the location of the problem detection. The question here is whether the nature of the problem-types relates to who detects these problem-types. The observation that a problem-type is for example almost systematically detected by the visiting committee could refer to a lack of attention or awareness of the importance of these aspects at the level of the programme. This could be a reason for the academic authorities to develop a specific policy in this field. On the contrary, when a problem-type attracts almost systematically the attention of only the evaluation committees, this could refer to a lack of interest by the visiting committees in these kinds of problems.

Figure 8.2 shows the extent to which problems are detected either by the (external) visiting committee or by the internal evaluation committee. The frequently appearing problems were put on a line from -1 to 1. The index specifies whether a problem is more often detected by visiting committees or by internal evaluation committees.

In the middle (point 0) the problem-types are located that are as frequently detected by the visiting committee and by the evaluation committee. This is the case for the problem-types regarding the adequacy of instructional methods, the extent to which exams assess students' comprehension and the computer infrastructure. Problems regarding the internal quality assurance, namely student involvement and the evaluation procedure, along with the educational training of the staff, which is closely related to quality assurance, are more often detected by the external visiting committees than by the internal evaluation committees. This is less so the case of problem-types with respect to the characteristics of the programme (problem solving, independent and critical attitude, self-activation and orientation of the programme to the profession) and study-advice.

With respect to the use of teaching methods, the extent to which the estimated study time corresponds to the actual study time, the assessment criteria and classroom facilities, the problems are more often reported by the internal evaluation committees than by the external visiting committees.

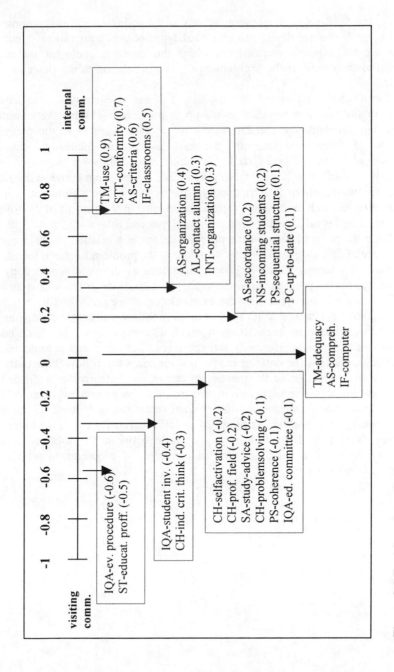

Figure 8.2 Problem detection

Follow-up

Finally, the third research question relates to the follow-up of evaluations. What types of problems are dealt with and what types of problems remain unaffected? There are two possible angles from which this question could be answered: in relation to the nature of the problem-types, and in relation to the detection of the problem.

The research data reveal that the nature of the problem-types can hardly be linked to the question whether follow-up is present or absent. With respect to almost any problem-type the data rarely reveal clear lines as to the presence or absence of follow-up. One of the rare exceptions relates to the entire professionalization of the staff. In this case follow-up consists almost systematically of a reaction by those responsible for the programme to the findings and/or recommendations that are mainly made by the visiting committee.

Further research on the data, especially oriented to the content of the follow-up activities, may reveal links between problem-types and follow-up.

From the point of view of the problem detection a relation between presence or absence of follow-up and the one who detects the problem has been found.

Table 8.4 represents the follow-up activities as they are reported by those responsible for the programme to the academic authorities in the follow-up report. This occurs about one year after the external committee published its conclusions of the external evaluation. With respect to these follow-up activities a distinction is made between measures (actions upon which a formal decision has been taken or actions that have been performed), intentions (one has the intention to decide or do something), reactions or nothing at all. In some cases the follow-up activity could not be qualified in one of the mentioned categories. Furthermore a distinction is made between the follow-up activities in response to a problem detected by the internal evaluation committee, by the external committee or by both. In some cases the action upon a problem consists of several activities, e.g. a measure and a reaction. Therefore distinction is to be made between the total of follow-up activities on the one hand and the total number of problems to which action occurred or did not occur.

Table 8.4 Follow-up activities

		Measures	Intentions	Comments	Unqual. follow-up	Total follow-up activities (a)	Problems without follow-up (b)	Sum (a + b)	Total probl.
Follow-up report	Detected by internal evaluation committee	3	/	1	/	4	178	182	182
	Detected by visiting committee	33	17	29	3	82	67	149	140
	Detected by both	40	15	31	/	86	26	112	100
	Total	76	32	61	3	172	271	443	422
Global report self-study		21	50	24	2	97	94	191	178

The research reveals that for 271 out of 422 problems (64 per cent) or in other terms 271 out of 443 follow-up activities (61 per cent) no follow-up activity is mentioned in the follow-up report to the academic authorities.

Of the follow-up activities that have been reported 76 (44 per cent) out of 172 relate to measures that have been taken, 32 (19 per cent) are still intentions – one year after the report of the visiting committee – 61 (35 per cent) consist of reactions to the findings or recommendations and three (two per cent) follow-up activities remain unqualified. Problems detected by both the internal evaluation committee and by the visiting committee are more often reacted upon than problems that are detected by the visiting committee alone ($x^2(8) = 193.78$, p < 0.001). In the first case the amount of measures within the follow-up activities is considerably higher than in the latter. As far as the follow-up reports to the academic authorities are taken into account the follow-up of problems that are detected only by the internal evaluation committees, is very problematic.

However, the question is to what extent follow-up reports give a correct view of the follow-up that has been given to problems that were detected by the internal evaluation committee but were not mentioned by the visiting committee. The data on follow-up activities that were found in the reports of the internal evaluation committees, the global report and the self-study, adjust the negative image drawn up by the follow-up reports. Table 8.4 represents the follow-up activities the internal evaluation committees report upon in their (internal) global report and in the self-study to the visiting committee.

The data reveal a more positive picture of the follow-up of problems that have been detected by the internal evaluation committee alone and are reported in the global report and / or in the self-study. Almost immediately after the detection of the problem 21 out of 191 (or 11 per cent) follow-up activities consist of measures that mean that formal decisions have been taken or action has been performed. A quarter of the follow-up activities relate to intentions. This relatively high percentage of intentions is not surprising given the fact that these reports follow the evaluation almost immediately. 24 out of 191 follow-up activities (or 13 per cent) regard reactions to the findings of the internal evaluation committee. Finally, 49 per cent of the problems stay without any measure, intention or reaction of the internal evaluation committee.

Although we do not know to what extent the intentions that were reported in these reports actually have led to measures, these data reveal that the follow-up reports to the academic authorities do not fully show to what extent follow-up has taken place, especially as far as the problems are concerned that are only detected by the internal evaluation committee. Still, at this stage of the research it is to be concluded that follow-up is more likely to occur in the case of problem detection both by the internal evaluation committee and by the visiting committee, or by the visiting committee alone than by the internal evaluation committee.

Towards an interpretive theoretical framework

The research results that have been presented so far reveal information on the absence or presence of follow-up in response to internal and external evaluations and on the types of problems that are to be dealt with in this respect. Our main research question was whether and to what extent follow-up takes place in response to educational evaluations. We gained insight into the types of problems that frequently appear during the evaluation processes, the relation between problem detection and the nature of the problems and finally the relation between problem detection and follow-up. We now need to interpret these results.

Only limited research has been carried out on the extent to which programme directors and faculty in general are able to make use of results of both internal and external evaluations (Westerheijden, 1999). Theoretical knowledge on this matter is scarce (Frederiks et al., 1994). Frederiks et al. developed a conceptual model in which the key dependent variable 'utilization' is influenced by contextual characteristics of actors and characteristics of the organization. In their search for explanations for the utilization of internal and external evaluations, they founded their hypotheses on the contingency and political economic approaches. The first concentrates on the conditions under which an organization functions most effectively, the latter is based on the maximization of utility and is related to the concept of power. The researchers found some partial support for the contingency and political economic hypotheses but concluded that further research is necessary to explain differences in utilization.

Brennan and Shah (2000) investigated the impact of quality assessment in terms of decision making processes through three mechanisms at hand (reward, structure and policies, cultures) and from the angle of four levels: the national system, the institutions, the basic unit and the individual. They concluded that impact through reward (status allocation, income, influence) is likely to be a function of the published outcomes of assessment. Impact through changing policies and structures occurs in response to the overall pattern of the internal assessment methodology and of the recommendations made by the external visiting committee. Finally, impact through changing cultures occurs in relation to the self-evaluation process and institutional quality assessment procedures. Although the insights of Brennan and Shah may contribute to a better understanding of the follow-up of evaluations, the difference in scope of their study still makes further exploration of possible theoretical angles worthwhile.

In relation to the lack of a workable theoretical framework directly related to the follow-up theme, it remains interesting to examine whether inspiration can be found in the innovation and the organizational literatures.

In spite of the massive knowledge that has been developed on strategic and cultural aspects of educational change, many change efforts do not meet expectations. One reason is that educational change is more than a strategic or cultural process. It is a multi-dimensional one (Hargreaves, 1997). Similar reasoning can be found in the organizational literature. Bolman and Deal argue that the complexity of organizations makes it difficult to understand organizations and thus organizational change. In order to appreciate the depth and complexity of organizational life one needs to look to an organization through frames. These frames are vantage points. They 'are both windows on the world and lenses that bring the world into focus' (Bolman & Deal, 1991, p. 11). The authors distinguish four frames, based on the major schools of organizational theory and research: the structural frame, the human resources frame, the political frame and the symbolic frame.

The structural frame illuminates two central dimensions of organizational designs: the division of labour through the creation of a variety of specialized roles, functions and units and the tightening-back of all these elements by methods of horizontal (a more informal coordination on an equal level) and vertical (coordination and control in a relationship of subordination) integration. From a structural perspective the follow-up in a university context will probably be influenced, amongst others, by variables such as the existence of common goals, the division and assignment of responsibilities (Mintzberg, 1979) and clear communication about these responsibilities (Frederiks, Westerheijden, & Weusthoff, 1993).

The human resources frame adds a new dimension, namely the interaction between the organization and the people who are functioning within. The quality of the interaction between individuals and within groups determine both the individual satisfaction and the organizational efficiency. One process that seeks some optimal 'tuning' between the organization and the individual is staff development initiatives. As is the case in other organizations, professional development may be one way to remove one's feeling of incompetence when introducing important changes that affect people's work in a university context. Also the attention paid to educational qualities for appointment, tenure and promotion, may be one of the variables that influence the follow-up that is given to educational evaluations. The existence of a teaching portfolio can be one of the elements.

The political frame 'views organizations as arenas in which different interest groups compete for power and scarce resources' (Bolman & Deal, 1991, p. 11). Persistent differences between individuals and groups as to values, preferences and scarce resources make conflict a feature of organizational dynamics. Bargaining and negotiating leads to the determination of goals and decisions. In a university context the struggle between divergent and even contradictory opinions, based on considerations of self-interest, about what educational quality is, might influence the eagerness to change educational practices after an evaluation. Also the division of scarce resources – such as time and money – between education and research or between departments probably affect the follow-up.

Finally, the symbolic frame 'seeks to interpret and illuminate the basic issues of meaning and faith that make symbols so powerful in every aspect of the human experience, including life in organizations' (Bolman Deal, 1991, p. 244). Absence of follow-up might be explained by variables that pertain to the way that faculty perceive their role as members of the academic staff and the way academic freedom is interpreted. Another important factor to consider is the way the academic culture supports collegial relationships so that talking about educational problems and matters becomes an aspect of daily life in the university.

We have selected a theoretical framework based on this multidimensional perspective. This is in line with a growing understanding that innovation in education ought to be seen as a multi-dimensional process. A university, and the processes within, can be looked at from these different frames. (Figure 8.3). Each frame has its own characteristics that influence as independent variables the presence or absence of follow-up of internal and external evaluations. The evaluation process is seen as an intermediate variable that strengthens or weakens the influence of the independent variables.

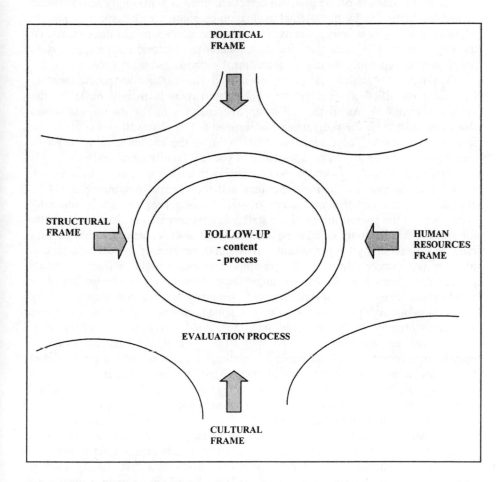

Figure 8.3 Conceptual model

Explaining divergence

In the previous section a theoretical framework was developed in order to interpret the results of the absence and presence of follow-up after educational evaluations. The question now is what can we learn when these results are looked at through the theoretical framework. The following section seeks possible explanations through the theoretical framework as we consider the findings about the locus of the problem detection (second research question) and about the relationship between the problem-types and the follow-up (third research question).

As to the location of the problem detection, there is a strikingly lower degree of problem detection by the internal evaluation committee with respect to aspects of internal quality assurance, namely the evaluation procedure and the educational training of staff. The same goes for the attention the external committee pays to problem-types regarding the use of instructional methods and study time.

The extent to which staff members attend faculty training programmes is frequently identified as problematic. This observation is mainly made by the visiting committees. As to the follow-up, the analyses of the documents shows those responsible for the programmes do respond to this observation, mainly in the form of a reaction. These reactions often refer to the existence of an offer of training programmes and to the attendance of younger faculty members.

From a structural perspective the unevenness in the locus of problem detection between the internal evaluation committee and the external committee might be explained by the fact that attendance of staff training programmes is internally considered as the responsibility of the staff members themselves. It is not a matter for which the collectivity is held responsible. In the same context the absence of a training plan set up by the permanent curriculum committee or the lack of attention of the programme director to training activities might influence actual participation. Seen from the cultural angle these observations can be explained by pointing out that in a research oriented university one cannot expect faculty members to put high priority on education oriented activities. Within the culture of a research oriented university traditional educational activities such as teaching, taking exams etc. are seen as an easy spin-off of research activities, not as a task with its own requirements and needs for professionalization. From a political and human resources perspective faculty probably have little interest in investing much time in attending educational training programmes as decisions regarding promotion are mainly made on the basis of research output of the faculty members. The external evaluation committee probably has a perception of the importance of professional development which is totally different from the internal evaluation committee. As a result the latter will not detect problems in that field as often as the visiting committee does. Furthermore the observation that mainly visiting committees detect these problems might explain why follow-up mainly consists of reactions. The faculty don't consider the problems to be theirs.

Besides the educational professionalization of the staff, the internal evaluation procedure is a topic where the external visiting committees are much more inclined to detect problems.

From a structural perspective these findings may be explained by the fact that the internal quality assessment procedure has been developed and decided upon on the top level of the university. The fact that the permanent educational committees, situated on the level of the programmes, are explicitly held responsible for permanent quality monitoring does not prevent them from perceiving the internal evaluation system as something alien to them, and for which they are not responsible. The fact that responsibility for the organization and co-ordination of the internal evaluations lies at the level of the programmes does not seem to influence this perception either. It seems that the internal evaluation committees do not approach the system critically and have little investment in changing the system.

Problems regarding the use of instructional methods and study time are often detected by the internal evaluation committee. In both cases follow-up seems to be difficult.

That educational evaluation committees are susceptible to problems related to the use of teaching methods might be explained by the fact that this is perceived as being at the heart of the educational quality. It is a vast topic in student evaluations of the teaching quality of the individual staff members and one that educational committees cannot ignore. But at the same time in reporting problems regarding the use of teaching methods, internal committees very often explicitly refer to their source ('according to the students...', 'untenured staff members feel that...'). For half of the problems found, none of the successive reports mentions any follow-up. If follow-up consists of a reaction it often refers to students as being responsible for the fact that some teaching methods do not meet expectations. In the few cases where intentions or measures are reported, these refer in general terms to new directions on the concept and implementation of the teaching methods within the study programmes, set out by the permanent educational committee.

From a structural perspective one might argue that there are clearly differences within the departments under scrutiny, and between these departments and the external evaluation committee about the qualities instructional methods should meet and the preconditions within which these qualities can be reached.

Considering the follow-up activities that are reported for the problems related to the study time, one may conclude that the responsibility for these aspects is situated, as was the case for educational professionalization, at the level of the individual staff members and not at the level of the collective. But in most cases problems related to study time remain unaffected or consist of a reaction in which the need for further investigation is emphasized.

Experience reveals that neither the average permanent educational committees nor the individual staff members are very concerned about the accordance between the predefined and the actual study time. But the universities are forced by decree to assess this accordance on a regular basis. Moreover, when study time is taken up in the internal evaluations, possible problems do easily come to the surface, within questionnaires or by measuring the study time itself.

Although problems come easily to the surface, the follow-up seems to be difficult. This might be explained by the lack of awareness of the implications of the introduction of the credit system as a whole and of the definition of study time for the individual courses and for the programme in particular. The notion of study time was formally introduced by decree in 1993. And although one of the main objectives pertained to the actual control of the study duration and the study load, the measure has been perceived by many faculty members as a purely administrative operation (Hulpiau and Waeytens, 2000-2001). From a structural perspective the introduction of the notion of study time (and credits) has been accompanied by clear prescriptions on how the study programmes might be formally brought into line with the regulations. From a human resources perspective it may be claimed that the introduction of the credit system has not been given sufficient attention, in a sense that the faculty may not have been thoroughly introduced to the underlying principles and mechanisms of the credit system.

The third research question pertains to the relation between the problem types and the follow-up. It has been observed that problem types detected by both the internal evaluation committee and the visiting committee are more often acted on than are problems that are detected by the visiting committee only. In the first case the amount of measures within the follow-up activities is considerably higher than in the latter. When only the follow-up reports to the academic authorities are considered the follow-up of problems that are detected only by the internal evaluation committee, appears to be extremely problematic. This picture has been corrected by the data that were found in the internal reports edited almost immediately after the internal evaluation and in preparation of the external evaluation. Nevertheless, at this stage of the research, it has to be concluded that follow-up is more likely to occur in the case of problem detection both by the internal evaluation committee *and* by the visiting committee, or by the visiting committee alone. Least follow-up has been found for problems detected only by the internal evaluation committee.

The results indicate a lack of follow-up for a majority of the problems detected in the course of an evaluation process. An external confirmation of problems that are detected at first by those responsible for the programmes seems to positively influence the follow-up. The lesser impact of problems only detected by the visiting committee might be explained by the lack of feeling of involvement in the problems.

The observation that follow-up occurs more frequently in the case of problems only detected by the external visiting committee than in the case that these are only detected by the internal evaluation committee might be (partly?) explained, from a structural perspective, by the fact that faculty interpret the follow-up procedure as set up in relation to the external evaluation, and not the internal one.

Conclusions

Considering the conclusions of an external audit committee the academic authorities of the University of Leuven decided that the ways in which the follow-up of educational evaluations could be strengthened needed to be investigated in order to develop a more efficient policy towards educational improvement.

Strengthening the follow-up of educational evaluations assumes knowledge about the strengths and weaknesses of the actual approach with respect to the follow-up. As research in this field is scarce this study had an exploratory character.

The research questions were the following: What types of problems regarding teaching and learning do systematically come up in the course of educational evaluations? Is there a relation between the nature of the problem-types and the one who detects these problem-types or in other words the location of the problem detection? What types of problems are dealt with and what types of problems remain unaffected?

More than a quarter of the possible problem-types do frequently appear, i.e. in four or more evaluations. These FAPs are of a pedagogical type or relate to educational and organizational conditions. The first category contains the highest number of FAPs. Many problem-types, 63 out of 87, only occur now and then or do never occur.

As to the location of the problem detection the lower degree of problem detection by the internal evaluation committee with respect to aspects of internal quality assurance, namely the evaluation procedure and the educational training of staff is striking. The same goes for the attention this committee pays to problem-types regarding the use of instructional methods and study time.

With respect to the follow-up, this study finally reveals that about 60 per cent of the problems remain without (re)action one year after the publication of the report of the visiting committee. 42 per cent of follow-up activities that have been reported relate to actual measures that have been taken. 18 per cent are still intentions and 39 per cent consist of reactions to the findings or recommendations.

In order to explain the findings that pertain to the locus of problem detection and the follow-up, and given the complexity of innovation and organizational processes a first attempt towards a fully-fledged multi-dimensional framework is presented.

The framework may be used to interpret the results that were presented (cfr. Explaining divergence). Furthermore the framework may be used to frame measures taken from a policy perspective and aiming to improve educational quality. Starting from a particular situation, i.e. the University of Leuven, a number of policy options are, illustratively, mentioned.

During the last few years the University of Leuven has improved the quality of its educational provision. The stimulus for these initiatives was the development of a vision in which the common goals for university education were made explicit. The educational concept that was introduced has been called 'guided self-study'. The explicit elaboration of this concept resulted in a policy blue-print. This blueprint contains a range of initiatives that each support the implementation of guided self-study.

The theoretical framework allows us to evaluate in a systematic way whether these initiatives might already be an answer to weaknesses that were detected in the previous part and were considered problematic in relation to an adequate follow-up of educational evaluations.

By means of illustration we first of all refer to a set of initiatives that pertain to the strengthening of the permanent educational committees. These committees operate at the level of one or more programmes and are responsible for the permanent monitoring of the educational quality.

The explicit assignment of responsibilities has been shown to be important. Vagueness about who is expected to do what often lies at the heart of inaction. Therefore one of the action items of the blueprint pertained to a clearer description of the responsibilities of the curriculum committee and its head, the programme director. This structural measure was accompanied by a political one: not only the responsibilities gained in clarity, but at the same time attempts were made to raise the power of the programme director, amongst others by giving him a voice in decisions about tenure and promotion. Although everyone, i.e. the policy-makers, the heads of the departments, the individual staff members, agreed upon the idea that the power of the programme directors should be strengthened, in a lot of discussions about actions taken into that direction, it remains a serious obstacle. Suggestions to strengthen the role of these programme directors in staff policy matters (promotion, tenure) remain a very delicate subject.

Turning to the human resources frame evolution towards greater emphasis on education certainly exists. The results of educational evaluations are more systematically taken into account in decisions that pertain to tenure and promotion. As a result it becomes worthwhile, even at a research-oriented university as the University of Leuven, to spend some of the scarce time on educational matters (cfr. political frame).

As another example we refer to the alignment of the staff development programme with the educational concept of guided self-study. One of the main objectives of this development programme is to create a common language so that staff could talk about education.

As these examples show, the framework used above allows links between measures taken to improve the educational quality, and possible explanations for the absence or deficiencies regarding the follow-up of educational evaluations. Continued analysis will allow persistent gaps to be identified and the development of further policy measures that lead to the strengthening of more educational evaluations.

References

Audit Commission (1998), 'Quality in the Flemish Universities, *Report of the Audit Commission on Quality Assurance in Academic Education in Flanders*', Ceuterick, Leuven.

Bolman, L.G., and Deal, T. (1991), *Reframing organizations: artistry, choice and leadership*, Jossey-Bass, San Francisco (California).

Boyle, P., and Bowden, J.A. (1997), 'Educational Quality Assurance in Universities: an enhanced model', *Assessment and Evaluation in Higher Education*, vol. 22(2), pp. 111-121.

Brennan, J., and Shah T. (2000), *Managing Quality in Higher Education. An International Perspective on Institutional Assessment and Change*, OECD, SRHE and Open University Press, Buckingham-Philadelphia.

Frederiks, M.M.H., Westerheijden, D.F. and Weusthof, P.J.M. (1993), 'Interne zorg en externe prikkel. Onderwijskwaliteitszorg in Nederlandse universiteiten en hogescholen (Internal concern and external stimulus. Educational quality assurance in Dutch higher education)', *Achtergrondstudies Hoger onderwijs en Wetenschappelijk onderzoek* 16, CSHOB, Zoetermeer.

Frederiks, M.M.H., Westerheijden, D.F. and Weusthof, P.J.M. (1994), 'Effects of Quality Assessment in Dutch Higher Education', *European Journal of Education*, vol. 29(2), pp. 181-198.

Hargreaves, A. (1997), 'Introduction. Pushing the Boundaries of Educational Change', in A. Hargreaves et al. (eds.), *International Handbook of Educational Change*, I., Kluwer, Dordrecht.

Hulpiau, V., Waeytens, K. (2000-2001), 'Studietijd en studietijdmetingen gewikt en gewogen (Study time and methods to measure study time)', *Tijdschrift voor onderwijsrecht en onderwijsbeleid*, vol. 4, pp. 272-280.

Krippendorff, K. (1980), *Content analysis: an introduction to its methodology*, Sage, Newbury Park.

Miles, M.B., & Huberman, A.M. (1994), *Qualitative data analysis: An expanded sourcebook*, Sage, Thousand Oaks.

Mintzberg, H. (1979), *The structuring of organizations*, Englewood Cliffs, Prentice Hall.

Westerheijden, D.F. (1999), 'Where are the quantum jumps in quality assurance? Developments of a decade of research on a heavy particle', *Higher Education*, vol. 38, pp. 233-254.

Chapter 9

Leading Change: African Conceptions of Leadership and Transformation in Higher Education in South Africa

David I. Bell

Reflection on Method: Personal Research Journeys

It is my contention that researchers conduct research in order to resolve the tension between what we know, and what we don't know. Research therefore primarily reflects our 'self' – our questions and our need to explore phenomena and find answers – and only secondarily, research attempts to find answers to broader social questions, and the questions of others. The science of research, and particularly qualitative research, is therefore not a neutral or objective process. It is a personal process. The questions we choose to ask (and more importantly, the questions that we choose not to ask) tacitly reflect our personal and our professional selves. Our questions, and by implication, our research interests, reflect our world-views, our beliefs and biases, and ultimately our identity. The kinds of phenomena that we choose to explore, and the modes and methods we choose to use help us to explore these, and the findings and interpretations that we make, all reflect facets of who we are as individuals and, how we choose to project ourselves to others – our identity. If this is so, it must also be assumed that others can infer from our research – some aspects of our identity and our beliefs – our prior constructions of the world. This study is an example of the sociological tensions and specifically, the issue of researcher identity and ethics, in conducting qualitative research. This research is, for me, a deeply personal process.

I identify as an African and the focus of this research is on Africa, on Africans. Ultimately, the research attempts to explore and affirm individual's conceptions of critical social phenomena from an African perspective. However, identifying as African – and being defined by others as African – is not a congruous reality. Identity is a highly subjective and political phenomenon and one that profoundly influenced the design and methodology of this research. Amongst a host of alternative definitions, the term African is a geographical construct relating to the African continent; it is a descriptive construct delimiting that which has emerged and evolved out of Africa; and, it is social and political construct that implies an identity. As an identity, it is often erroneously used to only imply ethnicity, usually black ethnicity. Being a white, male, South African connotes many things to many people. This research is an attempt to use the research process to explore and deconstruct the recurring tensions and issues that emerge when the ethnicity and social identity of the researcher plays a critical and determining role in the research. As a white South African conducting research into socially sensitive conceptions of phenomena expressed by influential black South Africans (Chancellors of Historically Black Universities), I was constantly aware of the impact of my identity on the process of collecting and making meaning of data – and on the socially sensitive nature of making the participants' personal conceptions public. This study acknowledges the tensions as critical factors that shaped the research design and the choice of methodology. Phenomenological phenomenography provided an epistemology and a research process.

Introduction

During the colonial and apartheid eras, higher education played an historically strategic and insidious role in shaping South African society. Today, higher education continues to play a significant role, as an agency of the state, and in helping to shape the social transformation process toward democracy. The current cadre of Vice-Chancellors of Universities, by implication, play a critical role in this process. However, in the light of democratic transformation and social transparency, their decisions and actions have become a matter of public scrutiny and they endure social, political and personal challenges to almost every action that they take.

While current higher education policy emphasizes the phenomena of institutional and social transformation and stresses the social accountability role of higher education in the national social change process, emergent policy simultaneously advocates for a change of governance from the traditionally centralized power of the Vice-Chancellery, to a more equitable and participatory mode of cooperative governance. Vice-Chancellors, particularly at Historically Black (disadvantaged) Universities are accountable both institutionally and socially to ameliorate the process, institutional and social transformation, while transforming their leadership roles in, and of this process. Vice-Chancellors are simultaneously advocates, agents and targets of transformation.

In political and social spheres, the term transformation has emerged as the popular mantra for almost all democratic processes and it has become a vague and rhetorical political term associated with an inordinately wide range of change processes. Understanding the phenomena of transformation and the role of leadership in higher education is critical to understanding the nexus between emergent higher education policy and the role of institutional leadership in the national social change process.

This study uses phenomenological phenomenographic methodology and in-depth interviewing to explore and graph the tacit conceptions of the Vice-Chancellors of Historically Black Universities in South Africa. The research focuses on the phenomena of transformation, leadership and social change. The research moves from the assumption that synergistically, Vice-Chancellors' tacit conceptions of these three phenomena will frame an understanding of their conceptions of institutional leadership and that a grounded African notion of Transformative Leadership of higher education will emerge.

The research findings reveal that although Vice-Chancellors share similarities in their broad conceptions of the phenomena, their conceptions are not sufficiently congruent to define a singular, homogeneous African mode of Transformative Leadership. Because higher education is a fundamental element in the process of social transformation, the research also assumed that the common mode of leadership of transformation in higher education would be transformational. This was clearly not the case. Participants emphasized that a single explicit mode of African leadership was not conceivable or desirable. The study also revealed that a tension exists between emergent higher education policy advocating a decentralization and devolution of decision-making power and a mode of institutional governance termed cooperative governance, and Vice-Chancellors' tacit positions relating to their perceived need to enact strong, centralized leadership within their democratically mandated positions of power in order to lead institutions and effect transformation in the current challenging social and political period of democratic infancy.

The role of the Vice-Chancellor in HBU's in South Africa is enormously complex and challenging and the new Ministry may need to re-conceptualize the role and function of the Vice-Chancellor in relation to current social and institutional realities in Historically Black Universities, and in relation to policies of institutional governance and leadership in higher education.

The social context of higher education in South Africa

> Africa needs change to ensure its development. Reform in education must be the starting point towards meaningful social change, not just for the sake of change, but in order to improve the quality of human life. (Julius Nyerere, 1974)

Nyerere's (1974) words capture an important facet of the process of decolonization that swept through Africa in the latter half of the 20th Century. His words succinctly assert a deeper conception of the role that education has played, and should continue to play in social reconstruction in post-colonial Africa. Sadly however, most African countries continue to struggle with the legacies of colonialism that pervade the structures and systems of society and that defile social reconstruction efforts. These legacies are most evident in the educational systems and administrative structures that remain as relics of the colonizing powers. Education reform is imperative to the post-colonial social and economic revival of Africa but the process of the renaissance in Africa will not be easy unless Africans can emancipate themselves from these legacies. For too long, non-Africans have spoken on behalf of Africa. For too long, decisions about the path of development and reconstruction of Africa have been imposed on Africans. The process of transformation must now be determined for Africans, by Africans, if it is to be authentically transformative.

Nelson Mandela's release from incarceration in 1990 is an icon of this process. His legacy symbolizes the liberation and emancipation of all Africans. However, it also ironically reflects a larger international trend, driven by the West, toward democratization and globalization. In Africa, African forms of democracy have existed for millennia. Most have emerged through bloodied struggles against oppressive systems of governance, not the least the past century of colonialism. These struggles have resulted in the evolution of indigenous modes of conceptualizing and structuring society and in most cases, indigenous systems of governance have emerged which do not resemble the egalitarian and participatory democracy assumed by the West.

The recent democratic process in South Africa has brought about renewed interest in the role of education as a major agency of the social change process. Consequently, it has also brought about a renewed focus on the critical relationship of leadership on the process of transformation toward democracy. The public and transparent nature of Western participatory democracy has induced a renewed, critical scrutiny of the actions of prominent political figures and leaders, not the least, educational leaders and specifically, the leadership of Historically Black higher education institutions.

Ironically, Professor William Makgoba (himself a recent target of racially induced critical public scrutiny at The University of Witwatersrand), argues that 'higher education institutions are the only major sector within South African society that have not been summoned to testify to its role in oppression, before the Truth and Reconciliation Commission, and that they have much to answer for' (Makgoba, 1997, p. 17). Because the previous cadre of higher education leaders and administrators played a strategic and sinister role in perpetuating colonial and apartheid political ideology through the implementation of discriminatory and repressive state policy, the current cadre of higher education leaders have a significant reparatory and transformative role to play in the transformation of a new South African society. Understanding the strategic leadership of their institutions will be an important facet of understanding the larger social transformation process.

Higher education institutions in South Africa are, by their legislative mandate, public institutions and therefore, assets of the state and the leadership of these institutions are employees and agents of the state. Vice-Chancellors are therefore simultaneously advocates of transformation, agents of transformation and targets of transformation. This sets up a tenuous relationship between the tacit and explicit goals of the state, the personal and professional actions of institutional leaders and the needs and expectations of those associated with higher education. It is imperative to the democratic transformation process that we understand their conceptions of policy and of critical social phenomena inherent in policy, both from their perspectives as institutional leaders and as prominent political figures.

As the legacies of the previous political era continue to frustrate even the noblest intent of transformers and institutional leaders, their actions are recurrently clouded in suspicion and challenge. Their attempts to enact strong centralized leadership in order to nurture the process of social transformation, at the expense of more time-consuming 'democratic' participatory processes of consultation and decision-making, has relieved and been lauded by the minorities on the political Right, and has bewildered and been lamented by the masses on the Left (Chisolm & Fuller, 1996). They are accused of mimicking neo-liberal western modes of leadership and reneging on the principles of People's Education. In order to better understand current notions of transformation and the role of higher education leadership in the process of facilitating change in South Africa, three critical questions emerge in relation to emergent Higher Education Transformation policy:

- How do the leaders of social and institutional transformation conceptualize the phenomenon of *transformation*?
- How do these leaders conceptualize the phenomenon of *leadership* of this critical institutional and social process?
- What are their conceptions of the role higher education should play in the current social transformation process?

Developing an understanding of the conceptions of Vice-Chancellors of Historically Black Universities and relating these to current policy, is the primary goal of this research. However Seepe (1998), a prominent Black South African scholar, educational leader and social critic, cautions that the debate concerning the meaning of leadership in the new South Africa cannot be complete without the authentic participation of African leaders. He argues that the rationale for such a process is to 'falsify the myth that Africa cannot make a meaningful contribution to universal human progress', and argues further that 'this process should provide both a critique of the dominant Western epistemological paradigm from an authentic, African perspective and an assertion of that which is African' (Seepe, 1998, p. v). It is therefore imperative that this research is contextualized within the social context of current higher education policy and that a research methodology and process be adopted that is respectful and affirming of that which is African.

Higher education policy

Current policy framework   The range of processes and policies directed at restructuring higher education, and specifically the most recent policy document entitled, *Towards a New Higher Education Landscape: Meeting the Equity, Quality and Social Development Imperatives of South Africa in the 21ˢᵗ Century* (July 2000), are an admirable testimony of the new Ministry of Education's intent to transform and rationalize higher education institutions in synchronicity with national processes of social transformation. These policy documents pose renewed challenges and ambiguous tensions for the process of higher education transformation, and in particular, for the leadership of higher education.

The recently appointed think-tank on higher education transformation, the National Commission on Higher Education (NCHE), uses the term transformation liberally in the various position papers and policy proposals. The NCHE *Policy Framework for Higher Education Transformation* (1996, p.1) proposes that:

> Higher education can play a pivotal role in the political, economic and cultural development and reconstruction of South Africa. To preserve what is valuable and to address what is defective requires *transformation*. The system of higher education must be reshaped to serve a new social order, to meet pressing national needs and to respond to a context of new realities and opportunities. (NCHE, 1996, p. 1)

Ironically, *The Policy Framework for Higher Education Transformation* (NCHE, 1997) also asserts the term *transformation* liberally but does not explicitly define or conceptually formulate it. Similarly, the concept of *cooperative governance* is explicitly advocated in a range of higher education policy documents, but it is tenuously defined. Vice-Chancellors therefore find themselves in the politically and socially contested positions of interpreting and enacting these ill-defined but critical policy concepts. The challenge of interpreting and enacting institutional transformation policy is further exacerbated by contradictions emerging from new higher education policy (including the Higher Education Bill of 1997) and which stand in contrast to traditional modes of strong, directive leadership of Universities. Current policy frameworks (*A Programme for the Transformation of Higher Education*, 1997, pp. 18-20) pose three dilemmas for Vice-Chancellors. Firstly, it mandates a particular conceptual mode of broad, inclusive and participatory institutional administration termed 'cooperative governance' – while simultaneously requiring rigorous administrative practices and rigorous levels of accountability in accordance with global and Western institutional norms and practices including such technicist modes as strategic planning, benchmarking, and fiscal viability. Secondly, the framework advocates further 'academic freedom, administrative autonomy and institution-level decision-making' – while mandating adherence to centralized ministerial decision-making and centralized policy formulation. This, in conjunction with the accreditation and curriculum frameworks of the National Education and Training Forum and the South African Qualifications Authority, makes the role of empowering and transformative institutional leadership a false assumption. Lastly, the framework advocates for the 'Africanization of institutions as agencies accountable for addressing pressing local community, social and cultural needs and acting as catalysts of broader social and political transformation' – while urging institutions to remain 'globally competitive' in terms of 'academic standards of teaching and research'. These laudable goals and objectives again stand in contrast to broader policy positions of educational equity, access and the redress of past academic imbalances, all of which Vice-chancellors are (unreasonably) expected to achieve.

Co-operative governance

Vice-Chancellors are primarily scholars and intellectual and social leaders, and secondarily institutional administrators. They have extensive scholarly records but few have formal administrative qualifications or experience at the institutional leadership level. Their challenges of enacting policy, maintaining scholarly autonomy and building institutional integrity is further framed by current policy pertaining to transformation and cooperative governance of higher education where the Higher Education Bill of 1997 explicitly emphasizes the term cooperative governance in preference to the term leadership.

HBU Vice-Chancellors are clearly scholarly leaders who also possess significant political leadership acumen, however, there is a lack of clarity of the specific role and function of the Vice-Chancellor, specifically as this relates to the intersect of the concepts of cooperative governance and institutional leadership. The Higher Education Bill (1997, p. 26) simply states, 'The principal of a public higher education institution is responsible for the management and administration of the public higher education institution'. The National Commission on Higher Education, by contrast, broadly defines the role of institutional leader as 'enacting the principles of cooperative governance' (NCHE, 1996, p. 4). Cooperative governance is further defined as 'an acknowledgement of the competing and complementary interests, interdependence and common goals of different role players ... balancing participation with effectiveness, while sharing power, responsibility and accountability ... requires negotiation of industrial relations within the framework of the labour Relations Act' (NCHE, 1996, p. 12). The outcome of this policy is that it presents a significant tension for Vice-Chancellors as they enact their roles as leaders of transformation within their institutions, while internalizing and actualizing governance policy that itself challenges their traditional power-base and personal styles of leadership, upon which much institutional transformation is currently dependent.

Transformation

In South Africa, the term transformation has become synonymous with processes of democratic change and has emerged as the popular mantra to describe all social change. It is used to define and validate an immense range of social and political change processes and as a result, it is fast becoming rhetorical and its semantic essence is vague. In its positive sense, transformation is a sweeping descriptor of positive democratic change and an affirming descriptor of those committed to the struggle. In its antithetical form (being not-transformative) it is asserted as a highly politicized juxtaposition to change and a typology of anyone perceived to be acting contrary to the mass democratic movement. It is also used to chastise those who legitimately oppose popular political positions and policy. Not transforming or being perceived as 'not transformative' is equated to capitulating to the principles of apartheid and oppression. The popular assumption is that there is either rhetoric or evidence of transformation, or there is capitulation to a previous era of social oppression.

Although the term has a sweeping social application, its lack of congruent semantic definition is problematic to understanding the various processes and policies that advocate transformation. The concept transformation and the process of leading change need to regain a grounded and popular semantic form that will have clarity, legitimacy and relevance to the process of social change.

The voices of Black Africans have however traditionally been disaffirmed and thereby neglected from the hegemonic higher education debate. Their conceptions should be central to re-conceptualizing the tenets of transformation, and it is argued that the appropriate place to begin the process of conceptualizing and defining the concept of transformation is from within the system of higher education.

Research focus and tensions

Conflicting epistemological paradigms   The concepts of transformation and leadership are explicitly at the heart of the movement toward the new social democracy and higher education leaders are a fundamental component of the process of conceptualizing and actualizing both social and institutional transformation.

The specific focus of this study places the research process and the findings, in a tenuous social and political relationship, in the light of Seepe's argument. Excluding the voices of Africans in favour of empirical research of transformative leadership would be a capitulation of the Western epistemological research paradigm of the other 'looking in'. Conversely, focusing exclusively on African voices and denying the existence of the Western epistemology would be similarly skewed. This study is an attempt to mediate the tension by acknowledging the Western theory-base traditionally associated with academic research while simultaneously attempting to remain sensitive to, and affirming of the African voice. The findings of the study are therefore not discussed comparatively or in relation to Western theory. They are offered as a legitimate alternate African perspective in the field of leadership, toward an alternate understanding of the process of leadership of transformation in higher education.

Focus of the study

This research explores the conceptions of transformation and leadership, not as an affirmation or as an alternative to Transformational Leadership (Burns, 1978, and Bass, 1981), but as a collective African perspective. It is assumed that the concepts of transformation and leadership synergistically merge to form the concept, Transformative Leadership (Tierney, 1989). The study is also primarily an attempt to describe and authenticate one source of an African perspective of leadership and transformation, as a means of understanding the process of institutional leadership, and secondarily, as a contribution to the existing theory-base of leadership, and specifically higher education leadership and administration. The narrow focus of the study therefore does not claim to represent the voices of all Africans, all Black South Africans, or the views of all leaders and administrators in higher education in South Africa. It is specifically contextualized within historically Black higher education in South Africa, and the findings are therefore limited to an understanding of one socially significant group's conceptions of transformation, leadership and the process of leading transformation.

Socio-political identity of the researcher

A tension inherent in this study arises out of the socio-political identity of the researcher, being a white, male South African researching the personal and professional notions of influential Black intellectuals. This, viewed from the perspective of the political history, socio-cultural context and social power legacy in South Africa, sets up a dynamic of the study which the researcher has contended with through the selection of phenomenography in preference to other qualitative or ethnographic methodologies. Phenomenography, both in its assumptions about the nature of reality and in the process of analyzing data and reporting findings (structural analysis and structural synthesis and graphing the range of perspectives of a particular phenomenon) provides a research methodology that mediates between the tensions created by the identity of the researcher and the necessary but sensitive nature of inquiry into the challenging and contested phenomena of this study.

Research paradigm

In an attempt to remain sensitive to the historical, social and political nature of education in South Africa and, while remaining congruent with Western norms and standards of research, the study utilized a phenomenological phenomenographic methodology. Phenomenography is a pragmatic methodology that has been used primarily to explore learner's conceptions of learning (Marton, 1988 and 1994). In its phenomenological form it has also been used to explore social phenomena (Lane, 1962; and, Theman, 1980) with the intent of identifying and delimiting the range of individual perspectives of a social phenomenon in order to better understand how a particular sector of people conceptualize a singular social phenomena. Data was analyzed on a descriptive level as opposed to a conceptual level as may be the case in pure phenomenological research. Phenomenography enabled the researcher to explore and describe the range of conceptions of critical social phenomena from a qualitative perspective while still maintaining a critical social distance between the data and the findings. It also enabled the researcher to explore and discuss these findings phenomenologically (as social realities of phenomena – as these appear to the subjects in the study).

Theman (1980) used phenomenography to study the social phenomenon of power and his study draws on an earlier study of social phenomena by Lane (1962), which explored the political ideologies of citizens in order to understand the relationship between the conceptual and descriptive nature of reality. Like the phenomena of power and political ideology, transformation and leadership are social phenomena that are used broadly and extensively, but which have inadequate semantic and conceptual definition in South Africa.

Phenomenography enabled the researcher to objectively delimit the range of conceptions of the social constructs (or phenomena) thereby defining a frame of reference for the phenomena as they related to the specific social context of higher education in South Africa and thereby facilitating the analysis in relation to emergent policy.

Phenomenography

Phenomenography is 'the empirical study of the limited number of qualitatively different ways in which various phenomena in, and aspects of the world around us, are experienced, conceptualized, understood, perceived and apprehended' (Marton 1994 p. 4424). Phenomenography is a theoretically deductive research paradigm that aims to produce elements of grounded theory and this paradigm stands in contrast to research paradigms that are theoretically inductive, causal-comparative or experimental by nature.

For the purpose of framing the methodology of this study, the definition of phenomenography of Gall, Borg and Gall, (1996, p. 602), is adopted as 'a specialized methodological process of inquiry for the study of the different ways in which people conceptualize the world around them and the analysis of data based on the assumption of a limited number of qualitatively different ways of perceiving a phenomena and grouped into categories of conceptions'.

Phenomenography is therefore the study of variation and congruence, between and among the different ways a group of individuals experience and conceptualize the same phenomenon. Phenomenography differentiates itself from phenomenology, in its philosophical assumption about research, i.e. the qualitatively limited number of ways of conceptualizing a phenomenon, termed 'outcome space'; and at the level of data analysis i.e. the analysis of data in terms of similar or different themes or conceptions as the units of analysis and comparison. In phenomenology, the individual in the study is the unit of analysis, and research comparisons are made across individuals and not within groups, as is the case of phenomenography.

Phenomenography and Social Phenomena

Phenomenography has not been used extensively in studying social phenomena but has found wide application in the study of student learning. An early milestone phenomenographic study of social phenomena by Theman (1980) serves as the core conceptual frame for this study. Theman studied how people viewed political power within the Swedish system, in response to a critical social moment where random citizens of Gottenburg were interviewed regarding their perceptions of a public demonstration in Gottenburg. Theman's study provides the methodological link between phenomenographic studies that have traditionally focused on learning in educational settings and the study of social phenomena in actual social settings. His study is both phenomenographically empirical and socio-contextually sensitive. This research attempts to emulate phenomenographic methodology and remain sensitive to and affirming of the social setting and power dynamics of the study.

Phenomenography and Higher Education

Recent phenomenographic studies point to its increasing frequency of use in studying phenomena pertaining to higher education (Attinasi, 1991). Most studies have concentrated on phenomena implicit in teaching and learning with little application of the methodology to higher education administration and policy-making. One series of studies by Breen (1999) has explored the efficacy of phenomenography as a tool in the process of institutional policy-making in higher education.

Phenomenography and the social outcome

From an epistemological perspective, and in the words of Ference Marton, 'phenomenographers do not make statements about the world as such, but about people's conceptions of the world' (Marton, 1988, p. 145) and these conceptions are assumed to contain qualitatively different ways that individuals think about and understand a phenomenon. Marton (1988) suggests that the structurally significant categorizations of descriptions are the research findings, and in turn, these categories are the research results. In the case of this study, phenomenography provided the range of categories of conceptions for the analysis of these in relation to policy.

Methodology and Design

This study highlighted a range of challenges including the socio-political historicity and context of the study; the focus on higher education and transformation in a transforming society; and, the racial identity and gender of the researcher juxtaposed against the racial, social and gender identity of the participants in the study and proposes phenomenography as the appropriate methodology for the study.

Modes of Phenomenography

A number of modes of phenomenography have been documented (Hasselgren, 1997), each of which is similar in respect of the phenomenographic manner in which data is analyzed and interpreted, but different in the specific research intent, the source of data, the conditions under which data is collected and, the mode of data collection. Experimental phenomenography is arguably the original form of phenomenography evolving in the 1970s and aims at using rigorous manipulated conditions to assess qualitative differences in learning outcomes, often using conventional, quantitative measures to delimit the qualitative differences in the learning outcomes among learners. Hermeneutic phenomenography is defined as the critical exploration and interpretation of a phenomenon through the analysis and interpretation of texts and statements not originally compiled for research purposes. Naturalistic phenomenography attempts to collect empirical material for phenomenographic analysis from uncontextualized, actual, lived experiences of people. Marton (1979) suggests that this form of phenomenography focuses on the world around us and aims to map the collective mind.

Phenomenological Phenomenography

Phenomenological phenomenography is a relatively more recent form of phenomenography and is best reflected in the work of Theman (Conceptions of Political Power, 1983) and Uljen (Phenomenological features of phenomenography, 1992). These studies are not typical of the other phenomenographic modes in that the outcomes of the learning are not the specific focus of the phenomenographic analysis as are the phenomenological experiences of the subjects. This mode balances phenomenographic research intent and data capture methods with phenomenological analysis, interpretation and discussion of the data. Van Kaam (1966, p. 46) suggests that phenomenological phenomenographic research 'sets the stage for more accurate empirical investigations by lessening the risk of premature selection of methods and categories'.

Phenomenological phenomenography, in contrast to pure phenomenological research, does not attempt to describe or discover what 'effective' leadership is or how leadership 'should' link to transformation or social change. Rather, it attempts to delimit the qualitatively similar or different categories and trends out of the various ways that leaders view a phenomenon, in this case, leadership and transformation. The range of conceptions could be hypothesized as an emergent 'African' notion of leadership and transformation or transformative leadership. Essentially, phenomenological phenomenographic research explores the 'conceptual' rather than the 'experiential' realities of individuals and attempts to find congruence (or categories) among the various interviewees' conceptions of a phenomena, in this case the phenomena of leadership and transformation.

Research design

Data gathering and interviews   Each of the ten Vice-Chancellors of the Historically Black Universities in South Africa were interviewed for approximately two and a half-hours. Interviews took place in the professional offices of each Vice-Chancellor and interviews were audiotaped with the consent of the interviewee. Each interview explored the broad and conceptual nature of the phenomena namely, transformation, leadership and the social juncture of institutional leadership in social transformation.

Interviewing took the form of in-depth (Seidman, 1998), elite or expert interviews (Marshall and Rossman, 1999). Elite or expert phenomenological interviewing is broadly defined as a specialized interview with individuals who are considered influential, prominent or well informed about a phenomena or area of interests, and on this basis, are selected for their assumed expertise in the area relevant to the research. It is assumed, for the purpose of this research, that Vice-Chancellors are influential and prominent and that they possess both a systemic 'macro' perspective of leadership and social and institutional transformation, as well as personal 'micro' perspectives of the phenomena.

Phenomenographic data analysis

Phenomenography is grounded in the position that conceptions and ways of understanding phenomena are not viewed as individual qualities. Phenomenographic research does not attempt to determine the objective nature of reality of each of the subjects' conceptions. Rather, phenomenographic analysis produces 'categories of description' and a 'range of conceptions' (Theman, 1980) of a single phenomenon across the subjects of a study. These form a frame of cognitive constructs with which to re-examine and thereby understand the conceptions that individuals in the study have of the particular phenomenon (Marton, 1981, p. 178).

The process of phenomenographic analysis initially seeks to identify and delimit the range of categories of description that individuals have of a central phenomenon, and then collectively the range of conceptions that the study group assigns to a particular phenomenon. Marton (1981) distinguishes the outcomes of the two levels of analysis as 'first order perspectives' and 'second order perspectives'. First order analysis aims to describe and categorize each individual's experiences that are then used in the second order analysis. Understanding the first order perspectives is therefore an essential first step of the analysis process in order to achieve the second order perspective. In phenomenographic research and analysis, the categories of conceptions are not pre-assumed and the process of analysis, both individually and collectively, does not pre-empt the research in order to prove or disprove a hypothesis or to link the findings to a particular theoretical point of reference. Rather, the conceptual categories that emerge out of the actual conceptions of the individuals in the initial phases of analysis are used to analyze and synthesize the research data at the secondary level of analysis and these findings ultimately become the research findings. In simpler terms, the research does not analyze data with pre-formed conceptual categories or theoretical constructs in mind – but rather allows the categories and themes to emerge from the initial analysis, and then uses these to explore the frequency and qualitative distinctions of these conceptual categories across the range of participants in the study. As a consequence of following this phenomenographic process of systematically analyzing data, a four phases process of analysis emerged comprising eleven distinct steps.

The data analysis process

The first phase of analysis (concretization of data) aimed to accurately and concisely capture and concretize the personal voices and dialogue of the interviews into workable text-as-data. The first step involved formalizing the interviews and personal reflections of the audio-taped interviews through *detailed transcriptions* capturing the exact words and verbal nuances in an attempt to capture the essence and implied contextual significance given to words by interviewees. The second step involved a *first, thorough reading* of the typed transcripts, checking for accuracy and omission between the transcriptions and the voice recordings. The original transcripts were then changed and corrected based on a simultaneous reading of transcripts and listening to the interviews. The corrected transcripts were then re-printed. The transcripts ranged from between fourteen and twenty-two pages of single line-spaced, ten point text per interview. The third step of this phase involved a *lay-off period of time* of about a month from the time that the transcriptions were corrected and read in this form for the first time, and the point in time when the transcripts were to be analyzed in the second phase of analysis. This was designed as a time for the researcher to place some conceptual 'distance' between the personal and interpersonal processes of collecting the data (interviewing) and transcribing the personal interviews, and the beginning of the process of detailed analysis of the interviews as data as opposed to individual personal statements. This can be described as a process whereby the researcher systematically de-personalized the data, from the interviews, through the transcriptions and eventually into anonymous text.

The second phase of analysis (textural analysis) (Borg, Gall & Borg, 1997) included a further three steps. Step four involved a *second thorough reading* of the transcripts. Each transcript was read following Gilligan's (1990) suggestion of repeated readings of the transcripts, interspersed with a period of time in-between each reading in order to allow the data to 'settle' in the mind of the researcher and to allow for natural – as opposed to imposed or 'forced' – trends and themes to emerge conceptually, and prior to the process of deliberately searching for themes and categories. Notes and comments relating to emerging themes and categories were inserted into the transcripts along with relevant information and reflections taken from the researcher's journal. Insert comments were italicized in order to distinguish between data and inserted comments. This was done in order to include into each data set, highlights and contextual nuances of each interview and as a means of keeping the emergent themes with the original data source. The fifth step involved *formatting each interviewee's transcript in a different type-font* and reprinting the transcripts. This allowed the researcher to *separate and re-collate the relevant pieces of transcripts according to the three phenomena*, without losing track of the source of the text, i.e. the text of each interviewee was identifiable through the specific type-font. This process of collation brought together the original individual conceptions (transcripts) into similar clusters of data relating to conceptions of a single phenomenon, allowing the researcher to view the collective range of conceptions as a single source of text and simultaneously able to determine the range of perspectives within the single cluster of text. This process of collation formed step six of the process.

The third phase (structural analysis) involved two further steps. Step seven captured the essence of the data for each interviewee by further refining each interviewee's transcript into *précis of each phenomena*. The words and phrases of the interviewees were used in constructing the précis. Non-essential and unrelated words, phrases and sentences were omitted in order to bracket and include only those essential thoughts and conceptions pertinent to the study questions and to the phenomena being explored. As is pertinent to phenomenographic analysis, iterations of words often reflect unclear attempts at conceptualizing unformed or emerging conceptions of phenomena and these are often expressed in unclear or repetitive word sequences and incomplete sentences. Clear, deliberate statements were interpreted as elaborations of pre-formed conceptions of phenomena. Each précis roughly follows the sequence of thoughts as they were expressed in the interviews. Précis are presented in the first person and the original tense of the interview is generically transferred into the present tense for ease of reading, analysis and comparison. Step eight involved *using the précis to delimit and define the categories and themes*. This process of defining themes and categories of description is referred to as creating the 'outcome space' (Marton, 1988) of the research that in turn determines the framework within which the fourth phase of analysis takes place. Themes were recorded and synthesized into categories, and then compared across participants and the thematic matrices are presented in section two.

Phase four (structural synthesis) (Borg, 1997; and Cresswell, 1998) *involved re-examining the original transcripts of all seven interviewees for frequency, congruence and divergence from the emergent conceptual categories* thereby graphing the range of conceptions of a particular phenomenon – as they emerged from within the sample group. This was done in step nine where the emergent categories of description are defined and delimited, and step ten where *the range of conceptual categories become the phenomenographic findings*. Step eleven involved the categorization of congruent themes and the presentation of matrices of themes across the interviewees and the process of constructing meaning from the findings.

The four phases of analysis provided a fluid yet distinct process that enabled the researcher to progressively lift out of each interviewee's verbalized conceptions, the essential structural elements of the particular phenomenon. This was done descriptively initially, and later, conceptually and contextually, a process described by Patton (1990, p. 393) as the inductive analysis of indigenous typologies. This process occurred in the first three phases of analysis and resulted in the 'outcome space' (Marton, 1981) and research categories. The fourth phase produced the structural synthesis or 'graphing' (Marton, 1981) of the range of categories of conceptions and the thematic matrices, and ultimately the research findings.

Marton refers to researchers' notions and preconceived assumptions as needing to be 'held in check' in the process of analyzing and synthesizing data. Marton (1988, p. 153) describes the process of phenomenographic research as 'bracketing the researchers' preconceived notions and depicting their immediate experience of the studied phenomenon through a reflexive turn, a bending consciousness back upon itself'. He further states that the aim of phenomenographic research is the 'studying of other people's experiences rather than one's own – a transcendence of one's own experience and phenomenological notions'.

Research Findings

Transformation

Modern South African society, and in particular, the education sector, uses the term transformation liberally but diffusely. The assumption of this research was that because the term transformation is extensively used, it would have a tacit common, generic or socially conceived essence. The assumption of this study was also that the process of exploring the tacit conceptions of Vice-Chancellors would produce a collective and explicit conception. This study indicates the opposite and the implications are important.

The Vice-Chancellors who participated in this study conceptualized the phenomenon of transformation in three distinctly different ways. One conceptual perspective is that transformation is a process of social change that is complex, amorphous and politically charged and highly contextual, and that transformation takes place on both a social and political level. A second conceptual perspective is that transformation is neither a process nor a single phenomenon, but rather that it is a descriptor of a wide range of social change phenomena. A third perspective is that transformation is a personal and internal process of change that is observable on the individual level of change, but is assumed to achieve impact at the collective level. What is central to all of the various conceptions of transformation is that it is a process, and that it implies universal and fundamental change (as opposed to sector specific change). Although not a remarkable finding, the significance of the lack of conceptual unity is important.

Vice-Chancellors who conceptualized transformation as a process of fundamental social change also tended to advocate for both a strongly social and political perspective of the broader change process. This group suggested that a close, positive relationship exists between higher education and government in facilitating the social change process. The group advocated for strong, charismatic and visionary leadership of the process of transformation. The implication of this frame of conceptualization of transformation is that Vice-Chancellors who perceived their roles to be agents of larger political and social change processes, by implication, also viewed their institutions as socially responsive catalysts of change that reciprocally initiated and were shaped by the larger political process. Vice-Chancellors operating from within this conceptual paradigm were generally less critical of the Ministry of higher education, and more accepting of emergent policy relating to higher education transformation and less critical of the notion of cooperative governance. In all cases, these Vice-Chancellors expressed that their leadership was political and that it was in-line with the emergent political goals of the current government.

The smaller group of Vice-Chancellors that conceptualized transformation as a rhetorical and descriptive term, as opposed to a positive but amorphous process, although diametrically opposite in their rationales of why transformation was rhetorical, tended to view the change processes with which transformation was associated as overly political and a process influenced by the state. This is an important distinction because it stands in contrast to the conceptual perspective of two Vice-Chancellors, who viewed transformation as a personal or intra-personal process and not a political concept. These two conceptual perspectives (rhetorical and semantic) suggested that higher education and in particular, higher education leadership had a minor role to play in the broader social change process and that their primary responsibility was as scholars and academics. The implication is that the Vice-Chancellors subscribing to this perspective may view the internal functioning of their respective institutions as more important than the social responsiveness of their institutions to the broader social and political process. In the two cases, policy relating to higher education transformation was not overtly endorsed and the process of policy formulation was viewed with mild cynicism. They viewed the catalyst of institutional transformation as coming from within the institution and not from external policy that mandated reform.

The third group that conceptualized transformation as a personal and intra-personal change process also conceptualized the leadership role of Vice-Chancellor as a strong, top-down, executive type leader. The implications of this conceptual position is that strong leadership is necessary to lead institutions and that individuals need to take responsibility for their own personal change. Institutional leadership was suggested as the process of raising individuals' awareness of the need to change. Vice-Chancellors subscribing to this conceptual perspective suggested and there was little or no social or political agenda to this mode of leadership. People-change was implied to be the catalyst for larger social change and higher education institutions therefore carried no broad social responsibility, but only responsibility to effect change in individuals. This is interpreted as a somewhat limited and socially acute perspective of the role of higher education and the function of leadership.

Leadership

A central synergy emerged in relation to conceptions of leadership as a style. However, the specific styles of leadership that emerged out of the various conceptions, did not have a strong transformative or empowering dimension. Vice-Chancellors conceptualized institutional leadership as inherently assertive, visionary and charismatic. In the majority of cases this was ironically juxtaposed with the expressed tension of not being able to lead institutions in strong, visionary and charismatic ways due to imposed policy that mandated a cooperative and shared form of institutional functioning. The most common tenets that emerged out of these conceptions of institutional leadership were that Vice-Chancellors felt compelled to operate in a political, lobbying and advocacy mode in order to persuade individuals to move toward goals that they as leaders saw as important and strategic for the institution. They felt that they were not empowered or supported by the higher education ministry or current political system to act as visionary leaders and therefore had to rely on a form of negotiated bargaining to move decision-making processes forward. This broad conceptualization of leadership suggests clear indicators of a transactional mode of leadership as opposed to a transformational mode (Burns, 1986) and for this reason, the conception of transformative leadership in HBU's in South Africa has more in common with transactional leadership than transformational leadership.

The implications of these conceptions are that leaders felt disempowered by the process of transforming higher education toward more democratic and cooperative modes of decision-making and tacitly implied that although mandated to function in a cooperative manner, they would continue to seek strategies to lead institutions in bold, visionary ways as they perceived to be congruent with their appointment as Vice-Chancellors. They did however express firm commitment to cooperative and consultative processes to achieve their leadership and institutional goals. This notion of explicitly advocating participatory modes of institutional administration while tacitly enacting strong leader-centered modes can be interpreted in relation to transformational leadership theory as a form of pseudo-transformational leadership (Bass 1996).

The juncture between higher education and social

It was assumed that collectively, conceptions of transformation and conceptions of leadership would merge into a collective, indigenous, empowering notion of transformative leadership and that this notion would have a contextual application in the juncture created between higher education's process of transformation and the process of social transformation. This assumption was skewed and presumptuous as is evident from the lack of clear conceptions relating to the socially transformative role of higher education. Conceptions expressed relating to this phenomenon were confined to two broad perspectives. The first related to higher education as an organ of the state. The other implied that higher education should play a role as social ombudsperson on behalf of society. Again, viewed in relation to transformational leadership (Burns, 1978 and Bass, 1981), the broad socially empowering role that is traditionally associated with the agenda of transformational leaders is clearly absent from the conceptions of the Vice-Chancellors in this study.

An African notion of transformative leadership

Although no single encompassing African style or mode of leadership emerged, a strong resistance to explicitly conceptualizing this phenomenon was expressed by all Vice-Chancellors. One central tenet did emerge. It was asserted that leadership, in an Afro-centric context, was highly contextual and firmly grounded in the need for relationships, both formal and informal. Vice-Chancellors however also acknowledged that, particularly in formal structures such as senate and council processes where formal authority and formal structure prevailed, the essence of effective leadership lay in the ability of leaders to nurture personal relationships outside of the formal structures and that the outcomes of informal relationships had an impact on their ability to lead and govern in formal contexts.

Discussion and Implications

Most current Vice-Chancellors are not specifically qualified to deal with the broad range of tasks and functions that present themselves in the current, tumultuous South African higher education context. Although all current Vice-Chancellors were appointed through rigorous and broad democratic and participatory processes of recruitment and selection, most achieved their social and scholarly status as scholars and academics in international institutions while in exile, or rose to notoriety through their participation in the struggle. Clearly, they are all accomplished scholars and it is fair to assume that their leadership should be endorsed and embraced by the widest range of stakeholders possible, but few had significant administrative experience in institutional leadership prior to their current appointments.

The administrative relics of the previous conservative and oppressive political eras litters their paths toward democratic and socially transforming modes of institutional leadership. Too often, their attempts to deal with these challenges are viewed with scepticism. When circumstances compel them to make critical decisions and enact seemingly autocratic leadership, they are viewed as capitulating to modes of leadership reminiscent of the previous political era. In cases where they act in accordance with the broad, participatory and democratic processes as prescribed in cooperative governance policy, they are deemed ineffectual in getting the job done and are considered weak leaders.

This, compounded by recent trends toward the centralized coordination of higher education policy (NCHE, 1996, p. 24) that advocates for the rationalization of higher education, and policy advocacy toward cooperative governance (NCHE, 1996, p. 12) of institutions, appears to support the suggestion by Scott (1996) that South African higher education is moving toward a predominantly Western democratic, managerial mode of administration and governance and that traditional forms of strong, centralized and charismatic institutional leadership, as conceptualized by Vice-Chancellors in this study, are becoming redundant. Appropriately therefore, the indigenous African mode of institutional and transformative leadership which is emerging, is being conceptualized and developed by African leaders who themselves are located within the process of transformation. However, no singular African mode of transformative leadership has emerged through this study and the implications are varied. Vice-Chancellors will continue to lead in modes that reflect both Western, democratic administrative styles and indigenous African elements of leadership. This will inevitably provide a context for the possible evolution of a grounded African mode of leadership that may inform, and perhaps rival current theories of institutional leadership and administration. What is certain however is that leaving the decision to Vice-Chancellors to adopt the particular style of leadership that they will utilize in any given context, which may range from the systematic, participatory and often public (transparent) mode of Western democratic leadership (read also governance), to the more individualistic, empathic, and private 'parenting' style of African leadership, will confuse and confound those on both the academic and political Left and the Right.

The overwhelming tendency to conceptualize the process of leadership of transformation as implying a fundamental shift away from the past, with no explicit construction of the future, is also significant. The informing principles of People's Education and The Freedom Charter which galvanized efforts and provided hope and direction for the masses during struggle for liberation, are explicit about transformation as a movement toward egalitarianism, access and redress. What is significant is that the process of conceptualizing transformational leadership primarily as a movement away from an undesirable past, is an indicator of the social and political tensions that emasculate Vice-Chancellors.

The current trend toward cooperative governance of institutions will prevail and the current cadre of Vice-Chancellors will play a significant role in shaping this process. Higher education will continue to serve as a significant social shaping agency and here too Vice-Chancellors will play a strategic role. However, the inevitable tension that arises when institutional leaders are publicly mandated (through centralized policy) to enact participatory modes of leadership and decision-making while tacitly they are expected to take strong, sometimes unpopular decisions, will ultimately perpetuate the current malaise among Vice-Chancellors and the inevitable short cycle of visionary and energetic appointees transform into disillusioned and burned-out early retirees within their current tenure cycle. Centralizing the process of policy-making for higher education is understandably necessary in the early stages of the evolution of any fledgling democracy. However, if the current process of policy procreation continues to advance non-indigenous notions and standards of leadership in deference to theoretical Western and funder-driven standards and styles of leadership and governance, not only will this signal, at the highest level, an end to current indigenous and affirming processes of evolution of African theory and practice, but it will also signal a capitulation to and a mimicry of neo-liberal institutional politics.

Conclusion

This study has provoked more questions than it has provided clear and simple answers. If the reasoning is followed that leadership and transformation collectively result in a form of transformative leadership, then this facet of leadership theory still has much to offer the process of leadership in higher education in South Africa. The hope that existing leadership theory would be directly relevant to the study and that the findings of the study would contribute an African perspective to the largely Western theory base of transformational leadership was idealistic.

A significant outcome of this research is the efficacy of phenomenography as an appropriate research methodology for the purpose of studying higher education from a structured but not impersonal perspective. Phenomenographic methodology enabled the researcher to mediate the process of inquiring into sensitive social phenomena across social and political divides by utilizing a person-centered mode of data collection and a pragmatic process for data analysis and presentation. It provided a framework that explored the congruence and diversity of individuals realities at 'conceptual' rather than the 'experiential' level thereby enabling university leaders (and administrators) personal, political and professional reflections to become a legitimate source for empirical research and for the development of leadership theory.

Acknowledgement

I am extremely grateful to the Vice-Chancellors of the Historically Black Universities in South Africa who were willing to participate in this study and who took time to share their thoughts with me. I am grateful too for their compassion, their interest and their support of my research. I trust that this study brings about a deeper understanding of the challenging and courageous leadership roles that these men and women play in the critical process of leading higher education and in shaping our new democracy.

References

Allen, K. E. (1996), 'Working toward transformational leadership in higher education', *About Campus*, July, 1996, pp. 11-15.

Avolio, B. J. (1999), *Full Leadership Development: Building the Vital Forces in Organizations*, Sage Publications, Thousand Oaks.

Bass, B. M. (1985), *Leadership and Performance Beyond Expectations*, Free Press, New York.

Bass, B. M. (1990), *Bass and Stodgills's Handbook of Leadership: Theory, Research and Managerial Applications*, Free Press, New York.

Bass, B. M. (1996), *A New Paradigm of Leadership: An inquiry into transformational leadership*, U.S. Army Research Institute for the Behavioral and Social Sciences, Alexandria, Virginia.

Bass, B. M. and Avolio, B. J. (eds.), (1994), *Improving organizational effectiveness through transformational leadership*, Sage Publications, Thousand Oaks.

Becher, T and Kogan, M. (1992), *Process and structure in higher education*, Routledge, London.

Bolman, L. and Deal, T. (1997), *Reframing Organizations; Artistry, Choice and Leadership*, Jossey-Bass, San Francisco.

Breen, R. (1999), *Phenomenography and Institutional*, Policy-Making in Higher Education.

Breen, R., Lindsay, R. and Jenkins, A. (2000), *Phenomenography and the disciplinary basis of motivation to learn, Improving Student Learning Through the Disciplines*, Oxonian Rewley Press Ltd., Oxford.

Brookfield, S. (1994), 'Tales from the Dark Side: A Phenomenography of Adult Critical Reflection', *International Journal of Lifelong Education*, Vol. 13(3), pp. 203-216.

Bryman, A. (1986), *Leadership and organizations*, Routledge and Kegan Paul, London.

Burns, J. (1978), *Leadership*, Harper and Row, New York.

Cameron, K. and Ulrich, D. (1986), *Transformational Leadership, Higher Education Handbook of theory and research*, Agathon Press, New York.

Chisolm, L. and Fuller, B. (1996), 'Remembering people's education? Shifting alliances, state-building and South Africa's narrowing policy agenda', *Journal of Education Policy*, Vol. 11, pp. 693-716.

Coombs, P. H. (1987), *Cost analysis in education: a tool for policy and planning.* Publication of the World Bank, Johns Hopkins University Press, Baltimore.

Dunlap, D. M. and Schmuck, P. A. (eds), (1995), *Women Leading in Education*, SUNY Press, Albany.

Gall, M. D., Borg, W. R. and Gall, J. P. (1996), *Educational Research; An Introduction*, Longman Publishers, New York.

Koehler, J. W. and Pankowski, J. M. (1997), *Transformational Leadership in Government*, Delray Beach, FL: St. Lucie Press.

Kotter, J. P. (1990). 'What leaders really do', *Harvard Business Review*, May-June, 1990, pp. 61-69.

Kozmetsky, G. (1985), *Transformational Management*, Ballinger Publishing, Cambridge.

Kuhn, T. S. (1970), *The Structure of Scientific Revolutions*, University of Chicago Press, Chicago.

Kuhnert, K. W. (ed.), (1994), *Developing people through delegation, Improving organizational effectiveness through transformational leadership*, Sage Publications, Thousand Oaks.

Lane, R. E. (1962), *Political Ideology. Why the American common man believes what he does*, The Free Press of Glencoe, New York.

Larsson, S. (1987), 'Learning from Experience: Teachers' Conceptions of Changes in Their Professional Practice, *Journal of Curriculum Studies*, Vol. 19(1), pp. 35-43.

Makgoba, W. M. (1997), 'Academia should also be made to face the music', *The Star*, 21 November 1997, p. 17 (Johannesburg, South Africa).

Mamdani, M. (1996), *Citizen and Subject. Contemporary Africa and the legacy of late colonialism*, Princeton University Press, Princeton.

Marshall, C and Rossman, G.B. (1999), *Designing Qualitative Research*, Sage Publications, Thousand Oaks.

Marton, F. (1981), Phenomenography - Describing Conceptions of the world around us. *Instructional Science*, Vol. 10, pp. 177-200.

Marton, F. (1994), 'Phenomenography', in: T. Hussein & N. Postlethwaite (eds), *International Encyclopedia of Education*, Pergamon, Oxford.

Maxcy, S.J. (1991). *Educational Leadership: A Critical Pragmatic Perspective*, Bergin and Garvey, New York.

Mbigi, L and Maree, J. (1995), Ubuntu: The Spirit of African Transformational Management, Knowledge Resources, Randburg.

Middlehurst, R. (1993), *Leading Academics*, Open University Press, Buckingham.

Minter, W. J. and Thompson, I. M. (eds), (1968), *Colleges and Universities as Agents of Social Change*, Western Interstate Commission for Higher Education, Boulder.

Mugler, F. and Landbeck, R. (1997), Learning in the South Pacific and Phenomenography Across Cultures, *Higher Education Research and Development*, Vol. 16(2), pp. 227-239.

Mungazi, D. A. and Walker, L. K. (1997), *Educational Reform and the Transformation of Southern Africa*, Praeger Publishers, Westport.

National Commission on Higher Education (1996), *Report; A Framework for Transformation*, CTP Book Printers, Parow.

Neumann, A and Bensimon, E. M. (1990), 'Constructing the presidency', *The Chronicle of Higher Education*, Vol. 61(6), pp. 678-701.

Plas, J. M. (1996), *Person-Centered Leadership, An American Approach to Participatory Management*, Sage Publishers, Thousand Oaks.

Ramose, M. B. (1998), *Black Perspectives on Tertiary Institutional Transformation*, Vivlia Publishers, Johannesburg.

Richardson, J. T. E. (1999), The Concepts and Methods of Phenomenographic Research, Review of Educational Research, Vol. 69 (1) pp. 53-82.

Rosener, J. B. (1990), 'Ways women lead', *Harvard Business Review*, Vol. 68, pp. 119-225.

Rossman, G. B. and Rallis, S. F. (1998), *Learning in the Field, An introduction to qualitative research*, Sage Publishers, Thousand Oaks.

Rost, J. C. (1991), *Leadership for the Twenty-First Century*, Praeger, Westport.

Scott, P. (1996), *The Meanings of Mass Higher Education*, Wiley, London.

Seepe, S. (1998), *Black Perspectives on Tertiary Institutional Transformation*, Vivlia Publishers, Johannesburg.

Seidman, I. E. (1991), *Interviewing as qualitative research*, Teachers College, New York.

Svensson, L. (1997), Theoretical Foundations of Phenomenography, *Higher Education Research and Development*, Vol. 16(2), pp. 159-171.

Theman, J. (1980), 'The Significance of Conceptions of Political Power', Paper presented at the *AERA*, April 7-11, 1980. Boston, MA.

Tichy, N. M. and Devanna, M. A. (1986), *The Transformational Leader*, John Wiley and Sons, New York.

Tierney, W. G. (1989), *Curricular Landscapes, Democratic Vistas; Transformative Leadership in Higher Education*, Praeger Publishers, New York.

Chapter 10

An Integral Part of the Local Community: Politicians' Perspectives on the Local University

Tony Potts

Reflection on Method: Consent

The chief research method used in this study was semi-structured interviews. Initially it was planned to interview all municipal, state and federal politicians who represented the Australian regional cities of Ballarat and Bendigo and who numbered 27 persons. Despite warnings to the contrary I believed that they would readily consent to be interviewed. However, this was not so. Whilst 12 of the municipal politicians finally consented none of the federal members of parliament and only two state members of parliament did. This lead to one of the main limitations of the study in that those with most responsibility for university education were not interviewed, those with the next most responsibility numbered only two and those with least responsibility made up the majority of persons interviewed.

Why were only 14 prepared to be interviewed? Firstly in the words of one municipal politician my research was 'a very low priority for them and for him personally'. Secondly the municipal politicians argued that university education was not one of their responsibilities and thus not their concern. Thirdly even many of those interviewed believed that they were unqualified to comment on matters connected with the local universities. Fourthly some were suspicious that my research was part of a government plan to shift more of the responsibility for the respective local universities to different levels of government. A number of the local councilors initially viewed the interview schedule as evidence that local government was going to be requested to assume responsibilities for the local universities. Fifthly some state politicians used the snap state election that was called during the research as an excuse to avoid being interviewed. Some of these claimed that party headquarters forbid talking to the press and other researchers during elections. Sixthly, as one of the city's mayors who was interviewed noted, the reluctance on the part of the state and federal politicians was probably because 'they may have thought I would catch them out and what they said would be used against them'. Seventhly my initial contact with the politicians probably caused some reluctance. Due to the demands of my university's ethic's committee the complete list of possible questions was sent to all the politicians I wished to interview. Some of those approached were overwhelmed when they received the permission letter and accompanying interview schedule. The secretary of one who agreed to be interviewed hinted at this.

On the other hand it needs to be strongly stated that the 14 who were interviewed were exceedingly helpful and went out of their way to assist with the research. However, there are important lessons to be learnt here. Despite the very best efforts to explain the aims of research, to guarantee anonymity and to conform to the guidelines of human ethics committees, the research can be viewed in a much different light by those who are the subjects of it. Simultaneously a range of other issues can unexpectedly come to influence how the research is viewed and how individuals react to it.

On a final note if I were to contemplate a similar study again I would obtain individuals' permission right at the start of the study and long before it had progressed to any extent at all. This would alleviate the anxiety that occurred in this study when at one stage it was feared that none of those approached would be part of the study.

Introduction

Throughout history universities have been connected with politics (Green, 1969: p. 245). Currently this is especially so for the success of the university system now depends on an informed and supportive public and this of course includes politicians (Benjamin, 1993: p. 277). Similarly universities must attend to public expectations about their performance because the public will be the source of their charter to continue operating (Theus, 1993: pp. 277-279). This chapter examines the perspectives of a group of Australian politicians on their regional university. It explores the extent to which these politicians understand the importance of higher education for economic and social prosperity and how much their understandings are influenced by misconceptions and prejudices. The chapter is structured as follows: theoretical considerations, methodological considerations, the social context of universities, the site of the case studies and finally an analysis of the politicians' perspectives on the university.

A note on theory

This chapter examines these politicians' perspectives using a framework based on notions of the self and identity in the network society. Postindustrial societies are characterized by various networks that embrace all parts of society and differentiate countries and people. The ability to produce and access knowledge depends on access to the flows of wider knowledge and information networks. Individuals derive their sense of identity from their network location. Yet the information age involves a 'fundamental opposition between *net* and *self*' (Castells, 1996b: p. 31). Thus there is a *reaffirmation* of basic identities and the search for identity is becoming the main and sometimes the only source of meaning with legitimizing identity being challenged by resistance and project identity (Castells, 1997: p. 7).

Regional loyalties have not disappeared however, because post industrial selves are more complex and find it possible to simultaneously maintain multiple identities (Hage and Powers, 1992: pp. 79-80). In the last 25 years expressions of collective identity have attacked globalization and cosmopolitanism to assert people's control over their own lives. Such expressions have included movements based on locality. Further there now exists 'the paradox of increasingly local politics in a world structured by increasingly global processes' (Castells, 1997: p. 61). Consequently local universities find themselves more than ever facing the local/global issue as they struggle to serve their local region and clientele in what is allegedly even more a global village.

The social context of the university

The historical and contemporary record underscores the social and political context of universities and their establishment and functioning. Accordingly the next section outlines this context in a number of countries so that the perspectives of these current Australian politicians can be better appreciated in a much wider context.

The Old World: Europe and the United Kingdom

Politicians and other civic leaders have always played key roles in the establishment of universities. For example, in the period 1500-1800 political power was important in approving the establishment of universities by regional and local communities and this was especially the case in Europe where municipalities founded universities (Frijhoff, 1996: p. 49).

For the first three centuries of its existence, Edinburgh was a civic university in the strictest sense of the term because Edinburgh Town Council exercised extensive regulatory powers over it (Phillipson, 1988: p. 100). These included controls over finances, building, the appointment of principals, professors, discipline and curriculum. Such wide ranging powers were a constant source of dispute between town and gown (Phillipson, 1988: p. 100).

Plans for a University of London originated in 1826 when various capital city interests combined to plan for a university which would have some of the status of Oxford and Cambridge (Rothblatt, 1988: p. 120). Civic leaders played important roles in the establishment of Britain's civic and red brick universities (Green, 1969: p. 100). Apart from London and Durham the new universities were the result of the civic initiative and generosity of rich manufacturers, often nonconformist in religious persuasion, who were reluctant to contribute to the traditional institutions (Green, 1969: p. 100). However, the advice provided by the local businessmen and administrators, who dominated their councils, often retarded their growth (Green, 1969: p. 130).

The University of Essex was the result of a recommendation of the Essex County Council in 1959 (Green, 1969: pp. 140-141). When the English 'New

Universities' were established the Universities Grants Commission took special notice of the case presented by the local community and its ability to raise private capital (Shattock, 1994: p. 105). Local communities founded Promotions Committees composed of prominent local individuals – the York University Committee was headed by the Archbishop of York and Warwick by Lord Rootes, a major industrialist (Shattock, 1994: p. 105). In the case of Warwick University its Promotion Committee was composed of industrialists, trade unionists and local politicians who had very definite views on the need to establish a university (Shattock, 1994: p. 110). These persons 'engaged in furious argument with academic members of the Planning Board whose priority was for the university to aim at international standards of research' while those on the Promotion Committee wanted a university that would firstly contribute to the local economy and to the social and intellectual life of the area (Shattock, 1994: p. 110). The effective gift of the site by the Lancaster City Council ensured the location of Lancaster University in that city (Wilson, 1995: p. 59). A somewhat similar situation occurred in Finland with the founding of a university in Vasa (Palomaki, 1997: pp. 311-315).

The New World: America and Australia

The establishment of universities in North America also attests to the importance of civic leaders and politicians in their foundation. It was wealthy persons who made possible the successful establishment of the University of Chicago in its first quarter of a century and they were important till after 1945 (Shils, 1988: pp. 214-216). Local businessmen endowed professorial appointments (and in areas where there was unlikely to be any personal or other economic return) and building funds (Shils, 1988: pp. 214-216). This was done from a sense of civic duty even though in many cases these individuals had little understanding of the university (Shils, 1988: pp. 213-219).

The idea for New York University appears to have resulted from the meetings of a small but influential literary society called The Club, which comprised three lawyers, three Columbia College professors, two ministers, two merchants and a medical doctor (Stevenson, 1988: p. 154). They were interested in civic betterment and raising the cultural standards of New York City (Stevenson, 1988: p. 154). During the 1890s the President of Columbia University, Low, transformed it from a small college into a major research university (Bender, 1988: p. 23). Low was not an academic but moved smoothly between the civic and academic world, coming to the presidency of Columbia after serving as reform mayor of Brooklyn and leaving to become mayor of New York City in 1901 (Bender, 1998: p. 23).

It was not just in the large cities of the United States that civic leaders and politicians were instrumental in the establishment and fostering of universities. The whole university tradition in America had a heavy rural bias (Barlow, 1998: p. 149). A number of factors were important in rural American towns desiring a college or university and one of the main ones was 'self-respect' (McGiffert, 1964: p. 3). This was coupled with the rivalries of competing communities whose leaders believed that a college or university would enhance the cultural standing and prestige of the town, increase the population and bring a variety of rewards

(McGiffert, 1964: p. 4). In America colleges and universities along with gaols, hospitals and the location of the state capitals were the rewards of politics (McGiffert, 1964: p. 5). Many regional colleges were established 'because small towns aspired to become large towns; the secret to growth was to acquire a railroad, a hotel or a college' (Riseman in Severino, 1996: p. 224).

In 1937 Australia's first regional university was established in Armidale. The University of New England owes its foundation largely to the work of the state politician Drummond, who held the rural electorate of Armidale for 22 years and the Education Ministry for 12 years – a period greater than any other minister of education in the history of New South Wales State Governments (Godfrey & Ramsland, 1997: p. 611). The establishment of the university was connected with efforts to decentralize educational provision in New South Wales (Drummond, 1959: Preface). Drummond (1959: pp. xi-xxi) acknowledges the assistance he gained from leading citizens of Armidale and northern New South Wales in his efforts to establish the university.

The establishment of Newcastle University in New South Wales, another of Australia's non-metropolitan universities, owed much to the 'work and commitment of many citizens of Newcastle and region' (Evatt in Wright, 1992: p. iv). Those who attended a public meeting to campaign for the establishment of the University on October 1, 1942 was a list of 'a Who's Who of Newcastle' (Wright, 1992: pp. 5-6).

In Australia some of the newer institutes of higher education established after 1965 owe their establishment to 'state political imperatives [rather than a] sober assessment of needs ... city-base politicians, campaigning in country towns prior to an election, had a standard proforma promise which ran "if it's got a river promise them a dam; if not, then promise them a CAE [college of advanced education]"' (Chipman, 1997: 10).

Universities do not simply come into existence in a vacuum. Their establishment is very much connected with the actions of civic leaders and other important political figures who have various social, political, economic and educational motives for their establishment.

The Cities of Bendigo and Ballarat

Both Bendigo and Ballarat are two of Australia's largest, most important and historic regional cities with histories extending to the world famous gold rushes of the mid nineteenth century. Their institutions of higher education have similarly long histories. Over a relatively long period there have been active campaigns by local politicians and civic leaders to secure universities in each respective city. Bendigo is situated 150 kilometres to the northwest of Melbourne, the capital city of Victoria. It is the second most populous municipality in regional Victoria (Victorian Department of Infrastructure, 1998: p. 71). Bendigo is a significant regional centre servicing a diverse rural hinterland (Victorian Department of Infrastructure, 1998: p. 71). Ballarat is located in the Victorian Central Highlands approximately 110 kilometres west of Melbourne. It is the third most populous municipality in provincial Victoria (Victorian Department of Infrastructure, 1998: p. 45). Like Bendigo it is one of the state of Victoria's major regional cities, with a historical importance based on its gold mining past (Victorian Department of Infrastructure, 1998: p. 45).

Ballarat's economy is founded on traditional manufacturing, information technology, education, health services and tourism – the latter based on the city's heritage and Sovereign Hill historical park (Victorian Department of Infrastructure, 1998: p. 45). The Australian Bureau of Statistics (Victorian Year Book, 1999: p. 6) states that the major employing industries in Bendigo are food processing, education, telecommunications, gold mining and tourism; while for Ballarat they are information technology, metals manufacturing, food processing, tourism and gold mining.

La Trobe University, Bendigo

La Trobe University commenced teaching in 1967. It was the third university founded in Victoria and now has six campuses across Victoria, including the one at Bendigo. The campus at Bendigo, 150 kilometres northwest from the main Melbourne campus, has approximately 4000 students and is located 3 kilometres from Bendigo's central business district. The Bendigo campus has a history extending to 1873 when the Bendigo School of Mines and Industry was established. La Trobe University, Bendigo (LUB) offers courses in arts, science, nature tourism, outdoor education, business, computing, education, engineering, health sciences and nursing, teaching and visual arts.

The University of Ballarat

The University of Ballarat (UB) is Australia's newest and smallest university. The history of UB extends to the Ballarat School of Mines founded in 1870. The University of Ballarat was established in 1998 as a new, multi-sectoral educational institution through the merger of University of Ballarat (established in 1994) with two Institutes of Technical and Further Education: The School of Mines and Industries Ballarat and Wimmera Institute of Technical and Further Education. The University has its main campus and its university division at Mount Helen, a site of 110 hectares, 10 kilometres from Ballarat's central business district. Total student numbers are 4,000 students enrolled in university courses and TAFE enrolments equivalent to 4,000 students. It has university courses in arts and visual arts, behavioural and social sciences, humanities, business, education, engineering, human movement and sport sciences, information technology, nursing and sciences.

Politicians' perspectives on the university

This chapter concentrates on the following components of these politicians' perspectives on their local university: part of the city's history, a city asset and a multifaceted identity. At the outset these politicians gave an indication that their perspectives rested on recipe knowledge that is 'knowledge ... automatically at hand' (Schutz, 1971: p.72). Consequently these politicians were quick to assert that they were not experts in this area and their knowledge was that of ordinary lay persons. Many stated that they were 'unschooled in the whole area'. However, what also appears in these politicians' perspectives as they contemplate the identity of the local university are notions of leadership that involve creative and forward thinking. These politicians display at various times transformational, visionary, transactional and managerial leadership traits (Gronn, 1996: p. 20). Consequently while relying on their own Socialization to help provide a non expert perspective these politicians have a vision for the local university, are able to see the transformations that the local university can enact in the region and also see the leadership issues that are often necessary for the university to realize its transformational and visionary potential. In the following discussion pseudonyms are given to the various local politicians.

Part of the city's history

The politicians interviewed were aware that Ballarat and Bendigo had a long and important history of higher educational provision. For over a century Ballarat and Bendigo both had schools of mines. These originated on their respective goldfields and provided geology, mining and engineering related courses. One politician, White, recognized that the Ballarat School of Mines had an illustrious history being 'the very first training school in Victoria'. The current universities in Ballarat and Bendigo had evolved from these schools of mines. Another politician, Millar, noted that there had always been a sort of university infrastructure in Ballarat 'and it had just been a matter of changing names'. Similarly, according to Troy, establishing a university was a 'natural progression in each city's educational history'.

From an early date each city had thus worked towards creating its own identity as a centre of higher education that was independent of those in the capital city. The politicians pointed out that Ballarat had subsequently established its own autonomous university that possessed its own unique identity. This action was a particular powerful expression of resistance identity. Bendigo, less driven by resistance identity, had opted for a campus of a larger metropolitan-based network university. Consequently university education had become part of each city's primary identity.

Troy, using recipe knowledge that utilized metropolitan universities as reference groups observed that the forerunners of the current UB and LUB 'may not have enjoyed the same status as the University of Melbourne and some of the more established universities'. However 'in terms of career and employment, the prospects of ... graduates in geology, mining and engineering and even in fine arts were excellent'. Thus while there was recognition that not all institutions in a knowledge network enjoyed the same status, and the same identities, it was also argued that graduates from both former local tertiary institutions were able to gain worthwhile employment in local and wider career networks. In so doing they challenged the belief that only metropolitan universities had legitimate identities.

Another respondent, Kersten, used the historical development of Australia's regional university network as a comparative reference to establish that Bendigo, and similar provincial cities, had developed successful universities. He claimed 'if you look at Warrnambool, Ballarat and Bendigo they have all proved that'. Hayman used international reference groups to expand the last observation to a global perspective. He argued that 'some of the best universities around the world are based in country towns or country cities'. Hayman meanwhile claimed that for universities in such locations there existed a greater opportunity for them to 'become part of the city and to "badge" the city'. This was especially the case where the university was centrally located in a large city. He observed that he 'came from England and if you think of London University it gets lost within the sort of metropolis, whereas places like Oxford and Cambridge, those cities, are known by the universities and nothing else'.

Hayman quickly added that he 'was not suggesting that Bendigo was in the same group' of such prestigious institutions as some other non-metropolitan universities. However one real advantage for universities located in a city like Bendigo was that they could identify with the community. Smaller regional universities facilitated much more intimate personal and educational networks and gave the towns and cities they were established in special identities. Having a university added to the status of a particular town or city in knowledge and other networks. Moreover without the local university the cities of Ballarat and Bendigo would find access to knowledge and other networks increasingly problematic. This was a critical problem in the information age.

A city asset

Ballarat and Bendigo had important geographic, social, economic, political and educational positions in their state. For both cities a university was an essential institution, as both were viewed by these politicians as being of sufficient population size, and with the necessary attributes, to host their own universities. Mellor encapsulated this when she noted that 'Bendigo was a major service centre, servicing not just itself but a far wider region and hence a university was essential'. Trewin argued that for Bendigo, as for any regional capital city, a university was a huge advantage. The local university was especially important in the network society for it provided access to knowledge generation and utilization and in addition provided an identity for the city. Without such access Ballarat and Bendigo would be cut off from national and global networks.

Trewin argued that LUB and BU were an 'an integral part of the local community'. This was for two main reasons. Firstly many of the cities' youth had previously left to attend universities in Melbourne. Not only had this been an educational necessity but local students had been attracted to the higher status knowledge networks there and also to their allegedly more attractive locations in capital city networks. This situation it was claimed had now altered. Bendigo and Ballarat politicians alleged that many persons, including those in Melbourne, now desired to attend the more friendly country campuses of the local university. Neil stated that in addition LUB and BU provided the opportunity for students who wanted to attend university but were not necessarily ready to leave their home city and the personal networks it provided for them. White observed that 'these days you don't take the people to education, you take the education to the people'. Thus UB and LUB provided access to knowledge and other networks without students having to move to other locations. For local students who would have in the past gone to Melbourne, UB and LUB reduced expenses associated with university education. The local university helped stem flows of students to other locations and to other network providers. In the reasoning above can be discerned notions of resistance identity. These politicians are not convinced that local students should have to leave their home city for university education in distant metropolitan centres.

Secondly UB and LUB were seen as assets in another equally important respect. This was connected with the continued growth of each of their respective host cities. Trewin was well aware that while a number of new enterprises had relocated to Bendigo it was still extremely difficult to attract high quality senior staff away from the capital cities because many educational, social, economic and other networks were centred there. He gave as an especially pertinent example the difficulty Bendigo experienced in securing medical practitioners. Trewin reinforced the seriousness of this by pointing out that Bendigo was not remote Australia but an important regional centre with access to a wide range of economic and social networks. A network of facilities, including a campus of a respected university, was for Trewin and Bendigo City Council, an important 'part of a good selling strategy to attract medical practitioners to the city'. A respected university campus gave the city an identity as an attractive place to live and work. In this example here we find not only perspectives that are derived from recipe knowledge but ones that also draw on more sophisticated notions of strategic and visionary leadership. The politicians note that a university is vital for the future growth and prosperity of their city.

Thus UB and LUB were intimately connected to the marketing of their respective cities and their continued growth and prosperity in an increasingly global world. Local politicians regularly spoke to business, professional and other persons contemplating business and other investment opportunities in Bendigo or Ballarat. On such occasions it was argued that there existed in the city high standard government and private schools, health and sporting facilities, library, art gallery, performing arts centre and in addition a respected university. The existence of UB or LUB aided such negotiations and was crucial in attracting staff. LUB and UB complemented education and other networks in each city. Neil for example noted that the LUB complemented 'the city's senior secondary college which had achieved state, national and some international prominence'. Trewin especially appreciated that in staff recruitment discussions LUB was an extremely important 'part of the total package'.

A multifaceted identity

Vocational and general education

According to Kersten there was a need for people not to be confused about the primary identity of LUB and UB. There was, he argued, a tendency for people wanting different things, not all of them complementary, from universities. But according to Kersten while people 'might want them to be all things to all people the primary aim is to educate people and if other things have a spin off well that was fine'. Hayman similarly appreciated that both institutions were 'first and foremost an educational facility'. Consequently for these politicians the chief but not exclusive identity of LUB and UB was as regional vocational educational providers. The primary identity of UB and LUB was to provide access to local, state, national and global knowledge networks.

Both UB and LUB had primary identities as centres of vocational education. Harding observed that LUB and UB could not ignore the fact that their graduates needed to be able to find employment. Perry saw this as the UB and LUB producing 'down to earth graduates'. Millar from his experiences as a student at UB readily understood that it concentrated on providing industry specific training for particular employment networks. Hence UB offered degrees in areas such as geology, food technology and environmental management. In so doing UB attempted to introduce students to industry networks where they would ultimately find employment. Using reference groups it was alleged that this approach contrasted with the orientation of some of the larger Australian universities who adopted a more generalist educational orientation. It was believed that in recent times the emphasis on vocational education had intensified. Harding recalled newspaper reports in *The Age* and *The Australian*, that suggested that UB and LUB needed to pay more attention to producing 'work ready students' for employment networks.

However these politicians argued that UB and LUB had to have identities broader than vocational educational institutions. Displaying resistance identity they were not content to accept government definitions of the role and status of the local universities and challenged the legitimacy of these. These politicians argued that the identities of UB and LUB should also derive from providing high quality tertiary education in a range of areas. Thus while Troy argued that the UB and LUB should provide both vocational education for specific careers and more general liberal types of education he 'had some difficulty coming to terms with university as vocationally oriented'. He believed that universities generally should provide a broad range of critical skills. Troy was concerned that universities generally appeared to have moved too far from a liberal education that provided a range of such critical skills that allowed legitimate and accepted notions to be challenged. They were now overly concerned with vocationally specific education and career networks.

Liberal and general education were especially important as they contributed to the city's intellectual networks and, in Harding's words, to 'the vivacity of the city's thinking'. However, trying to strictly differentiate between vocationally oriented and liberal education was very difficult. Kersten realized 'these things are mixed [and] I actually don't think there is an easy answer'. While there was always a need for general education in areas such as classics and liberal arts courses there was simultaneously the need for more vocationally specific courses for engineers, lawyers and architects. Getting the correct balance was not easy.

Both LUB and UB faced difficulties with having identities focused exclusively on vocationalism. This was because in the informational age accepted notions of careers and career structures were quickly becoming redundant. In this respect Mellor observed that individuals 'no longer knew if they would have a career from one year to the next [and] hence education had to change with that'. Neil added that education that was provided by LUB and UB needed to be much more 'rounded [as] there were going to be jobs in 9-10 years that had never been heard of'. One of the big tasks that the LUB and UB had to undertake was in Mellor's words to help students understand what was 'happening in the world'. Hence LUB and UB needed to provide students with the ability to cope with an uncertain global future and to move away from role scripted performances to more strategic ways of thinking.

For Millar UB had a particular regional identity and provided education especially for the people of Ballarat and the Western District of Victoria. However there was a realization, expressed by Staley, that if LUB and UB had only a regional vocational identity then some individuals would be forced to attend Melbourne based institutions which offered a wider range of courses. But at the same time he foresaw that ultimately LUB and UB would not be able to offer a complete range of courses and programmes. What LUB and UB should attempt to offer were courses allied to major service industries and networks in the city. These networks included those focused on education, health, engineering, sport and leisure. Similarly Rogers argued that the LUB and UB should aim to establish an identity as a centre of excellence in some key disciplines and develop those. In this respect Trewin noted specialisms provided by the LUB assisted it to in his words, 'badge' and niche market itself and thus to identify the city.

Research and consultancy

An important role of LUB and UB in the network society was research and consultancy. Research was primarily important because it established the core identities of UB and LUB as reputable universities and located them in legitimate university networks. In addition research by LUB and UB gave an added dimension to the respective identities of the cities of Ballarat and Bendigo. Hayman for instance, argued that LUB and UB should be involved in both pure and applied research. This was because one of the identifiers and strengths of a real university 'is in pure research and you need that'. While Hayman recognized that it was not always possible to put a measure on the outcomes of research he noted it would be ideal if the local city benefited and if the results were internationally relevant as 'that is another element that assists Bendigo being recognized'.

There were also more immediately pragmatic reasons for UB and LUB to be involved in research. Both Ballarat and Bendigo and their respective regions provided a range of social, economic, environmental and developmental problems that UB and LUB could investigate and solve. For example, in both Ballarat and Bendigo agriculture and food technology were major industries with major issues and problems. Thus agriculture was seen as an obvious area of research endeavour for both UB and LUB. Hayman noted that for example, Bendigo City Council had been involved in examining the economic potential of olive trees and LUB could play a role in this investigation. Harding argued that the food industry research was a natural one for UB. Ballarat was the location of McCains, the multinational food company, who sourced potatoes from the Ballarat region. Millar observed that in addition to this Ballarat was the location of Mars, the multinational food confectionery giant. Troy noted that UB was involved in survey design, conducting surveys, data analysis and so forth. UB had also conducted research into environmental issues such as heavy metal pollution of Lake Wendouree.

Particular social problems of Ballarat and Bendigo were also seen as important for UB and LUB. Advocating such research displayed resistance identity, as its purpose was to challenge the legitimizing policies of government and other organizations. Mellor argued strongly that LUB needed to redefine its educational identity by broadening its focus on the kinds of community relevant research it did. One particularly pressing issue that could profitably be investigated, she argued, was the lack of proper psychological support services in Bendigo. Research could assist in determining whether the new model of psychological support services advocated and enacted by government agencies 'where people had been released out of psychiatric centres' was better for them and those they associated with. Mellor stressed the need for research into this area, as there appeared to be a huge community problem caused by the implementation of the new mental health services provisions. People were being threatened, terrorized and having their quality of life undermined. Mellor thought that this was especially the case in the central business district of Bendigo where there were 'mentally disabled people in the Mall [central business district] sexually terrorizing people, women in particular'. She stated that there was a need for this research to explore the ramifications of this policy. Staley similarly noted research into the impact of the government's gambling policy on residents was urgently needed.

These politicians were thus cognisant of the kinds of research being undertaken at UB and LUB. They stated, as Hayman did, that they were for example 'aware of the work that [LUB] had done in the past on water and sewerage treatment', its international significance and potential to assist Bendigo's economic development. Perry was familiar with similar developments at Ballarat where UB had been involved in research developing Austrac – an electronic surveillance and positioning system. They realized that these examples represented leading edged, internationally recognized research, which they were keen to highlight, wherever they went. Such endeavour assisted in providing identities for LUB and UB as legitimate universities and for Bendigo and Ballarat as university cities. However there were three areas of concern with respect to the research profiles of UB and LUB.

Firstly Perry from his involvement in business ventures in North America and consequent associations with Mississippi State University and Iowa State

University noted that he believed that Australian universities did not have the same levels of commitment to agriculture. Thus personal involvement in overseas business and knowledge networks lead to the use of overseas reference groups. This resulted in less than favourable comparisons with local developments and undertakings.

Secondly Troy and Mellor thought that what was 'lacking though is the UB being involved in some of the big issue debates'. These included particular local and regional responses to important problems such as transport and unemployment. Troy was of the opinion that engineering and economic experts from UB were not involved in these debates but should be. Rogers thought that LUB could provide more visionary and strategic leadership for Bendigo. He argued that LUB needed to construct a more regional identity and 'plug some of the gaps in the educational and social infrastructure' of Bendigo and region. Rogers reasoned that LUB could do this by firstly becoming more involved in some of the important debates concerned with, for example, the decline of rural Victoria and the effects of globalization on regional and rural Australia. However, Troy wondered if university staff were so affected 'by workloads that did allow them to do that'. Again we see evidence of resistance identity with these politicians arguing that the local university should be much more involved in questioning legitimizing identity fostered by other individuals and organizations.

Thirdly these politicians were well aware that UB and LUB faced major impediments to research. Kersten saw that research involvement depended on a critical mass of researchers but he added that as LUB was now attached to La Trobe in Bundoora the 'opportunities are now a lot greater'. Thus there was a realization that being involved in larger and wider knowledge networks, while reducing local community identity, did have other benefits. White added that while any university should engage in research it was not possible for them to be involved in research in all areas. There was a need for UB and LUB to specialize in certain fields and to construct an identity concentrated on a limited number of areas. White used external reference groups by noting the prohibitive costs of medical research to make his point. He recounted how the government had prepared a budget paper on the cost of medical research to the state of Victoria. He had been amazed at what seemed to him the stupid competition for the same sources of funding for similar research. White suggested that one area where UB could concentrate its research expertise was in the field of information technology because of the location of the Ballarat Technology Park next to UB.

Economic

These local politicians appreciated the economic contribution of UB and LUB to the wider financial networks of both Ballarat and Bendigo. It was recognized that LUB and UB were focal points of the respective economic networks of both cities. Torr stated that UB was one of Ballarat's biggest industries along with the multinational confectionery and food firms, Mars and McCains. Harding was aware of the exact direct economic contribution of UB at $A87 million (taking the figures from UB budget papers on her desk during the interview). White noted that

UB's budget was 'bigger than the city council budget'. Troy too was cognisant that UB employed 500 staff and 200 of these were academic staff. He added that its economic contribution to Ballarat was substantial as it 'was one of the biggest generators in the Ballarat economy' and along with health and welfare accounted for the largest proportions of employment. Bendigo politicians fully appreciated that LUB was one of Bendigo's major industries. Hayman pointed out that it 'would be second only to the health group in terms of employment'. Neil recalled that council was well aware of the economic contribution and for that reason always wanted to support LUB. However, she also argued that LUB needed to support the city by supporting local businesses.

Other respondents stressed the contribution of UB and LUB to particular economic networks in each respective city. Troy realized that many Ballarat individuals were involved in housing market developments and depended heavily on the student housing market. He further observed that students were just like any other low-income earners in that they generally spent 100 per cent of their income on consumables. In that respect they were a big impetus for the local economy. Hotels, Troy added, were especially appreciative of the economic importance of students! Millar argued that simply having a large number of staff and students in the city ensured the economic importance of the UB and LUB. Hayman noted that the LUB was in fact a major employer and this gave it a vital economic role in the city.

While it was well understood that LUB and UB could be important generators of economic activity in a range of areas doubts were expressed by these politicians over some economic aspects of LUB and UB. Some politicians wondered if functioning as an economic incubator was a fit and proper role for LUB and UB. Were UB and LUB undertaking a role that was more the responsibility of local government? Some thought this role could lead to inappropriate subsidization of industry by taxpayers. Rogan was especially concerned about this. However, he added that the Vice Chancellor of Ballarat University 'would tell me different'. Here there is an indication of very decisive signs of leadership being exercised by key university personnel at the local university. Such leadership certainly moves away from 'cook book notions' to more strategic and visionary forms.

Lastly there were concerns that Ballarat and Bendigo would become too economically dependent on UB and LUB and construct primary identities as university cities. It was again reiterated that there was a need for balanced economic development in Ballarat and Bendigo. Each city needed to be located in a number of economic networks. Each city should also have good health facilities for its high proportion of aged citizens, and tourist attractions such as Sovereign Hill or Central Deborah Gold Mine. Rogan suggested that what was needed was a 'dynamic balance' in the overall economic development of each city. Lastly from a somewhat different angle Harding wondered whether some citizens perceived UB to be obtaining preferential funding treatment from Ballarat City Council compared to other needy areas in Ballarat. If this were the case she feared this would not be to Ballarat City's overall advantage and there would be strong resistance from the local citizens.

Community identity

The presence of university staff and students, especially in a provincial city such as Ballarat and Bendigo, gave both communities special identities. Kersten was especially aware that the presence of LUB and UB 'just made a difference to the city'. This was because the universities meant that there were young people in the cities. He pointed out that that 'you only have to look at the way the world is and if you have not got a university in your town young people leave. You notice in my electorate they turn 18 years of age and they clear off, which is the case across the whole of Victoria'. Troy saw this special identity as deriving from students simply 'injecting a lot of life' into the life of the city. These politicians believed that the community identity of UB and LUB stemmed from the active participation of youth in various city and community networks. Students contributed to a wide range of city networks especially sporting ones. Trewin observed that citizens needed to realize that

> a university city, with students in it, lends a heck of a lot of life to it. All that expertise, and young people living here, it flows back into the community in terms of ... sporting talent, not only in the actual playing side but in terms of advice and expertise that was provided to sporting committees and associations by students and persons associated with the university.

In both Ballarat and Bendigo there were joint city and university initiatives that generated wealth and provided employment. Both UB and LUB helped to provide an increased range of sporting facilities that Ballarat and Bendigo would not otherwise have had. In Ballarat the university contributed to the development of the Technology Park and the Greenhill Enterprise Centre. Staley highlighted the recent establishment at LUB of the Centre for Sustainable Development. This was a multidisciplinary and networked centre, with links to a number of organizations. Staley believed that this body would be important in increasing LUB's identity in the city and regional networks. Additionally the centre would play a part in influencing and informing key decision-makers in a range of government and policy-making networks.

However, doubts were expressed about some aspects of UB's and LUB's community identity. Rogan wondered if the primary identity of UB should be more exclusively focused on being an academic institution. According to him it was possible that UB could easily duplicate the efforts of other Ballarat networks for example, in the provision of sporting facilities. Again, according to Rogan, there was a fear that the UB could come to dominate local sports and community networks and overwhelm community identity. It could be the case that the only legitimate involvement would come to be seen as that which originated from university networks. Similarly, while acknowledging LUB's important social and cultural identity in Bendigo, Hayman observed that 'universities were tending to lose sight of what university is all about'. He believed that a university was

> an educational centre but it was much more than that; it was a way of life, in that it provides an area for research and development that you do not get anywhere else ...

you have to be careful that we don't end up with universities that are really only other tertiary colleges rather than what a university in my view is supposed to be about.

Staley too supported these latter notions by noting that while LUB should have a community identity it should primarily be an institution that provided opportunity for free thinking, for reflection, for writing and for the sorts of things that make for a better society.

Conclusion

These Australian regional politicians' perspectives on their university have similarities with those of other civic leaders in various periods and countries. Their perspectives were grounded in the histories of their universities. They viewed their regional university as 'being an integral part of the local community' that gave a special identity to its host city. These Australian politicians viewed their university as an extremely important city asset fulfilling a multifaceted role. This included providing vocational and general education (and the latter was given much prominence), research and consultancy, and providing an important economic stimulus to the local community along with important economic contributions to the city.

Most importantly the perspectives of these regional politicians were based on sophisticated notions of leadership and less on 'knowledge automatically at hand' (Schutz, 1971: p. 72). These politicians fully realized that, in the global world of the informational society, a regional university enabled their city and its citizens to access global knowledge and other networks. Access to such networks was seen as essential for survival and prosperity. In addition it was also realized that their regional university linked local and community networks with the national and global networks. These politicians' perspectives finally contained evidence of a tension between expecting their local university to plug them into the wider network society but simultaneously to give expressions to issues of local identity. Whether they realized the implications of this was not clear. Again this perspective was not something that was either new or unique to Australia at the present time.

This chapter by focusing on the interaction between the university and its broader social context and highlighting groups that are often ignored in studies of universities has sought to aid understanding of the cultures and contexts involved in shaping universities (Friedman, 2000: p. 2). Furthermore it has revealed the diversity and complexity of individual institutions and attempted to counter the monolithic mythologies and idealized archetypes that exist in university histories (Friedman, 2000: p. 3). This chapter has allowed for some appreciation of the *local* dynamics of contextual meanings (Friedman, 2000: p. 18). Furthermore the chapter highlights the local-global axis (Deem, 2001: p. 1). It illustrates the importance of local and regional influences on universities and how these are not subordinate to more global forces (Deem 2001: pp. 17-18). Regional universities, while part of wider global university networks, must still serve their immediate and local regions even if in so doing they take account of wider global influences. This is simply because their local public will be their first source of their charter to continue operating.

Simply focusing on a few prestigious institutions, whether Berlin, Cambridge, Paris or Harvard, is scarcely valid (Friedman, 2000: p. 38). Local conditions are important in all universities, and it should not be assumed that the developments in mainstream institutions are somehow 'natural' (Friedman, 2000: p. 38). Studies of peripheral institutions such as in this chapter can enable us to examine the local and provincial as informing elements (Friedman, 2000: p. 39). This can assist us to determine the extent to which universities develop as part of local variations (Friedman, 2000: p. 39). For example, what is the connection between the social landscape in such peripheral outposts and the features of these universities? (Friedman, 2000: p. 40). This chapter investigates the interplay between the university in its broader local, national and international and contexts (Friedman, 2000: p. 43).

References

Australian Bureau of Statistics. (1999), Victorian *Year Book*, Government Printer, Melbourne.

Barlow, M. (1998), 'Developing and sustaining an urban mission: Concordia University in Montreal', in H. van der Wusten, (ed.), *The Urban University and its Identity*, Kluwer, Dordrecht.

Bender, T. (1988), 'Introduction', in T. Bender (ed.), *The University and the City*, Oxford University Press, New York.

Benjamin, T. B. (1993), 'Public Perceptions of Higher Education', *Oxford Review of Education*, vol. 19(1), pp. 47-64.

Castells, M. (1996a). *The Information Age: Economy, Society and Culture, Volume 1. The Rise of the Network Society*, Blackwells, Oxford.

Castells, M. (1996b), 'The Net and the Self - Working notes for a critical theory of the informational society', *Critique of Anthropology*, vol. 16(1), pp. 9-38.

Castells, M. (1997), *The Information Age: Economy, Society and Culture, Volume II The Power of Identity*, Blackwells, Oxford.

Chipman, L. (1997), *The Modern University and the Moulding of Character*, Central Queensland University, Rockhampton.

Deem, R. (2001), 'Globalization, new managerialism, academic capitalism and entrepreneurialism in universities. Is the local dimension still?', *Comparative Education*, vol. 37(1), pp. 7-20.

Drummond, D. H. (1959), *A University is Born: The Story of the Founding of the University College of New England*, Angus and Robertson, Sydney.

Friedman, R. M. (2000), *Integration and Visibility: historiographic challenges to university history*, University of Oslo Forum for University History, Oslo.

Frijhoff, W. (1996), 'Patterns', in H. De Ridder-Symoens. (ed.), *A History of the University in Europe*, Vol. II, Universities in Early Modern Europe (1500-1800), Cambridge University Press, Cambridge.

Godfrey, J. R. and J. R. Ramsland. (1997), 'The Drummond influence on state education and child care in 20th century New South Wales', *Australian and New Zealand History of Education Society Conference - Old Boundaries and New Frontiers in Histories of*

Education - Collected Papers, The University of Newcastle, Australia, 7-10 December, Volume 2, 609-618.

Green, V. H. H. (1969), *British Institutions - The Universities*, Pelican, Harmondsworth.

Gronn, P. (1995), 'From transactions to transformations - a new world order in the study of leadership?', *Educational Management and Administration*, vol. 24(1), pp. 7-30.

Hage, J. and C. H. Powers. (1992), *Post-Industrial Lives - Roles and Relationships in the 21st Century*, Sage, London.

McGiffert, M. (1964), *The Higher Learning in Colorado-An Historical Study, 1860-1940*, Sage Books, Thousand Oaks/London.

Palomaki, M. (1997), 'New universities and their cities, the case of Vassa, Finland', *GeoJournal*, vol. 41(4), pp. 311-318.

Phillipson, N. (1988), 'Commerce and culture: Edinburgh, Edinburgh University, and the Scottish Enlightenment', in T. Bender (ed.), *The University and the City*, Oxford University Press, New York.

Rothblatt, S. (1988), 'London: A metropolitan university?', in T. Bender, (ed.), *The University and the City*, Oxford University Press, New York.

Schutz, A. (1971), *Collected Papers: Studies in Social Theory*, Vol. II, Martinus Nijhoff, The Hague.

Severino, C. (1996), 'The idea of an urban university - A history and rhetoric of ambivalence and ambiguity', *Urban Education*, vol. 31(3), pp. 291-313.

Shattock, M. (1994), 'Balancing priorities in the foundation of a new university. The experience of British universities founded in the 1960s', in Dahloff, U. and S. Selander, (eds), 1994. *New Universities and Regional Context*, Acta Universitatis Upsaliensis, Upsalla.

Shils, E. (1988), 'The university, the city and the world: Chicago and the University of Chicago', in T. Bender (ed.), *The University and the City*, Oxford University Press, New York.

Stevenson, L. L. (1988), 'Preparing for public life: the collegiate students at New York University, 1832-1881', in T. Bender (ed.), *The University and the City*, Oxford University Press, New York.

Theus, K. T. (1993), 'Academic reputations: the process of formation and decay', *Public Relations Review*, vol. 19(3), pp. 277-291.

Victorian Department of Infrastructure. (1998), *Regional Victoria in Fact*, Department of Infrastructure Research Unit, Melbourne.

Wilson, C. 1995, 'A district council perspective from Lancaster', in H.W. Armstrong, T. Bruce, B. Jackson, (eds.), *Cities of Learning? Papers from a Conference held on 20 and 21 April, 1995*, Committee of Vice-Chancellors and Principals of the Universities of the United Kingdom, London.

Wright, D. (1992), Looking *Back - A History of the University of Newcastle*, The University of Newcastle, Callaghan.

Index

214   *Realizing Qualitative Research into Higher Education*